DOING
COACHING
RESEARCH

edited by

Peter Jackson & Elaine Cox

Los Angeles | London | New Delhi
Singapore | Washington DC | Melbourne

Los Angeles | London | New Delhi
Singapore | Washington DC | Melbourne

SAGE Publications Ltd
1 Oliver's Yard
55 City Road
London EC1Y 1SP

SAGE Publications Inc.
2455 Teller Road
Thousand Oaks, California 91320

SAGE Publications India Pvt Ltd
B 1/I 1 Mohan Cooperative Industrial Area
Mathura Road
New Delhi 110 044

SAGE Publications Asia-Pacific Pte Ltd
3 Church Street
#10-04 Samsung Hub
Singapore 049483

Editor: Susannah Trefgarne
Assistant editor: Ruth Lilly
Production editor: Rachel Burrows
Copyeditor: Joanna North
Proofreader: David Hemsley
Indexer: Gary Kirby
Marketing manager: Dilhara Attygalle
Cover design: Naomi Robinson
Typeset by: C&M Digitals (P) Ltd, Chennai, India
Printed in the UK

First published 2020

Library of Congress Control Number: 2019954004

British Library Cataloguing in Publication data

A catalogue record for this book is available from the British Library

ISBN 978-1-5264-5946-6
ISBN 978-1-5264-5947-3 (pbk)

Contents

About the editors and authors   iv

Part I   Introduction to coaching research   **1**

1   Introduction   3

2   Theoretical foundations of research   17
    Peter Jackson

3   Designing your research project   33
    Elaine Cox

Part II   Research strategies   **51**

4   Grounded theory   53
    Teresa Carmichael and Natalie Cunningham

5   Phenomenological approaches   74
    Tatiana Bachkirova, Alison Rose and Roger Noon

6   Autoethnography   93
    Juliette Koning and Liam Moore

7   Quantitative and statistical approaches   112
    Christine Davies and Annette Fillery-Travis

8   Case study research   128
    Andrea D. Ellinger and Rochell R. McWhorter

9   Action research   148
    Elaine Cox, Hany Shoukry and Janice Cook

Part III   The impact of research   **169**

10   The experience of research   171
     Elaine Cox and Peter Jackson

11   The dissemination and implementation of research-based
     coaching knowledge   181
     Peter Jackson and Elaine Cox

Index   195

About the editors and authors

Dr Peter Jackson is deputy director of the International Centre for Coaching and Mentoring Studies at Oxford Brookes University (UK). He teaches on the MA programme in Coaching & Mentoring Practice, the professional doctorate in Coaching, and on the Centre's professional development programme in Coaching Supervision. He has published on reflective practice, coaching supervision and physicality in coaching. His coaching practice has a particular focus on the challenges of general management and the dynamics of individual change within organisations.

Dr Elaine Cox is a senior lecturer within the International Centre for Coaching and Mentoring Studies at Oxford Brookes University. She is an experienced researcher, author and editor and also supervises doctoral students.

Elaine has a comprehensive knowledge of research approaches and methods and their application to coaching research and her current research projects are focused upon aspects of managerial and leadership coaching. In addition to authoring a number of books and research articles, Elaine is the founding editor of the *International Journal of Evidence Based Coaching and Mentoring*.

Tatiana Bachkirova is Professor of Coaching Psychology and Director of the International Centre for Coaching and Mentoring Studies at Oxford Brookes University, UK. She is a recognised author, international speaker and a coaching supervisor.

Teresa Carmichael. At Wits University in South Africa, Teresa's scholarly focus on the discipline of qualitative research (particularly grounded theory and action research) means that she teaches and supervises students at MBA, specialist master's and PhD levels. She is an active researcher and widely published across a variety of disciplines, and rounds off her academic activities with MOOC development and facilitating student writing programmes.

Natalie Cunningham enjoys a multiplicity of roles: Research Associate at GIBS, University of Pretoria; a coach and leadership development educator, coach practitioner, researcher and author.

Christine Davies is Programme Director for the Doctorate in Professional Practice programme at UWTSD, and a doctoral supervisor. An experienced education professional, she was initially a researcher in biomedical sciences, and continues to teach and promote a quantitative approach to research.

Andrea D. Ellinger recently retired as a Professor in the Department of Human Resource Development in the Soules College of Business at The University of Texas at Tyler where she remains affiliated. Her research interests include informal learning, organisational learning and learning organisations, managerial coaching, mentoring, employee engagement, organisational change and development.

Annette Fillery-Travis is a senior academic, doctoral supervisor and coach educator with an original background as a research scientist in biophysics. She is the Head of the Wales Academy for Professional Practice and Applied Research where she works with seasoned professionals wishing to take their practice to a more flourishing and innovative level.

Juliette Koning is Professor in Organisational Studies and Director of the Research Centre for Business, Society and Global Challenges at Oxford Brookes Business School, Oxford Brookes University. She has a PhD in social anthropology and a keen interest in ethnography to understand the complexities and dynamics of 'how things work'.

Rochell R. McWhorter is an Associate Professor of Human Resource Development in the Soules College of Business at The University of Texas at Tyler. Her research interests include adult learning, virtual human resource development, virtual scenario planning, and qualitative research methods.

Liam Moore is a Learning and Development practitioner with a particular interest in coaching and mentoring. He has previously published research exploring the professional development of trainee coaches.

Roger Noon is an executive coach and independent culture change consultant. He holds a master's in executive coaching (2013) and a doctorate in coaching and mentoring (2018).

Alison Rose is a leadership development specialist and executive coach, with 20 years' experience in senior roles in organisations such as RSA, Prudential UK, Santander and BAA. In 2016 she completed her doctorate on the topic of coaching in talent development programmes.

Hany Shoukry is an honorary research associate at Oxford Brookes University. He is interested in participatory research to understand coaching from a social perspective, and to develop coaching approaches that support emancipatory development in individuals, as well as social change.

PART I

INTRODUCTION TO COACHING RESEARCH

1

Introduction

Purpose of the book

This book contributes to a growing collection of SAGE books which concern the practical challenges of doing research in a particular context. It aims to support students carrying out research projects in the field of coaching on master's and doctoral programmes which include the completion of independent research projects (MA, MSc, DProf, DCM, PhD).

While there is an extensive and mature literature in social research methods as well as excellent manuals describing how to carry out research projects, research students also experience particular difficulties applying this knowledge to their specific research projects. The existing methodology literature tends to explain approaches in ideal terms. In carrying out real research, researchers have real questions that are not answered in these textbooks. In this book we intend to outline the dimensions and challenges of researching in the field of coaching and demonstrate how researchers have engaged with them. It is about researchers sharing their practical experience of doing research.

This is why we called it *Doing Coaching Research*.

As the prevalence of coaching as a legitimate organisational and work intervention has grown, so too has the demand for a specific body of knowledge to understand the practice, its place in human endeavour, what it means to those affected by it, and how best to do it. A growing number of practitioners are now interested in extending their knowledge, skills and contribution to the field through advanced educational programmes, including those at postgraduate and doctoral level. Various such programmes at universities around the world have now been in place for around two decades, each growing out of different disciplinary roots, especially psychology, education and business, but with legitimate influences drawn also from other fields such as philosophy and sociology, and extensively from counselling and psychotherapy. We feel that doing coaching research has specific challenges and to some extent these challenges are related to the very same influences that give the field its great sense of vibrancy and opportunity. The diversity of theoretical and practice roots has presented both opportunities and challenges. On the one hand it enables a wide range of approaches, perspectives and interests expressed through research in coaching. For new researchers, moreover, the opportunities to contribute useful knowledge through their work are an exciting prospect. On the other hand, coaching research has struggled to date to establish a unique character and identity. Consequently, the reassurance of norms and standards of a disciplinary culture that may be more available to researchers in more established disciplines, are not so clear to coaching researchers.

With this in mind, we are faced with a choice of taking one of two generalised stances. Do we attempt to pin down the discipline, its precepts, its reference points in an ontological exercise to frame what could and should be done? Or do we engage with uncertainty from a more critical perspective to explore what might be there and hold open the creative opportunities of such a complex domain? It will be no surprise to learn that we feel that the most appropriate help to provide in these circumstances is to combine an explanation as best we can of the challenges that face coaching researchers, with some clear accounts of the challenges faced and negotiated by our peers in the field. It is a pragmatic and constructivist programme which is entirely in keeping with both our own philosophy of practice (see for example, Cox, 2013; Jackson and Cox, 2018) and our philosophy of coach education (see Bachkirova et al., 2017). There is some overlap here between our values and interests as coaches and our values and interests as researchers and academics. That said, we strongly believe that methods of research can be entirely independent of the methods of the coaching being investigated. Many a student, for example, has tried to argue that as emotion is ontologically subjective it cannot be researched in an objectivist manner (it seems entirely possible to us). Or, has asked us whether it is appropriate to carry out face to face interviews in an investigation into telephone coaching (again, yes, it may well be). As I commented to a colleague recently, I can study kangaroos without learning to hop (though I may be asking a different question)! Consequently (and notwithstanding that Elaine Cox has a specific interest in action research which is reflected in her contribution to Chapter 9 in Part II of the book), our approach to learning should not be taken to mean that we favour the presentation of pragmatist and constructivist research. Our intention has been to present a range of research perspectives that closely reflects the current state of diversity of coaching research agendas. In summary, we wish to make as many opportunities available as possible to researchers seeking to produce excellent work.

In this introductory chapter we set out first the structure of the book as a whole and how the parts fit together. We then discuss how research contributes to professional practice. This is an important premise for *Doing Coaching Research* in the first place. Finally, there is a short introduction to the features of the book under the heading 'How to read the book'.

The structure of the book

The book is structured in three parts. In Part I we attempt to establish a shared basis and vocabulary for the discussion of the specific application of different research strategies. The current introductory chapter, in addition to an overview of the purpose and contents of the book, includes a discussion of how research knowledge contributes to the development of professional practice. While coaching may be an interesting site for other disciplinary theorising, its uniqueness springs from the practice that it encompasses. The strong link with this practice motivates and enables research. Two further chapters deal with the theoretical foundations of research and with establishing an outline structure for the research project itself. The first of these chapters is included because we feel very strongly that the discussion of research paradigm, ontology and epistemology is presented in confusing and contradictory ways in the research literature. Perhaps reflecting the cross-disciplinarity of the coaching field, this can leave the coaching research student bewildered. An outline of the history of the paradigm argument in social research, and a comparison of some of the language used for different concepts, is intended to help the reader make sense of their own research outlook. Later chapters also refer to relevant paradigmatic, ontological and epistemological stances in the process of situating and legitimising the research approaches under discussion. We have not imposed on contributing authors a single framework or vocabulary for these discussions and they therefore reflect the diversity of terminology in the field. We intend that Chapter 2 will help the reader to develop a constructive understanding of these issues and in doing so better connect with the richness of this diversity. Chapter 3 outlines the underlying framework of the research process, identifying areas where coaching research presents particular challenges, or suggests particular ways of doing things. It will be presented in two sections. First, there is a discussion of the framing of the project (formulating a research question, developing and gaining approval for the research proposal, carrying out a literature review). Second, there is a discussion of research ethics and ethical research practice (as distinct from the professional ethics of coaching practice – in particular in relation to 'insider' research), and the mechanics of approval. This leads on to Part II: 'Research strategies'.

Part II consists of six chapters dealing with different research strategies. These chapters have been written by researchers active in using the methodological strategies they discuss. They each explore the distinctive features of the strategy, the role of the researcher, the relationship with participants, and the types of questions best handled by the particular strategies. While the theoretical frames within which the strategies sit are explained, there is an equal emphasis on the practical issues and the particular challenges of using the strategy in the context of coaching. For this reason, many of the chapters have been co-authored by recent doctoral graduates who discuss the particular challenges they experienced in their research. We see these chapters as complementary to more detailed works on the strategies themselves that can be found elsewhere. Such works will be recommended in each case.

One of the motivations for embarking on this project was the observation that while there is an infinite range of research questions, our set of established methodologies is more limited. It may seem paradoxical, therefore, that we should concentrate on a limited number of approaches. By concentrating on the strategies most frequently encountered in coaching research, however, we hope to illustrate the creativity in methodological problem-solving that advanced research demands. The creation of knowledge will always be a meeting between the researcher, the research question, the common understandings of the research community and the reality of the domain under study. For this reason, no collection will be exhaustive of all possibilities. We have therefore sought to make the selection of research strategies as useful as possible whilst keeping the collection to a reasonable length.

In Chapter 4 Teresa Carmichael and Natalie Cunningham explore the history and development of grounded theory. From the foundations established by Barney Glaser and Anselm Strauss, they explore both 'classic' and Kathy Charmaz's 'constructivist' forms of the approach. Grounded theory's strongly inductive and exploratory ethos lends itself, they argue, to the demands of investigating a domain where there is a paucity of theory. The challenges of designing and carrying out effective grounded theory are amply illustrated from the experience of the authors as researchers and research supervisors as well as with the voices of other doctoral students.

As noted by Willig (2008: 45), grounded theory was originally intended to map social processes. Its methods have been co-opted to the exploration of inner worlds, either in more or less their original form, or following Charmaz's (2014) adaptation to a constructivist foundation. In contrast, phenomenology – the central concept of Chapter 5 by Tatiana Bachkirova, Alison Rose and Roger Noon – arises from Husserl's philosophical exploration of experience. In this chapter the authors outline the assumptions behind phenomenological research, highlighting the alignment of phenomenological method to coaching practice. They describe key phenomenological research approaches in coaching. The challenges and rewards of investigating the world-as-it-is-experienced are both discussed and illustrated by Rose's investigation into coaching in high potential development programmes, and Noon's exploration of presence in coaching. The most common practice in textbooks and course materials is to differentiate phenomenological approaches at the highest level as descriptive (or transcendental) and interpretive (or hermeneutic), following the respective philosophical grounding in the thought of Husserl and Heidegger. We are reminded of this division, but Noon's account highlights the alignment of Conceptual Encounter (de Rivera, 1981) as another approach to the study of experience. The example brings into focus the paradox of knowing and not-knowing in phenomenological research.

Ethnography and autoethnography, explored in more depth in Chapter 6 by Juliette Koning and Liam Moore, engages explicitly with the researcher's relationship to the cultural context within which the research question is being explored. The impossibility of the 'view from nowhere' (Nagel, 1989) is introduced in the previous chapter, but ethnography represents perhaps the most self-conscious challenge to it, engaging explicitly and intentionally with the researcher's experience. In keeping with this ethos, the chapter is written partly as an autoethnographic vignette, bringing the challenges of research to life through Moore's account of his own investigation of being a developing coaching professional. Koning and Moore point out the greater opportunity for coaching research to be carried out in this way: an observation that resonates with ideas of professional knowledge, the practitioner-researcher and evidence-based practice that we will expand on later in this introduction.

In Chapter 7, Christine Davies and Annette Fillery-Travis explore quantitative and statistical approaches. Quantitative research presents particular problems in the coaching field that can deter researchers and students: how can an emergent, individualised, meaning-making process be both reduced to numerical descriptions and sufficiently controlled to establish reliable outcomes? In the process of outlining the principles and distinctive features of quantitative research Davies and Fillery-Travis highlight the kinds of questions to which the approach is well suited. What the researcher has chosen not to do can be as significant a part of the rationale for their approach as any other argument. Not only should this chapter enable and encourage researchers to engage with this type of research for its own strengths and advantages, it also provides an important insight for researchers following different methods.

The research strategies explored in the final two chapters of Part II stand in our view slightly apart from the preceding chapters. Both case study and action research might be carried out in any number of ways, incorporating methods of data collection and analysis associated with the full range of other methodologies. We often encourage our students to think of case study and action research as frames rather than methodologies: case study characterised by its framing of the unit of analysis; action research characterised by its conceptualisation of knowledge as embedded in practice. While both invite the consideration of mixed methods, it is not a necessary strategy for either.

In the first of these chapters – Chapter 8 – Andrea Ellinger and Rochell McWhorter undertake a careful articulation of what constitutes case study. They highlight important considerations in relation to the validity and power of case-based research, including a mixed reputation arising from an erroneous association with the anecdotal reporting of practice cases. They outline the different contribution of realist, relativist and interpretivist modes of inquiry within the frame of case-based research and describe specific examples of how case studies have contributed to our understanding of the discipline. Similar to the previous chapter, this chapter is a valuable resource for any researcher to understand the value of small-n research, even if they are not choosing to pursue such a strategy themselves.

In Chapter 9, Elaine Cox, Hany Shoukry and Janice Cook explore the particular relevance of action research for investigation of practice. Action research in its many various forms represents a break from other research approaches in its pragmatic commitment to *working with* the processes of interest, rather than *looking at* them. Morgan's (2007) position on pragmatism and paradigm is discussed in Chapter 2 ('Theoretical foundations of research'). Rather than positing pragmatism as an additional research paradigm, Morgan argues that a pragmatist stance, following the great figures of Dewey, Peirce and James, rejects the very premise of anchoring paradigm in epistemology and ontology. In Chapter 9, Cox, Shoukry and Cook extend the pragmatist premise. Through the analysis of specific examples of coaching research, the authors have re-cast different approaches to action research according to the dimensions of collaboration and theory-building in the particular project. This in turn opens up the possibility of an emancipatory, *critical* action research, which is also illustrated from research practice. This version of the discussion has been rewritten for this collection by the first two authors and builds on work undertaken previously by Cox and Cook (2010, 2016). Janice Cook sadly died in 2017. Her contribution to the field of coaching and action research is greatly appreciated and is still very much evident in the chapter.

In Part III we return to more general topics of coaching research. Where in Part I we looked at the premises and planning of research, here we look at the impact of research.

First, in Chapter 10, we look at its impact on researchers themselves. We have gathered first-hand accounts of how doctoral students have made sense of their experience as researchers. This has helped uncover the ways in which this experience and the knowledge and personal development gained through their studies have affected their practice, their engagement with the discipline and their identity as practitioners.

Finally, in Chapter 11, we return to the theme of impact that we will expand in the following section of this introduction. Now in the light of the collective experience recorded in the various accounts in the book, we return to the question of how researchers might disseminate the knowledge created through the research process and how practitioners might use research in their practice: how do we make research matter?

The role of research knowledge in the development of professional practice

Many readers of this book will be practitioners coming to coaching research for possibly the first time. They may be familiar with the term evidence-based practice. Certainly, they want to be trusted to do the best possible professional work with their clients. In this section, we explain the value of research to coaches and the coaching profession. We begin by highlighting discourses such as professionalisation and professionalism, and the role of professional bodies, moving on to discuss the importance of evidence-based practice and the concept of the practitioner-researcher.

Professionalisation, professionalism and the coaching professional

The process of professionalisation traditionally involves pursuing, developing and maintaining the particularity of an occupational group, in order to protect occupational self-interest in terms of jurisdiction, status, power and salary.

Thus, scholars of professionalism define it as a set of externally set boundaries – Evans, for example, suggests: 'professionalism may be interpreted as what is effectively a representation of a service level agreement, imposed from above' (2008: 4). This idea was earlier illustrated by Carr (2000), who described professionalism as the provision of an important public service, the existence of theoretical and practical expertise, an ethical code of practice, a regulatory organisation, but with a significant degree of autonomy for individuals.

However, this interpretation has shifted recently as various groups critique the notion of a profession. According to Evetts (2011: 3), *professionalisation* continues to be an important consideration for newly emerging occupations which, she says, are 'perhaps seeking status and recognition for the importance of the work, often by standardization of the education, training and qualification for practice'. However, contrasting with the discourse of professionalisation is the idea, or ideology, of *professionalism* where dedicated service and autonomous decision making provide an appeal (Evetts, 2011). According to Evetts, the notion of service and autonomy are 'what make professionalism attractive to aspiring occupational groups'. She argues that when discourse is 'constructed "from above", then often it is imposed and a false or selective discourse, because autonomy and occupational control of the work are seldom included'. The discourse of professionalism on the other hand is welcomed by the occupational group: 'It is a powerful ideology and the idea of becoming and being a "professional worker" has appealed to many new and existing occupational groups particularly during the second half of the twentieth century (e.g. social work and social care occupations throughout Europe and North America)' (Evetts, 2011: 6).

In relation to coaching, Lane (2010: 158) describes how, due to the growing demand for coaching in all sectors, 'both consumers and educators of coaching have been advocating the professionalisation of the industry to ensure the quality of coaching services'. Lane follows Spence in outlining the features of a profession which include: 'formal academic qualifications; adherence to an enforceable code of ethics; practice licensed only to qualified members; compliance with applicable state-sanctioned regulation; and a common body of knowledge and skills' (Spence, 2007: 261). It follows that if, as coaches, we want to be considered professional, then a well-researched theoretical understanding of the body of knowledge that underpins coaching is important and this would usually be acquired through qualifications and some form of recognition or accreditation by a professional body.

Lane et al. (2018) also confirm how over the last few decades the idea of a profession has become 'fragile'. They say the main reason for this is the loss of monopoly of knowledge by any particular profession or group of professionals. This is particularly evident in the field of coaching where knowledge has become something that has evolved through communities of practice. Lane et al. have pointed out that knowledge is not fixed or stable, but it is contextualised and relational: 'knowledge is democratized by being accessible through channels open to everybody, mainly through the internet. In that sense there is no profession that has exclusive ownership over the knowledge base in specific areas of expertise' (Lane et al., 2018: 419).

The word 'professional' has traditionally been used to denote people in occupations such as the law or medicine. However, Evans suggests the criteria for being a professional have now shifted. Professionalism within any profession may be viewed primarily as incorporating a range of 'professionality orientations' which underpin 'outlook, attitudes, values, ideologies and approaches to the job' (2008: 9). This suggests that the homogeneity and consensus that were seen to be essential to professionalism have become less justifiable.

This emphasis on orientation is evident in the coaching field itself. Ellinger and Kim (2014) refer consistently to coaches as professionals. For example, they suggest that coaching can be delivered by 'coaches who work in the organization as either line managers or human resource professionals (internal coaches) or by professional coaches/consultants brought in from the outside (external coaches)' (2014: 131). Gray et al. also write about the use of external professional coaches, arguing that coaching 'is becoming one of the fastest growing interventions in the professional development of managers' (Gray et al., 2011: 863).

Referring to professionalism in a wider sense, Evans (2008) raises the question of how we ought to evaluate professions. If we can no longer assess on the basis of how long it takes to qualify or the level of difficulty of training, Evans suggests the introduction of 'developmentalism' as a concept: the natural development that forms the basis of professional practice. This commitment to self-development she suggests ought to be the new criterion for professional quality. Practitioners will need to be analytical and self-critical in evaluating their own practice, problematising all aspects of practice, through intensive reflection: 'The developmentalist individual is likely to be predisposed towards perfectionism and to strive continually for excellence, according to her/his own definition and measurement of it' (Evans, 2008: 4). This approach to professional practice would seem to sit well with coaching. Bachkirova et al. (2017) have further articulated how a developmentalist approach can be taken to coach education.

Lane et al. (2018) suggest that although the practice of coaching is widespread, its recognition as a profession is contentious, despite the growing awareness of the benefits to the industry of professional status. Similarly, Bennett (2006: 241) had earlier argued that coaching could not be described as a profession because of crucial gaps in the criteria: no generally accepted, identifiable and distinct skills for coaches; specific training/education not required before someone can practise as a coach; the public and related professions do not recognise coaching as a profession; no established community of practitioners; and a lack of theory on which coaches can base their practice.

However, Palmer and McDowall (2010) consider that coaching, at least in the UK, already meets the criteria for being a profession. They point out that we have:

national and international professional bodies providing members with codes of ethics and practice, supervision recommended for practitioners, national and international registers of practitioners, accreditation and certification of courses and practitioners, professional qualifications such as membership grades, university or exam board accredited courses, peer reviewed academic and practitioner journals abstracted in psychological databases such as psycINFO, and in some countries such as the United Kingdom, they have National Occupational Standards developed by national training organisations. (2010: xiv)

The role of professional bodies

A number of professional bodies have emerged to support the growing coaching profession, each following the requirements of professionalisation by providing members with codes of practice and codes of ethics as well as the usual member benefits. These bodies also support research in various ways. The European Mentoring and Coaching Council (EMCC) for instance support an annual research conference and a research journal in order to encourage members to undertake research. The International Coaching Federation (ICF) also have a research focus. Their website claims research enables coaches to 'separate fact from fiction, reach sharper conclusions and ultimately make better decisions' and they have a separate research portal which provides access to a wide range of coaching research and resources (https://coachfederation.org/research).

The International Coaching Research Forum (ICRF), which is now part of the Research Division at the Institute of Coaching (IOC) at Harvard McLean, aims to promote the value of research, critical self-reflective practice and the development of a coaching knowledge base. In 2008, the ICRF generated 100 exemplar research proposals through a multi-disciplinary forum of coaching experts from across global regions, disciplines, roles and perspectives. Since that time researchers have continued to use the proposals as a guide for informing and framing research topics. The IOC itself now sponsors and funds coaching research at academic and practitioner levels.

Bachkirova and Smith highlight how 'Without the active contribution of researchers and conceptual thinkers professional bodies risk developing policies and procedures based on the old paradigms of knowledge unchallenged by current thinking' (2015: 131).

Building the profession through practitioner research

Belli (2010) explains how over the last forty years there has been increasing recognition of the gap between research and practice across a significant range of disciplines. Belli suggests that the cause is a dichotomy between two cultures. 'On one side are the researchers, intent on the rigors of sound academic research but divorced from the ongoing concerns of practice, and who are dismayed about the fact that practitioners are not reading or using their research results. On the other side are the practitioners, concerned with relevance in terms of bettering their practice but not interested in theoretical reasoning, and who claim that research results do not address existing problems and practical needs' (2010: 2). This situation is very obvious in the coaching field where practitioners could be described as action-oriented. Kotte et al.

(2017) argue that we need to pay attention to the inherent logic of the two systems of practice and research in the area of coaching so that we begin to understand the relationship between these two worlds and identify how to develop a way of working between practice and research that benefits coaching research. This is discussed further below.

What it means to be a practitioner-researcher

We would argue that there are (at least) two types of research active coaches. The first is the researcher-practitioner, who uses evidence-based coaching to underpin and inform his/her practice. The second is the practitioner-researcher, who undertakes research on his/her practice to examine aspects of that practice and inform others.

According to Cox and Ledgerwood (2003: 1) 'evidence-based' practice is not just trendy educational jargon: 'It is an approach which claims that practice should be capable of being justified in terms of sound evidence: it is the process of methodically searching out, evaluating, and utilising up-to-date research findings to support decisions about practice. It is only by grounding the practice of coaching and mentoring in this way that the necessary credibility will be achieved.' Garvey similarly defines evidence-based coaching as 'an approach to coaching that emphasis [emphases] the importance of only using approaches and techniques that are validated by research and that are grounded in empirical data' (2011: 66). *Researcher-practitioners*, then, use the skills of evidence-based practice to ensure a professional approach to their coaching work.

Like other practice-driven areas such as education or nursing, much coaching research is conducted by *practitioner-researchers*. Practitioner-researchers have agency over their own research agenda, unlike some professional researchers in academic institutions and, as Kemmis et al. (2014: 180) explain, they are required to engage in 'systematic self-critical inquiry that is *publically shared*' (our emphasis). Kemmis et al. cite Lawrence Stenhouse's (1979: 7) definition of research as 'systematic enquiry made public' and elaborate on this as follows:

> Research practices are consciously undertaken, identifiable, deliberate, planned, data driven, analytical, interpretive, oriented towards reflection and action, and directed towards communication with others (including a range of people from peers in a setting to researchers in a discipline or professional field). (Kemmis et al., 2014: 180)

Recently, Van Veggel (2017: 7) has discussed the narrow and exclusionary view of what constitutes evidence and highlights another interpretation that takes account of interactions between research evidence and practitioner-generated evidence. Van Veggel supports the argument that *all* evidence-based material, regardless of source, 'may be included if found trustworthy and relevant' but highlights how positivistic research is frequently valued above phenomenological research, which we would argue limits the impact of evidence-based research. The methodology for evidence-based research depends on the question being asked, the context and the practical outcome.

Fillery-Travis and Cox (2014) have discussed how coaching research has lagged behind practice but that coaching research is maturing and so becoming more authoritative on topics such as coaching effectiveness. This is good for practitioners. They point out that 'maintaining the dialogue between practice and research is critical to producing a robust body of evidence' and cite the growing number of coaching journals that publish practitioner-based research and which are 'excellent sources of evidence-based practice' (Fillery-Travis and Cox, 2014: 454).

Fillery-Travis and Cox (2014) also identified a number of important areas for future coaching research suggesting that research should not be an end in itself, but a way of constructing the evidence base for practice. They concluded that: 'Getting to grips with such a range of variables to study coaching is a mighty task and one that requires a range of methodological approaches' (2014: 455).

How to read the book

We said earlier that our aim is to support students carrying out research projects in the field of coaching on master's and doctoral programmes which include the completion of independent research projects. Though we have presented the material in what we think is a logical order, we do not imagine for a moment that what someone in this position needs is another thick volume that they must read cover to cover. Each of the chapters does stand in its own right. In particular, readers may wish to focus on the chapters in Part II which deal with strategies closest to their methodological choices. Each of these chapters has been presented with some features in common. You will find a general structure of the narrative (an introduction, distinctive features of the approach, practical issues and evaluation). In each chapter there will be suggestions for further reading as well as questions for discussion and reflection. These section headings may be useful to the reader looking to compare quickly different strategies. The researcher looking to follow one of these specific strategies is strongly urged to consult with the specialised literature in the area. We have intended to give you *different* insights than the ones available elsewhere. By the same token, this implies that you should not rely on these chapters to replace more in-depth descriptions of methodologies and their procedures. They should serve as a useful introduction.

We have also highlighted wherever possible three aspects of the description of each strategy. These we have labelled 'key concepts', 'doing coaching research', and 'case studies'. The 'key concept' boxes introduce important foundations such as definitions or descriptions of purpose. They may often be in the form of brief quotations from significant contributors to the field. In the 'doing research' boxes, we have provided short vignettes illustrating researcher challenges. Where a longer account of doing coaching research has been useful, we have used the heading 'case study'.

We hope these will help readers to orient themselves quickly within the respective chapter.

We would encourage less experienced researchers to read Chapters 2 and 3 in their first year of study. Not all institutions or examiners insist on a discussion of paradigm; where it is the normal expectation we feel that Chapter 2 will serve as very useful orientation. Where it is not the normal expectation we still feel that researchers should be self-aware and reflexive with regard to the generation of knowledge, so it is recommended all the same. We have tested the main content with both doctoral and general research audiences for whom it has proved useful. Chapter 3 is a very useful outline of the research project as a whole and will support researchers' planning early in the process.

Despite sitting at the end of the collection, Chapters 10 and 11 may be useful to practitioners and aspiring and active researchers at any time. We are very aware of how the pursuit of an individual research programme can demand a lot of the researcher's personal resilience. It may be a useful resource to be reminded of the importance and value of the project. Chapter 10 may also give prospective doctoral students a useful insight into the rewards of advanced study, while Chapter 11 is just as relevant to practitioners as it is to researchers.

Most of all our aim is to inform and enable. We would be delighted to hear from readers with their stories of where this has been achieved and how.

References

Bachkirova, T., Jackson, P., Gannon, J., Iordanou, I. and Myers, A. (2017). 'Re-conceptualising coach education from the perspectives of pragmatism and constructivism'. *Philosophy of Coaching: An International Journal* 2 (2): 29–50.

Bachkirova, T. and Smith, C. L. (2015). 'From competencies to capabilities in the assessment and accreditation of coaches'. *International Journal of Evidence Based Coaching and Mentoring* 13 (2): 123–40.

Belli, G. (2010, July). 'Bridging the researcher-practitioner gap: Views from different fields'. ICOTS8 Invited Paper. In C. Reading (ed.), *Data and Context in Statistics Education: Towards an Evidence-Based Society*. Proceedings of the 8th International Conference on Teaching Statistics (ICOTS 8), pp. 11–16.

Bennett, J. L. (2006). 'An agenda for coaching-related research: A challenge for researchers'. *Consulting Psychology Journal: Practice and Research* 58 (4): 240–49.

Carr, D. (2000). *Professionalism and Ethics in Teaching*. London: Routledge.

Charmaz, K. (2014). *Constructing Grounded Theory: A Practical Guide through Qualitative Analysis* (2nd edition). London: Sage Publications.

Cox, E. (2013). *Coaching Understood: A Pragmatic Enquiry into the Coaching Process*. London: Sage Publications.

Cox, E. and Cook, J. (2010, May). 'Action research as a strategy for researching coaching and mentoring'. Paper presented at the 4th Annual EMCC UK Coaching and Mentoring Conference, London.

Cox, E. and Cook, J. (2016, June). 'Action research: Four directions for developing evidence-based coaching practice'. Paper presented at the International Research Conference, Faculty of Business, Oxford Brookes University.

Cox, E. and Ledgerwood, G. (2003). 'Editorial: The new profession'. *International Journal of Evidence Based Coaching and Mentoring* 1 (1). Available at: https://radar.brookes.ac.uk/radar/items/ce783bb6-e49e-478c-aee8-b9a1c1bdd466/1/ (accessed 1 February 2018).

De Rivera, J. (1981). *Conceptual Encounter: A Method for the Exploration of Human Experience*. Washington, DC: University Press of America.

Ellinger, A.D. and Kim, S. (2014). 'Coaching and human resource development: Examining relevant theories, coaching genres, and scales to advance research and practice'. *Advances in Developing Human Resources* 16 (2): 127–38.

Evans, L. (2008). 'Professionalism, professionality and the development of education professionals'. *British Journal of Educational Studies* 56 (1): 20–38.

Evetts, J. (2011). 'Sociological analysis of professionalism: Past, present and future'. *Comparative Sociology* 10 (1): 1–37.

Fillery-Travis, A. and Cox, E. (2014). 'Researching coaching'. In E. Cox, T. Bachkirova and D. Clutterbuck (eds), *The Complete Handbook of Coaching* (2nd edition). London: Sage Publications, pp. 445–59.

Garvey, B. (2011). 'Researching coaching: An eclectic mix or common ground? A critical perspective'. In R. Wegener, A. Fritze and M. Loebbert (eds), *Coaching entwickeln. Forschung und Praxis im Dialog*. Wiesbaden: VS Research, pp. 65–76.

Gray, D. E., Ekinci, Y., & Goregaokar, H. (2011). 'Coaching SME managers: Business development or personal therapy? A mixed methods study'. *The International Journal of Human Resource Management* 22 (4): 863–82.

Jackson, P. and Cox, E. (2018). 'Developmental coaching'. In E. Cox, T. Bachkirova and D. Clutterbuck (eds), *The Complete Handbook of Coaching* (3rd edition). London: Sage Publications, pp. 215–30.

Kemmis, S., Wilkinson, J., Edwards-Groves, C., Hardy, I., Grootenboer, P. and Bristol, L. (2014). *Changing Practices, Changing Education*. Singapore: Springer Science & Business Media.

Kotte, S., Oellerich, K., Hinn, D.E. and Möller, H. (2017). 'The ambivalent relationship between coaching research and coaching practice: Discreetly ignoring, critically observing or beneficially cooperating?' In A. Schreyögg and C. Schmidt-Lellek (eds), *The Professionalization of Coaching*. Wiesbaden: Springer, pp. 23–45.

Lane, D.A. (2010). 'Coaching in the UK: An introduction to some key debates'. *Coaching: An International Journal of Theory, Research and Practice* 3 (2): 155–66.

Lane, D.A., Stelter, R. and Stout-Rostron, S. (2018). 'The future of coaching as a profession'. In E. Cox, T. Bachkirova and D. Clutterbuck (eds), *The Complete Handbook of Coaching* (3rd edition). London: Sage Publications, pp. 357–68.

Morgan, D.L. (2007). 'Paradigms lost and pragmatism regained: Methodological implications of combining qualitative and quantitative methods'. *Journal of Mixed Methods Research* 1 (1): 48–76.

Nagel, T. (1989). *The View from Nowhere*. New York: Oxford University Press.

Palmer, S. and McDowall, A. (eds) (2010). *The Coaching Relationship: Putting People First*. London: Routledge.

Spence, G.B. (2007). 'Further development of evidence-based coaching: Lessons from the rise and fall of the human potential movement'. *Australian Psychologist* 42 (4): 255–65.

Stenhouse, L. (1979). 'The problem of standards in illuminative research'. *Scottish Educational Review* 11 (1): 5–10.

Van Veggel, N. (2017). 'Evidence-based professionalism in small specialist HE course management: Reflexive thoughts on ongoing research'. *WBL e-journal international* 7 (1).

Willig, C. (2008). *Introducing Qualitative Research in Psychology: Adventures in Theory and Method* (2nd edition). Maidenhead: Open University Press.

2

Theoretical foundations of research

Peter Jackson

Introduction

Postgraduate and research students in applied social disciplines are often required to examine and explain their epistemological and ontological positions underpinning their research strategy. As a tutor, I have found myself working with students who have produced a whole range of responses to this requirement in the methodology chapter of dissertations and theses. Some of these responses are excellent, some are cursory, some are inquiring and some are conventional. There is a lot to think about in creating your own research outputs for the first time and many students find it easier to deal with the more concrete problems such as data collection and analysis. Generally, people find it hard to discuss ontology and epistemology and hard to make them relevant to their research process.

This chapter explores the value of such discussions and also seeks to make the task of discussing methodology at the theoretical level both easier and more productive.

In order to do this I intend to

- Highlight the role of theoretical thinking in the construction of research.
- Clarify various uses of key terms such as ontology, epistemology and paradigm, and how these are described in the research methods literature.
- Present a brief recent history of the use of these concepts in research, including some points where there is disagreement between different perspectives.
- Identify some debates and anomalies that confound attempts to describe theoretical foundations effectively.

The sections that follow are presented in this order.

In this chapter I make only brief mention of the meaning of different philosophical stances, doing so where it is necessary in order to progress the argument. General methodology texts such as those cited in this chapter, amply provide more specific guidance and, in turn, refer to more specialised texts that provide comprehensive treatment of the theories concerned.

The role of theoretical thinking in the construction of research

As outlined in Chapter 1, this book is aimed at researchers relatively early in their research career, particularly those looking at issues in the field of coaching. You may be undertaking a research project as a 'capstone' stage of a master's-level qualification, working on a doctoral thesis, or perhaps undertaking research outside of a formal qualification as part of your own practice development. For people in this situation, there are three main reasons to think about the theoretical underpinnings of research, though there may be a slightly different emphasis for different people depending on their rationale for undertaking the research in the first place. Those three reasons to think about theoretical underpinnings relate to:

- The *legitimacy* of knowledge claims.
- Criteria for understanding the *quality* of the research.
- Demonstrating *mastery* of research as an activity in its own right.

These criteria are important because they relate very directly to the principle of research supporting practice. As regards this overall objective, it follows that knowledge becomes useful when it emerges from the private space into some kind of shared space. Such sharing also implies some form of negotiation or agreement around what constitutes knowledge: about what is 'good' knowledge, and what its limitations are. Without this scrutiny, a knowledge claim is no more than a personal belief. And when it comes to advanced study (and the commitments and sacrifices that often entails), why would we want to plough on into a research process without knowing what counts?

However, an intention to examine our theoretical foundations is not necessarily a call to work from first principles on every occasion. There are a certain number of textbook (or cook book) approaches to these questions that represent a distillation of a research community's approach. This can be a useful shortcut for the novice researcher. For some purposes, it is quite reasonable to pick up an established recipe and to follow its instructions. Some institutions and some disciplines might teach in this way, specifying on the students' behalf what constitutes a reasonable strategy and what would conform or not conform to the standards of that strategy. (I have completed such a programme myself as a student.) These standards may also be very widely agreed. Indeed, many published research papers leave their discussion of methodology at quite a practical level precisely because there is a wide consensus around a particular strategy. However, not only is it a reasonable expectation of many programmes that postgraduate (particularly doctoral) researchers should develop more insight into the research process, but it is also the case that the same insight will help the researcher address the methodological problems that often crop up in the course of producing research. As noted in Chapter 1 to this volume, the discussions in Part II outline some of the issues that do crop up in the course of producing research; in many cases it is precisely an understanding of the basic assumptions of the particular research strategy that has enabled the researcher to overcome problems when they have arisen.

Confusingly, different research communities have formulated the characteristics of legitimate knowledge in slightly different ways, reflecting different areas of interest as well as fundamental philosophical tenets. The research strategies outlined in Part II of this book reflect some of those different formulations: ethnography, for example, is associated with an interest in meaning through social interaction; phenomenology is more interested in understanding the immediate lived experience of individuals; natural science-influenced approaches using quantitative techniques are interested in what can be understood as the most probable causal relationship between different regular events, characteristics and phenomena. So such strategies represent a pairing of theoretical underpinnings on what constitutes knowledge, along with specified ways of producing knowledge that conform to those theoretical underpinnings. The work these communities have already put in place for researchers, therefore, can be seen as immensely powerful, providing some of the 'recipes' mentioned earlier. They can also create naïve adherence to methodological authority, as well as some rather fixed attitudes and misunderstandings of other communities (the so-called 'paradigm wars'). We would like students and researchers to use the body of methodological work constructively and critically and we believe that this both enhances research and renders entrenched methodological positions unnecessary.

Elements of the theoretical landscape (and their nomenclature)

One of the most confusing things about exploring the theoretical underpinnings of social research is that there are so many different terms used and different writers have historically used them in different ways. For example, does the term 'realism' refer to an ontological position (answer: it can do), or a paradigm (again, it can do)? What then does realism contrast with? It might be 'anti-realism' (e.g. Searle, 1995), idealism (e.g. Howell, 2013) or relativism (e.g. Guba and Lincoln, 1994) depending on how each of these terms are understood.

It seems useful at this stage to set out some of these possibilities so that researchers can make an informed choice. I will return to some of the debates and controversies about the use of these terms in a later section of this chapter.

These discussions regularly rely on the following key terms which I will define briefly first, and then return to in relation to social research:

1. Ontology – ontology is 'The branch of metaphysics dealing with the nature of being' (*Oxford Dictionaries | English*, n.d.), or 'the study of what things exist' (Effingham, 2013: 1). The essential ontological question is 'what exists?'

2. Epistemology – in contrast to ontology, epistemology is 'The theory of knowledge, especially with regard to its methods, validity, and scope, and the distinction between justified belief and opinion' (*Oxford Dictionaries | English*, n.d.). The essential epistemological question is 'how do we know?'

3. Paradigm – the term research paradigm is sometimes used to describe, 'overarching philosophical systems denoting particular ontologies, epistemologies, and methodologies' (Denzin and Lincoln, 2013: 11). The essential question for paradigm is 'what kind of research do we do?'

4. Methodology – methodology refers to the broad collection of methods and principles inherent in particular research approaches or strategies. Crotty (1998: 3) calls methodologies, 'research designs that guide a researcher in choosing methods and shape the use of the methods chosen'. There is variation in the extent to which particular methodologies emphasise underlying principles as against the actual techniques used. Hence we come across questions in discussion forums asking, 'is such and such an approach a methodology or a paradigm?' The boundaries may be porous, but it is reasonable to say that it is more than just a method.

5. Methods – methods are the things the researcher ultimately does to create knowledge from their engagement with the world (such as interviewing, or measuring, or using statistical tests on data). Methods may pertain primarily to how data is collected, or how it is analysed.

These concepts can be seen as building blocks progressing from the theoretical foundations of research to the actions to be taken. Some elements are open to debate, and different writers on methodology populate this framework using different terms and sometimes different concepts. I will describe some of these variations after an outline of the concept of paradigm, which has become quite pivotal in thinking about methodology.

The development of the concept of research paradigms

The discussion of the theoretical foundations of research in theses and in other reports tends to centre around the research paradigm; the idea of paradigm is often used as an agglomeration of ontology, epistemology and methodology. A review of the development of the concept of paradigm in research will be helpful in setting a clearer framework for researchers' decision making about how they address the issue. It also opens the possibility (to be discussed in the following section) that the construct of paradigm itself can, and perhaps should, be problematised.

The idea of research paradigms became an issue of debate in the late twentieth century as researchers sought to legitimise approaches to social research that did not rely on dominant assumptions that surround the scientific method. In particular, Lincoln and Guba (1985) adopted the term to present such research from the perspective of its own frame of reference, rather than as something that did not meet the strictures of 'science'. The term itself is drawn from Kuhn's (1962) *The Structure of Scientific Revolutions.* Kuhn argued that the work of science takes place in a framework of consensus about fundamental principles (paradigm). However, scientific advancement proceeds in discontinuous ways, with incremental change progressing within the paradigm, alternating with more radical jumps. Such jumps occur when, through an accident of evidence or imagination, the existing framework of understanding is shattered. The result is scientific 'revolutions', 'the tradition shattering complements to the tradition-bound activity of normal science' (Kuhn, 2012: 6). At this point, the paradigm changes. Imagine the impact of the Copernican revolution, relativity and quantum theory: these are points where scientific revolution changes the paradigm.

Lincoln and Guba (1985) use Kuhn's concept of paradigm, not to describe a shift in the state of a discipline, but as way of legitimising the possibility of different worldviews. They presented an extensive critique of positivism and post-positivism – the dominant paradigm of natural science – and formulated alternative principles to guide the kind of social research they were interested in. They labelled this alternative paradigm, 'naturalist'. By contrasting attitudes to key issues such as the neutrality of the observer, generalisability, causality, and the presence or absence of theory in observation, Lincoln and Guba constructed an alternative set of qualities and criteria for creating knowledge about human behaviour in its natural setting.

In later work Guba and Lincoln (1994) formalised a systematic description of the features of the research paradigm. Here they argued that paradigms can be differentiated by their adherence to particular theories of existence and reality (ontology), to theories of knowledge and truth (epistemology), and their position on questions of how best this knowledge/world should be explored (methodology). Although the term 'constructivism' only appears in passing in Lincoln and Guba (1985), in their later work it is the preferred label for the naturalist paradigm. Now, between positivism and constructivism at opposite ends of their table, Guba and Lincoln placed post-positivism and critical realism. The terms they used to describe ontologies and epistemologies are set out in Table 2.1.

Table 2.1 Competing ontological, epistemological and methodological positions according to Guba and Lincoln (1994)

	Positivism	**Post-positivism**	**Critical theory***	**Constructivism**
Ontology	Naïve realism; objective external reality	Critical realism; objective reality which can be apprehended only imperfectly	Historical realism; a reality 'consisting of historically situated structures that are … as limiting and confining as if they were real' (p. 111)	Relativism; 'multiple, apprehendable, and sometimes conflicting, social realities' (p. 111)
Epistemology	Dualist, objectivist	Modified dualist, objectivist, embracing the uncertainty of apprehension	Transactional/ subjectivist; 'knowledge is value-mediated and hence value dependent' (p. 111)	Broader transactional/ subjectivist; knowledge 'created in interaction among investigator and respondents' (p. 111)
Methodology	Experimental; verification of hypotheses	Modified experimental; falsification of hypotheses	Dialogic/ dialectical; reconstruction of constructions	Hermeneutic/ dialectical; reconstruction of constructions

*In full, Lincoln and Guba label this category 'Critical theory and related ideological positions'.

More recently, Lincoln, Lynham and Guba (2018) have identified the growth of a number of different interests that might sit within the 'critical theory' column (such as feminist studies and queer theory) as well as further alternatives to positivism and post-positivism, adding participatory research to their table. The comparison in this later edition has become extensive and the elaboration of the different positions more descriptive. At the high level, the differentiation along ontological, epistemological and methodological lines remains essentially the same. The descriptions of positions relating to participatory research generally reflect a stance of co-creation and co-construction.

If the three versions of the discussion of paradigm that have been outlined here, give something of the sense of how ontology and epistemology are related to paradigm, it should also be noted that they also express something more than simply a choice or preference. Rather than a linear, hierarchical relationship, methodological, epistemological and ontological questions can be seen as a kind of system, located around the nexus of key characteristics of the research. I referred earlier to key issues discussed in

Lincoln and Guba (1985) such as the neutrality of the observer, generalisability, causality, and the presence or absence of theory in observation. By exploring these issues the authors are able to assert other important characteristics of paradigm (focusing in their argument in this case on naturalist research). Therefore:

> N (the naturalist) elects to carry out research in the natural setting or context of the entity for which study is proposed because naturalistic ontology suggests that realities are wholes that cannot be understood in isolation from their contexts. (Lincoln and Guba, 1985: 39)

With respect to the role of the researcher:

> N elects to use him- or herself as well as other humans in the primary data-gathering instruments ... because it would be virtually impossible to devise a priori a non-human instrument with sufficient adaptability to encompass and adjust to the variety of realities that will be encountered. (Lincoln and Guba, 1985: 39)

Key debates and differences

The brief history above sets out the logic of the concept of paradigm. However, on closer inspection, a number of complexities arise for developing researchers. Firstly, reading more widely, we come across a large number of different terms used to describe different elements of the paradigm, including labels for the paradigms themselves. Some terms overlap; some terms are used in conflicting ways or with conflicting meanings. I will outline, in turn, how different terms are used to describe ontology, epistemology and paradigms. I will then outline questions raised about the structure of 'paradigm' itself. Finally, there is an important debate, specifically from a pragmatist perspective, that the concept of paradigm is not itself useful. It is important to set out these complexities to help avoid the risk of picking up parts of arguments, or idiosyncratic uses of terminology which confuse the researcher and their readers.

The use of terms in methodological literature to describe ontologies

Methodology literature presents to readers a confusing array of terminology. It would do well to establish what is meant by different authors in their use of particular terminology to describe differences of approach. Let us deal first with ontology.

Table 2.1 offers the terminology used by Guba and Lincoln (1994) with some indication of their meaning. Bryman (2015: 29) echoes these essential positions contrasting, in his section on ontology, 'objectivism' on the one hand, with now 'constructionism' on the other. Bryman says that objectivism 'implies that social phenomena confront us as external facts that are beyond our reach and influence' while constructionism, 'asserts that social phenomena and their meanings are continually being accomplished by social actors', noting that this position is 'often also referred to as constructivism' (Bryman, 2015: 29).

Howell discusses the problem of reality with reference to historical positions in Western European philosophy. Adopting the terms more commonly used in philosophy, Howell outlines that, after Hume, 'realism identified that the object existed without the subject' (Howell, 2013: 5), while, drawing more from Kant and Schopenhauer, idealism considers 'the world and mind to be intrinsically linked' (Howell, 2013: 4). It is important to note that this explanation of idealism does not imply a full blown relativism whereby every individual lives in a world of their own mental projection. Such a position has severe limitations and contradictions for the researcher in any case. Johnson and Duberley (2000: 150) argue that, 'Relativism may well have the laudable aim of opposing positivists' naïvely objectivist epistemology, but the resultant sceptical alternative is devoid of any possible grounds for critique or intervention.' For the time being, let us take idealism as at least allowing for the existence of 'things' in the mind rather than a more encompassing position that things are *only* in the mind.

Another strong influence on the way terms are used is the early work of Burrell and Morgan (1979) who use the terms realism and nominalism (where nominalism refers to the structuring of reality through language) and of Morgan and Smircich (1980). Morgan and Smircich describe six different positions along an axis of objective–subjective. At one extreme, they report 'reality as concrete structure' and the other, 'reality as a projection of human imagination'. It is helpful to note the number and progression of intervening points. These are set out in Table 2.2.

Table 2.2 Different ontological positions along an axis of objective–subjective after Morgan and Smircich (1980)

Reality as a concrete structure	Reality as a concrete process	Reality as a contextual field of information	Reality as a realm of symbolic discourse	Reality as a social construction	Reality as a projection of human imagination

A broad range of terms, then, are used to describe ontological positions (summarised in Table 2.3). Students may wonder why so many different formulations persist and which ones to use in their own work. Crotty (1998: 10–11) argues that it is because writers on methodology tend to collapse ontology into epistemology. Indeed in the examples discussed above, we might detect some elasticity in the concepts being used. For example, the idea of an 'objective external reality' (see Table 2.1) uses a term – 'objective' – which appears to relate to the apprehension of that reality (an epistemological question) rather than its existence (the ontological question). Bryman uses the term 'objectivism' as an ontological position in its own right. Crotty cites a number of such examples, and on the basis of this presents a brief but interesting argument that the ontological question can be dispensed with. This is a discussion we will return to shortly.

Table 2.3 Different terms used to describe the range of epistemological stances

Sample of terms used in ontological discussions		
Realism	Nominalism	Burrell and Morgan (1979)
Objective/concrete	Subjective/imagined	Morgan and Smircich (1980)
External/realism	Multiple/relativism	Guba and Lincoln (1994)
Objectivism	Constructionism	Bryman (2015)
Realism	Idealism	Howell (2013)

Yet despite Crotty's argument, it is possible to extract a logical structure to this variation of use of ontological terms. In order to do so, it is useful to attend to these labels ('-isms'), not necessarily as schools of thought, but as ways of referencing the nature or substance of what is real. In Table 2.4, I have extracted what might be considered the substance of each term. Hence, for example, ontological 'objectivism' can be seen to refer to reality being made of real objects rather than referencing the neutrality of the observer. The two concepts of 'object' (as substance) and 'objective' (as perspective) are closely related, and for this reason the use of 'objectivism' may be ambiguous, yet this simple analysis demonstrates its legitimacy as an ontological term.

Table 2.4 Core concepts and defining qualities referred to by ontological terms

Core substance of terms used in ontological discussions	
Material	Immaterial
Object	Construct
Real	Idea (idealism)
	Name (nominalism)
Other implicit and defining qualities	
External	Projected
Extra-mental	Imagined
Independent of experience	Bound with experience
Independent of language	Languaged

The use of terms in methodological literature to describe epistemologies

The previous discussion demonstrates an underlying problem which is reproduced in the terminology used to describe competing epistemologies in the research literature. For ease of comparison, I will refer to the same authors as previously (see Table 2.5).

Guba and Lincoln (1994) describe the epistemological positions relating to their four paradigms as ranging from 'dualist/objectivist', which expresses the possibility of understanding reality from a neutral stance, to 'transactional/ subjectivist', which expresses the dependence of knowledge on an interaction between the observer (subject) and the world. We can see here that Guba and Lincoln use different vocabulary for epistemology than they do for ontology, but at the same time, their usage seems to cross over with other authors' usage (for example Bryman's use of 'objectivist' as an ontological stance). It is also worth noting that these epistemological stances are to some extent conceptually independent of the ontological stances, though they tend to become bundled together.

Burrell and Morgan (1979) had earlier used positivism to describe a group of positions that stress causality, the incremental growth of knowledge through the testing of hypotheses, and the possibility of a neutral observer: 'Positivist epistemology is in essence based upon the traditional approaches which dominate the natural sciences' (1979: 5). These positions are opposed by 'anti-positivists' who are both engaged in the world they research and see it as an essential position in order to develop an understanding of the social world. Objectivity is not possible. Burrell and Morgan discuss this under the rubric 'the epistemological debate'.

Bryman (2015) similarly uses the term 'positivism' to describe the collection of principles that characterise natural science, similarly to Burrell and Morgan, under the heading 'Epistemological considerations'. Bryman contrasts positivism with interpretivism: 'a view that the subject matter of the social sciences – people and their institutions – is fundamentally different from that of the natural sciences', and that 'therefore requires the social scientist to grasp the subjective meaning of social action' (Bryman, 2015: 26).

Howell describes a range of different positions under the terms correspondence, coherence, pragmatic and consensus/constructivist. Correspondence theory of truth aligns to Guba and Lincoln's use of 'objectivist'. The term correspondence expresses the idea that truth and knowledge correspond with reality. By implication, knowledge claims can be tested by how well they fit, or correspond to, reality. It follows that particular notions of validity and reliability in the research context fall out of this position. A coherence theory of truth requires that 'truth, knowledge and theory fit with a coherent system' (Howell, 2013: 15). This position therefore allows for multiple legitimate conceptualisations. A pragmatic epistemology reflects the claims of pragmatic philosophers such as Dewey and Peirce who argued that knowledge claims were valid only insofar as they had the potential for impact in the world of action. Finally, according to a constructivist perspective, 'knowledge, truth, reality and theory are considered contingent and based on human perception and experience' (Howell, 2013: 16).

Morgan and Smircich (1980) plot different epistemological stances along the same objective–subjective continuum as they used to differentiate ontological stances. In their discussion, they refer to the 'objectivist view of the social world as a concrete structure' which 'implies a need to understand and map out the social structure, and gives rise to the epistemology of positivism' (1980: 493).

In opposition, they describe a 'phenomenologically oriented perspective' (1980: 493) which rejects the externality of the thing to be known and focuses rather on, 'understanding the processes through which human beings concretize their relationship to their world' (1980: 493).

Table 2.5   Different terms used to describe the range of epistemological stances

Sample of terms used in epistemological discussions		
Positivist	Anti-positivist	Burrell and Morgan (1979)
Objective/positivist	Subjective/phenomenological	Morgan and Smircich (1980)
Dualist/objectivist	Transactional/subjectivist	Guba and Lincoln (1994)
Positivist	Interpretivist	Bryman (2015)
Correspondence		Howell (2013)
→Coherence	→Pragmatic	→Constructivist

The use of terms in methodological literature to describe paradigms

I turn to descriptions of paradigms last because some of the terminology makes more sense in the light of the preceding discussions. As noted previously, Lincoln and Guba's (1985) original contrast was setting naturalistic against positivist inquiry. Guba and Lincoln (1994) preferred 'constructivism' and added post-positivism and critical theory, with Lincoln, Lynham and Guba (2018) adding different strands of critical theory and participatory research. Other authors, however, have found different divisions and used different terms.

Thomas (2013: 111) makes a similar contrast, but uses the terms positivism and interpretivism. For interpretivists, the research aim is to 'understand the particular, contributing to building a framework of "multiple realities"' identifying that the terms naturalistic, qualitative and idiographic are sometimes used 'often inaccurately' to describe different aspects of the approach. It is notable that these are the same terms, under the heading of paradigms, as those used by Bryman under the heading of epistemology. Furthermore, they are used to express largely the same idea.

Crotty (1998) does not refer to paradigm, preferring to talk about 'theoretical perspective'. Under this heading, Crotty mentions positivism, interpretivism (specifying symbolic interactionism, phenomenology and hermeneutics as subdivisions), critical inquiry, feminism and postmodernism. This inclusion of postmodernism by Crotty is significant in that he associates it with a subjectivist rather than constructionist epistemology. He differentiates these with reference to the object: construction implies that the subject makes sense through their relationship with the object; subjectivism denies the engagement with any external object. Hence, in this model, postmodernist approaches are more interested in how people create social objects rather than how they make meaning of them.

Saunders, Lewis and Thornhill (2015) use the term 'paradigm' for a different purpose, but describe five 'major philosophies' consisting of positivism, critical realism, interpretivism, postmodernism and pragmatism. Critical realism is not the same as the critical inquiry delineated by Crotty, or critical theory in the earlier frameworks of Lincoln and Guba (and later editions). Critical theory is a perspective that highlights power and its maintenance. In this sense 'critical' research may seek to enable the emancipation of those seen as oppressed. It may take a strong interest in discourses as a mechanism of power (overlapping with some postmodernist research) or in the ways communities make sense of the world (overlapping with social constructionist research). In critical realism, it is the realism rather than the structure of society that is effectively questioned. Critical realism represents a stance that accepts a realist ontology, but questions the possibility of an objective experience of it. Thus the 'objectivity' of ontology and epistemology are delinked. As Searle (1995: 165) puts it, 'The fact that alternative conceptual schemes allow for different descriptions of the same reality, and that there are no descriptions of reality outside all conceptual schemes, has no bearing whatever on the truth of realism.'

The final term suggested by Saunders et al. is pragmatism. Pragmatism's driving principle is that truth and meaning are only relevant insofar as they are enacted in the real world. Abstract discussions of epistemology and ontology are argued to be irrelevant (indeed some pragmatists reject the very idea of paradigm) and the aim of research is to make a difference. These pragmatist positions and their impact will be described further in the next section.

The reason for outlining these overlapping and contradictory systems of reference is to provide researchers with some kind of map. It is easy to refer to a textbook that describes things in a certain way, then to become extremely confused when other terms – or other meanings of terms – are introduced into the debate. I resist the temptation to present a 'preferred' structure here. The intention is to help researchers find their way, not to impose yet another structure.

In this search for clarity there is a final question that lurks behind the discussion of foundations. Whether it is a useful or meaningful discussion at all.

Why not paradigms? Critiques from pragmatist and critical realist perspectives

A pragmatist perspective has been mentioned in the preceding sections on the nomenclature of both epistemology and paradigm. An adherence to the ideas of pragmatic philosophers such as Dewey, Peirce and James could suggest an altogether different framework to that proposed by Guba and Lincoln: one that recognises the paradigm model itself as one of many ways of seeing things. Fishman (1999: 118–19) refers to the relativity of paradigms from a 'perspectivist' stance: '[The] idea that we are always looking at the world through a particular pair of "glasses" that creates a particular perspective.' Rather than offering a better worldview, Fishman positions pragmatic relativism as a stance which holds that different perspectives may be more or less useful for different purposes.

Morgan (2007) argues that there are inherent conflicts in the way paradigms have been conceptualised, emerging from Guba and Lincoln's focus on ontology and epistemology. Morgan labels this view of paradigms as a 'metaphysical paradigm' (that is, a metaphysically-based construction of the concept of paradigm). It is in the nature of the metaphysical paradigm that it is essentially foundationalist – that the frame of reference is built up from indisputable stages of logical inference (see Hughes and Sharrock, 1997: 4–5). Yet the process of successively revising the structure of paradigms itself undermines the foundationalist logic. Morgan also argues that it follows from this stance that logically paradigms should be entirely incommensurable. Yet at the level of data and methods this appears not to be the case. Indeed proponents of the metaphysical paradigm consistently argue that methods spring from the research question. For Morgan, this demonstrates that questions of ontology and epistemology do not provide answers to questions of method.

A different position can be seen in the critical realist literature which nevertheless results in a similar relativising of the status of paradigm. (Note that in the literature this is often labelled simply 'realism', creating yet another confusing overlap with terms used to refer to specifically ontological positions.) In various ways a number of critical realists suggest an understanding that makes use of the idea that the ontologically 'real' may arise in different ways. Common to these approaches is a commitment to treating social patterns of different types as real in their own right.

Maxwell (2012), for example, argues that the quality of the 'real' is not substance, but causality. Hence accounts of the world can legitimately include the influence of material and mental phenomena on each other, including cultural practices, meanings, and social structures. The legitimacy of this position is supported by two related ideas. Firstly, that immateriality and externality are not incompatible: 'people's interpretations and social practices themselves can be seen to constitute a "reality" that exists independently of what the researcher may have to say about it' (Willig, 2016: 34). This principle is referred to in other realist works as 'intransitivity'(for example, Sayer, 2000). And secondly, that critical realism separates the 'real' expressing the potential for events, from the 'actual' expressing what happens, and also from what part of the actual might be experienced, namely the 'empirical' (Sayer, 2000). Willig expresses the way in which this more complex understanding can undermine the paradigm concept altogether:

> It seems to me that realism and relativism are much more closely intertwined than we tend to acknowledge. They are wrapped around each other in a way that suggests that it is hard to exclude one or the other entirely from a research project. (Willig 2016: 36)

Conclusion: Where does my paradigm come from?

The intention of this chapter has been to provide readers with a map rather than a destination. In it I have examined the history of the idea of being guided by paradigm in social research, highlighted the inconsistencies and complexities of the terminology used in discussions of research paradigm, and introduced some critiques. My hope is that readers are better able to articulate the three outcomes of this theoretical thinking which are mentioned in the introduction to this chapter:

- the *legitimacy* of their particular knowledge claims
- meaningful criteria for understanding the *quality* of the research produced, and, where appropriate
- *mastery* of research as an activity in its own right

Doctoral supervisors regularly rehearse the mantra that methodological questions can only be answered with reference to the research question. This casts doubt on whether abstract questions such as 'what exists?' and 'how do we know?' are the right (or useful) points of departure. Gergen and Gergen's (2003: 8) description of paradigm highlights both the strength and the limitation of this approach:

> One of the things a scientific community acquires with a paradigm is a criterion for choosing problems that, while the paradigm is taken for granted, can be assumed to have solution. To a great extent these are the only problems that the community will admit as scientific or encourage its members to undertake.

This seems to limit legitimate questions to those that fit a paradigm rather than those that occur in the world. Emerging from the discussion of pragmatism and critical realism in the previous section, I would suggest that there are two different ways of looking at the questions of ontology and epistemology that are more helpful. Firstly, we can address the questions not from a foundational position – that these must be resolved before moving forward – but from a more systemic position. This would suggest that such questions are important alongside other issues relating to the context of the study: its aims; the researcher's commitments to the discipline in question; the researcher's values. Secondly, they can be seen not as fixed rules but as ways of thinking about a problem. This sense of paradigm as a more holistic outlook can be seen in descriptions of philosophical underpinnings such as Duberley, Johnson and Cassell's (2012) review. Duberley et al. focus on research 'traditions' and the ontological and epistemological commitments they reflect, referring only in passing to paradigms in their suggestions of further readings.

Research students often find their curiosity frustrated by a complexity around the rationale for different research philosophies that increasingly seem to be, themselves, constructed. Nonetheless, the process of navigating a way through that bewildering literature can be satisfying in its own right. Not least because it can enable the student to arrive at a methodological strategy that feels right for the research question they wish to investigate. It can also provide a touchstone for methodological decision making, allowing the student to ask, 'if this is how I have framed the question, does it make more sense to use strategy A or strategy B in practice?' I hope that the exposition in this chapter will help readers to find their own routes through this bewildering landscape and to make these decisions for themselves.

References

Bryman, A. (2015). *Social Research Methods* (5th edition). Oxford: Oxford University Press.

Burrell, G. and Morgan, G. (1979). *Sociological Paradigms and Organisational Analysis*. Farnham: Heinemann Educational Books.

Crotty, M. (1998). *The Foundations of Social Research: Meaning and Perspective in the Research Process*. London: Sage Publications.

Denzin, N.K. and Lincoln, Y.S. (2013). *The Landscape of Qualitative Research*. London: Sage Publications.

Duberley, J., Johnson., P. and Cassell, C. (2012). 'Philosophies underpinning qualitative research'. In G. Symon and C. Cassell (eds), *Qualitative Organizational Research: Core Methods and Current Challenges*. London: Sage Publications, pp. 15–34.

Effingham, N. (2013). *An Introduction to Ontology*. Cambridge: Polity Press.

Fishman, D. (1999). *The Case for Pragmatic Psychology*. New York: New York University Press.

Gergen, K.J. and Gergen, M. (2003). *Social Construction: A Reader*. London: Sage Publications.

Guba, E.G. and Lincoln, Y.S. (1994). 'Competing paradigms in qualitative research'. In N.K. Denzin and Y.S. Lincoln (eds), *Handbook of Qualitative Research*. London: Sage Publications, pp. 105–17.

Howell, K.E. (2013). *An Introduction to the Philosophy of Methodology*. London: Sage Publications.

Hughes, J.A. and Sharrock, W.W. (1997). *The Philosophy of Social Research* (3rd edition). London: Routledge.

Johnson, P. and Duberley, J. (2000). *Understanding Management Research: An Introduction to Epistemology*. London: Sage Publications.

Kuhn, T. (1962). *The Structure of Scientific Revolutions*. Chicago, IL: University of Chicago Press.

Kuhn, T. (2012). *The Structure of Scientific Revolutions* (50th anniversary edition). Chicago, IL: University of Chicago Press.

Lincoln, Y.S. and Guba, E.G. (1985). *Naturalistic Inquiry*. Thousand Oaks, CA: Sage Publications.

Lincoln, Y.S., Lynham, S.A. and Guba, E.G. (2018). 'Paradigmatic controversies, contradictions and emerging confluences, revisited'. In N.K. Denzin and Y.S. Lincoln (eds), *Handbook of Qualitative Research* (5th edition). London: Sage Publications, pp. 108–50.

Maxwell, J.A. (2012). *A Realist Approach for Qualitative Research*. London: Sage Publications.

Morgan, D.L. (2007). 'Paradigms lost and pragmatism regained: Methodological implications of combining qualitative and quantitative methods'. *Journal of Mixed Methods Research* 1 (1): 48–76.

Morgan, G. and Smircich, L. (1980). 'The case for qualitative research'. *The Academy of Management Review* 5 (4): 491–500.

Oxford Dictionaries | English (n.d.). 'epistemology'. Definition of epistemology in English by Oxford Dictionaries. Available at: https://en.oxforddictionaries.com/definition/epistemology (accessed 23 May 2018).

Oxford Dictionaries | English (n.d.). 'ontology'. Definition of ontology in English by Oxford Dictionaries. Available at: https://en.oxforddictionaries.com/definition/ontology (accessed 23 May 2018).

Saunders, M.N.K., Lewis, P. and Thornhill, A. (2015). *Research Methods for Business Students* (7th edition). Harlow: Pearson Education.

Sayer, A. (2000). *Realism and Social Science*. London: Sage Publications.

Searle, J.R. (1995). *The Construction of Social Reality*. New York: Simon & Schuster.

Thomas, G. (2013). *How to Do Your Case Study* (2nd edition). London: Sage Publications.

Willig, C. (2016). 'Constructivism and the "real world": Can they co-exist?' *QMiP Bulletin* 21: 33–7.

3
Designing your research project
Elaine Cox

Introduction

In this chapter, I explore the challenges of designing a coaching research project, identifying areas where the design phase has presented particular difficulties for researchers. The structure of the chapter tracks the traditional research process, but also features the particular trials and tribulations that can arise at each phase when designing a research project in a coaching context. I begin by examining the importance for students of finding a research focus and describing the problem to be researched. This is followed by an exploration of other challenges in the process such as formulating a research question; developing the research proposal; setting the aim and objectives; defining terms; channelling the literature review; deciding on a research approach; the issues surrounding gaining access to participants and some of the ethical challenges that face coaching researchers.

Finding focus and describing the problem

Many students of coaching have a desire to make a real difference in the world through their research and as a result they often formulate a very wide, all-embracing research topic. However, the importance of finding a manageable and motivating research question early on in the process cannot be over-stressed. Students sometimes find this difficult and struggle with finding a clear focus that will guide the creation of a problem statement. A clear focus also assists with setting a research aim and scoping the literature review, as well as helping shape the research design. Therefore, when students have a number of topic areas that they are interested in, or they have a list of sub-questions that shift the focus in subtle ways, it can cause delays and confusion. So, one of the first things that I ask new researchers is 'What do you really want to find out?' In order not to stall right at the outset they need to select one question that will drive the study and sustain their motivation over the period of the research as well as making a useful and original contribution, however small, to theory and professional practice (their own and that of other coaches).

One of the next questions students need to answer, in order to test for contribution and impact, is whether this research is important and who it is important to. The next step therefore, is to develop the problem statement. This statement, containing perhaps five or six main paragraphs, is the first opportunity for the researcher to articulate the gap in current knowledge and explain why, where and to whom the proposed research will be significant. It guides the research question and the research design, and provides a foundation for research conclusions to be drawn. It also introduces the research topic to the university research committee and supervisors, and ultimately to the examiners and other readers of the dissertation or thesis.

A good problem statement may begin by highlighting something topical or contentious, or with something significant from the current research on the topic. It should be a clear, focused statement about an area of concern to the coaching profession, or something that is disconcerting about the pre-existing scholarly (or practitioner) literature. Students find it takes a little time to create the problem statement succinctly and not make generalisations or offer an evaluation or solution to the problem. They are rewarded by a well-defined description of the contemporary context of the problem and the significance of the study.

The problem statement addresses the question of why the research question is important in relation to theory and practice and includes a summary of what theories, research findings and/or practical issues have prompted interest in the study. The statement should conclude with a note about how the study will augment or challenge understanding about the topic. The need to explain the impact of the study can be testing for students, and it may take some effort to justify the importance of the research question and the contribution to new knowledge that the study will make. This will be a work in progress until submission.

From the problem statement, it should be possible to refine the working title. A good title is a little like a good elevator pitch. It should be quite brief, interesting and describe accurately what the research is about. Often it helps to phrase the title as a question in order to sharpen the focus and students are advised to work on a research question early and to revisit it often. In devising a question, students should make sure there are no superfluous, ambiguous or confusing words, but instead should include key words that will help future researchers find the work.

Once the question is decided, it is helpful to revisit the problem statement yet again and work on it to reaffirm the coaching issue that is being addressed, identify gaps or deficiencies in the literature and end the statement by stating the aim of the study. In the example in Box 3.1 the student begins by identifying a gap in the coaching research, using references to support the claim that there is little research discussing what happens between coach and client in the first session, especially from a client perspective. The student then goes on, in the second paragraph, to look at research in other fields and again finds little focus on the topic of the study. In the third paragraph the student can then build a robust justification for undertaking the study in this area.

Box 3.1   Example of a problem statement

Title

First coaching sessions from the executive client's perspective and their influence on the coaching process (Karboul, 2014).

Problem statement

The number of executive coaching studies published has accelerated in the last decade (Passmore and Fillery-Travis, 2011) and global revenue in the coaching profession has been cited as high as $2 billion (International Coach Federation, 2012). However, firstly there has been less focus on the process itself; namely what happens between the coach and their client (Day et al., 2008) particularly in the first session and secondly until recently the current literature on the executive coaching relationship was predominantly written from the perspective of the coach (Feldman and Lankau, 2005).

Looking at neighbouring fields such as psychotherapy or mentoring can add value to this research. In the therapeutic field, several authors have described the first 10 or 15 minutes as vital to therapeutic success, even in a long-term setting (Bachelor and Horvath, 2002; Odell and Quinn, 1998). The first session itself has also been described as pivotal to the success (Coleman, 1995) or predictive concerning the following therapeutic process (Odell and Campbell, 1998; Sexton et al., 2003). In psychotherapy research, there has been some discussion of the skills necessary to conduct a first interview (Cabie and Fride, 1990; Heller, 1987; Paterson Williams et al., 1998; Weber et al., 1985) and key abilities to build rapport with clients (Haley, 1980). Hartzell (2010) conducted an explorative grounded theory approach exploring children's and parents' perspectives on first sessions in psychiatry, concluding that for children the act of being actively listened to and experiencing the therapist in a dynamic role switching between active questioning and passive but alert

(Continued)

listening roles were appreciated. Harari and Waehler (1999) found that counsellors who included the topic of termination of the counselling relationship within their first session were perceived and rated as more influential. However, surprisingly Hartzell et al. (2009) stress that on the whole, little research exists on first encounters in therapeutic settings and that the client's perspective got too little attention.

Some recent studies from 2010 and 2011 did focus on the client perspective on the coaching process, for example De Haan et al. (2011) found in a quantitative study focusing on the executive coaching clients' perspective of helpfulness a confirmation of another finding in psychotherapy (Horvath and Marx, 1990; Tallman and Bohart, 1999), namely, that the perspectives of clients and their therapists (in this case clients and their coaches) on the process are quite different. To bridge this gap, they suggest further research to look closer at what is the language or conceptual model that best describes the coaching from the perspective of the client? After all, the whole coaching journey is undertaken for the benefit of the clients, so it is certainly worthwhile to understand their perspectives as deeply as possible (De Haan et al., 2010b). Palmer and McDowall noted that it became clear that the coaching relationship that is referred to by scientists and practitioners for over a decade has been based on limited research (Palmer and McDowall, 2010, preface). The lack of knowledge about what executive clients experience in their first coaching session warrants an exploration.

It should also be recognised that a research topic will be difficult to study if it is too broad and so ways need to be found to limit the topic. For example, if the topic of interest is 'what is the client's experience of executive coaching?' it could be limited by sector – 'What is the client's experience of executive coaching in the public sector?' or by gender – 'What is the female client's experience of executive coaching?' Searching for ways to limit the topic can lead to a more motivating, focused and well-defined research project.

Writing a research proposal

Once a problem statement has been drafted and a research question decided, the research proposal can be properly developed. The proposal stage can be a significant milestone in the research journey, particularly at doctoral level where it is usually a formal university requirement.

A proposal typically begins with the title and then asks for the aim of the study and a number of objectives. The aim is normally very similar to the title and the objectives are numbered statements of intention about how the research process will achieve the aim. This is followed by a clear explanation of the research design, including ontology and epistemology, the research strategy and the planned data collection methods. The approach to data analysis is also included and this leads into some indication of the expected contribution to knowledge and, in the case of professional doctorates, professional practice. In some proposals the timescale for completion of the study is also expected.

An example of how an aim and allied objectives might be developed is given in Box 3.2.

Box 3.2   Example of aim and objectives

Title of the research programme

First coaching sessions from the executive client's perspective and their influence on the coaching process.

Aim of the investigation

The aim of this research is to explore what happens in first coaching sessions from executive clients' perspectives and understand how the first session influences the coaching process.

Objectives

1. To critically review literature on first sessions in helping relationships, drawing on research from coaching, mentoring, psychotherapy, counselling, and relationship building.
2. To explore what happens in the first coaching session in a way that gives voice to the executive client.
3. To analyse how the first session influences the coaching process.
4. To contribute to a theoretical understanding of first coaching sessions that will enhance knowledge within the coaching profession.

Students often find it a challenge to create the aim and specific objectives for the research early in the process. However, it is important to have clarity right at the beginning of any proposal. The aim sets out the intention of the research – and emphasises what is to be accomplished. It reflects the aspirations and expectations of the research topic, but does not set out how the research is to be accomplished. The objectives on the other hand are the specific list of tasks needed to achieve the aim. They must be highly focused and feasible and must be precisely described. Objectives are usually numbered so that each objective reads as an individual move towards the completion of the research.

There are a number of challenges that students encounter when preparing research proposals. These may include:

- More than one aim identified, leading to confusion about where the research is focused.
- Objectives not explicit enough. The list of objectives should be the blueprint for action.

- Too much rhetoric leading to the proposed research not being described with sufficient precision and detail.
- Lack of a clear relationship to and grounding in current research literature in the field. The proposal should set out the gap in the literature that will be filled by the planned research.
- Methodology not geared effectively enough to the research being proposed. The research design needs careful thought and planning. Part II of this book is intended to help students think through the design issues of various research approaches.
- The proposal is not focused enough: it needs to give the detail of how work will be carried out; the methodology to be adopted and how this is linked to an appropriate ontology and epistemology; the data collection and analysis methods chosen in order to resolve the research question.
- Finally, it is important to spend time thinking about how to articulate the tangible benefits, originality or significant contribution to knowledge and/ or professional practice.

Literature review

The design of any research project hinges on the quality of the literature review. The aim of the review is to locate all relevant research undertaken on the chosen topic to date and to marshal it into a useful review that exposes a gap in the research.

Sometimes the literature review incorporates a review of definitions, especially where the research question contains ambiguous or complex terms: an example would be 'What is the role of the Aha! moment in transformational coaching?' In this question, it is necessary for extensive literature exploration encompassing a variety of definitions of both the 'Aha moment' and 'transformational coaching'. In the earlier example (Box 3.1), where the concept seemed less ambiguous, a straightforward discussion of the definition of 'first meetings' and 'client perspective' as pertaining to the current study would probably be included in the introduction to the study, and the research on each aspect followed up in the literature chapter.

The literature review process involves three iterative stages:

1. Ongoing literature searches using key words to locate articles and texts that are of current relevance to the research.
2. Clustering the research and reporting it so that that research gaps can be exposed. These gaps may relate to research content or to methodology.
3. Summarising the theoretical or conceptual framework.

1. Ongoing literature searches

The review begins with carefully choreographed literature searches, using key words identified from the research question. All researchers are advised to keep track of the words that are used to describe their topic:

- Look for words that best describe the topic or those that are in common use in the field.
- Look for them when reading articles, or background and general information.
- Find broader and narrower terms, synonyms, key concepts for key words to widen your search capabilities.
- Make note of these words and use them later when searching databases and journals.

The challenge for students during the search process is the ability to stay focused in the midst of reading so much interesting research. One student suggested the discipline involved 'training my butterfly mind'. She asked how she could approach the literature in order to establish a solid foundation for the study going forward.

One way of doing this would be to follow a fairly strict literature search protocol such as that proposed by Booth, who points out that 'standards for reporting literature searches must acknowledge the demands of both quantitative and qualitative systematic reviews' (Booth, 2006: 421). Booth introduces a mnemonic, 'STARLITE', which stands for sampling strategy, type of study, approaches, range of years, limits, inclusion and exclusions, terms used, electronic sources. This can be useful for guiding (and reporting) the literature search process – and for keeping on track. The STARLITE process involves identifying criteria for the literature search that help narrow the type of study and impose inclusion and exclusion criteria. For example, the study of 'first meetings' (Box 3.1) might well have excluded first meetings within a romantic relationship. Booth suggests that a thorough approach to explaining the literature search methodology can add rigour and replicability to the process, adding that 'systematic reviews draw strength from the fact that they claim to be both explicit and reproducible' (2006: 426).

2. Clustering the research

Having just suggested that rigour and structure are necessary for a robust literature search, I now want to suggest that researchers allow room for creativity and serendipity! Montuori, for example, warns about using a purely 'reproductive approach' where the review merely 'regurgitates' the study under review. This, he says, may lead to 'reviews that are generally as deadly to read as they are to write' (Montuori, 2005: 374). Rather, Montuori suggests, the literature review should be approached as a 'creative inquiry' where students envisage themselves in dialogue with the research community: 'A literature review can be framed as a creative process, one in which the knower is an active participant constructing an interpretation of the community and its discourse, rather than a mere bystander who attempts to reproduce, as best she or he can, the relevant authors and works' (2005: 375).

Once students begin to see themselves in dialogue with a specific research community they can go deeper into that community. They can begin to explore the underlying assumptions of the knowledge claims presented. Montuori distinguishes three different levels of what he calls the deeper 'underground network' (2005: 378):

i. Discipline

Boundaries are set by the (sub-)disciplinary nature of knowledge and Montuori gives the examples of psychology and sociology. Psychology is defined as the study of the human mind and has different underlying assumptions than sociology: 'Psychologists generally assume that the individual is the unit of analysis, and sociologists in general assume that society is the unit of analysis' (Montuori, 2005: 388). Within each discipline there are sub-disciplines. In psychology for example, phenomenological psychology makes different assumptions than social psychology, and this affects how they approach their research. In coaching, the contexts and genres, for example those identified by Cox et al. (2018), may have a similar consequence. Students benefit from immersing themselves in the disciplinary dialogues.

ii. Culture

In the same way as there are disciplinary differences, there are also different ways in which research is addressed across cultures: Montuori outlines how 'social research in the United States, Northern and Southern Europe, and Japan, for example, originates in different cultural contexts that leave their mark on the underlying assumptions of the researchers, and this shows up in interesting and informative ways' (2005: 388). Students of coaching can take account of such cultural nuances when reviewing the literature.

iii. Paradigm

Another level of underlying assumptions stems from the organisational logic or 'paradigm' used to construct knowledge. By observing an author's attitude to reality and knowledge creation and noting the methodology used students can add depth to their review.

The literature review process therefore invites students to engage in a truly creative process involving finding their own voice through explorations of context, ideas, social and methodological trends, offering an opportunity to find their own original niche through in-depth academic enquiry (Montuori, 2005). This is not an easy task and it can be helpful for students to think of themselves as the conductor of an orchestra, with other authors and researchers as the instrumentalists: sometimes the conductor wants to hear from a soloist, but more often the task is to make the sections of the orchestra talk to each other. Similarly, students can compose an analysis where researchers talk to each other about the topic under review. A literature review of this type is always interesting to read.

3. Summarising the theoretical framework

The key purpose of the literature search is to enable the researcher to show the relationship of the study to previous work. Showing the relationship enables the problem to be located within the context of what is often called a *conceptual* or *theoretical framework*: a framework is created by organising relevant literature into useful categories that highlight the gap in the research. Typically, students find it helpful to create a diagram to illustrate the framework that orients the research.

The emerging framework contributes to both quantitative and qualitative research: by establishing research variables and identifying the relationships between them in quantitative studies and in qualitative research by helping refine theoretical gaps and identify a specific research question that will drive the research. In both qualitative and quantitative research, the review enables a contribution to be made to contemporary debates that surround the research question.

A theoretical framework always underlies the research question, even if it is not evident from the problem statement. In our example, the question initially appeared quite practical: 'What happens in first coaching sessions from the executive client's perspective and how does it influence the coaching process?' However, the literature review revealed a body of literature relating to first experiences in areas such as memory and skill acquisition, to first sessions in therapy as well as in popular coaching models, and also revealed

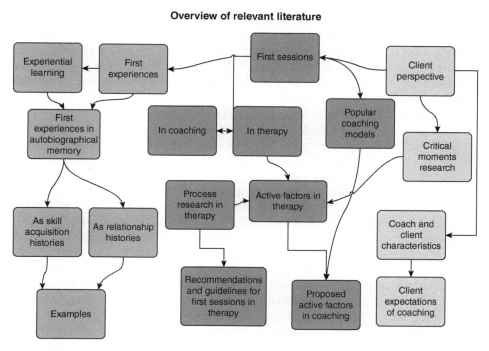

Overview of relevant literature

Figure 3.1 A student example of mapping relationships between themes in literature. Arrows indicate relationships between literature themes

Source: Karboul, A. (2014). 'Experiencing coaching for the first time: First coaching sessions from the executive client's perspective'. Doctoral thesis, Oxford Brookes University.

studies where the client perspective had been highlighted, especially in studies of client expectations of coaching. Figure 3.1 illustrates the resultant literature framework and shows how the student identified various strands of literature that 'spoke' to other strands, thus building the creative dialogue so desired by Montuori (2005).

Theoretical frameworks are commonly more detailed when the researcher traces significant academic strands of work, for example by drawing on psychology or sociology in order to embed their empirical study in well-established theories as well as including the coaching specific research.

The importance of the research approach in qualitative research

As discussed in Chapter 2, ontology (fundamental beliefs about whether reality exists in its own right) is mediated by the researcher and influences the choices made during the research design. Similarly, epistemology (the way in which we claim meaning is created and how we create knowledge) links with the design: do we extract knowledge from the real world (via experiment and discovery), or do we construct it ourselves or with others and thus have to interpret our constructions in order to convey meaning? Together, the researcher's ontology and epistemology suggest a research approach that then becomes the foundation of the research design. The ontology/epistemology combination heralds a coherent research design which is fundamental to the research outcome: as Yin recognises, 'the design is the logical sequence that connects the empirical data to a study's initial research questions and, ultimately, to its conclusions' (2003: 19).

By 'research approach', I therefore mean the adoption of a coherent framework that ensures the cohesion of the research from paradigm through to conclusions. Popular examples of research approaches are provided by Creswell (2013) who gives worked examples of narrative, phenomenology, grounded theory, ethnography and case study; other approaches commonly used in coaching research are interpretive phenomenological analysis (Smith et al., 2009), mixed methods (Creswell and Plano Clark, 2017), and action research (Coghlan and Brannick, 2014). Denzin and Lincoln explain how each of these strategies is 'connected to a complex literature, each has a separate history, exemplary works, and preferred ways for putting the strategy into motion' (Denzin and Lincoln, 2005: 21). In Part II of this book the frequently used research approaches in coaching are problematised and discussed.

According to Denzin and Lincoln, a research approach or strategy incorporates 'a bundle of skills, assumptions and practices that the researcher employs as he or she moves from paradigm to the empirical world. Strategies of inquiry put paradigms of interpretation into motion' (Denzin and Lincoln, 2005: 21). In effect, the approach operationalises the chosen paradigm.

Bauwens et al. (2013: 29) argue that a paradigm is 'constituted by answering three questions':

1. The ontological question, which as we have already noted, relates to the nature of existence.
2. The epistemological question or how the researcher sees the nature of the relationship between the knower and the known – that is, how it is possible to gain knowledge.
3. The methodological question that links the ontological and epistemo-logical decisions to the practical research through appropriate bound-ing of the study via the research approach. This, in turn, informs the choice of data collection methods and analysis approaches.

The vital thing to remember is that if researchers go straight from paradigm to data collection without considering the approach, they reduce two vital elements of research design: legitimation and representation (Denzin and Lincoln, 2005: 21). If, for example, the researcher jumps from a discussion of paradigm to the descriptions of data collection methods then the proposed treatment of context within the study can be lost. It is important, particularly for qualitative researchers, to explain how, although the methods they use produce inherently subjective data, the findings will still be valid and transfer-able. Part of this legitimation is usually done through contextualising the research and describing the research approach in detail in order to tell the reader more about what is involved in the research process and what is impor-tant. Information about context and process is given in the articulation of a research approach and representation is addressed in the faithful inclusion of participant and researcher voices. These aspects will be slightly different in each approach as discussed in Part II of this book.

Thus, in all qualitative research the setting of the research is important – it forms a contextual boundary to the research enabling stakeholders to under-stand participants' perspectives and their meaning in relation to the phenom-enon under study. Figure 3.2 illustrates common types of coaching questions and some of the research approaches most suited for their study.

As intimated by Bauwens et al. (2013), each research approach will have links with certain epistemological assumptions and so choice of a research approach makes the link between the epistemology and the data collection methods. For example, grounded theory can be adopted to support a construc-tivist epistemology when studying an area where little or no previous research has been undertaken. Interviews may be the main data collection method, and they are analysed to construct knowledge in that little-known context. Similarly, interviews can be the main data collection method in a case study approach, but here the contextual boundary is all important. A case study involves recognising the circumstances of the research that may impose limits on the transferability of the knowledge uncovered (Stake, 2008). Action research is usually chosen when there is little or no implementation evident and the researcher needs to make something happen. In action research knowledge is created through making an intervention, often within a prag-matic perspective – again interviews may be the main source of data collection following the intervention.

PEOPLE'S EXPERIENCE	CONCEPTUALISATION OF A PHENOMENON	UNDERSTANDING/ IMPROVEMENT OF A PROCESS	OUTCOMES OF A PHENOMENON
What is the experience of a phenomenon? How is it perceived by the participants?	*How can we conceptualise a phenomenon? What are useful explanations or interpretations of it?*	*How does a phenomenon unfold as a process? What facilitates? What inhibits?*	*What are the outcomes or consequences of a phenomenon?*
Phenomenology (IPA)	Conceptual Analysis	Action Research	Quasi-Experimental
Heuristic	Grounded Theory		Survey
Life History/ Narrative	Discourse Analysis		Organisational Case Study
Individual Case Study	Hermeneutic		
Ethnography			

Figure 3.2 Qualitative research questions and choice of research strategy

Linked to the legitimation provided by contextual discussion of design, as discussed above, is a need for other types of legitimation within the research. Fundamental to all research are the issues of truth value, applicability, consistency and neutrality (Lincoln and Guba, 1985). These issues can all be addressed in qualitative research during the discussion of research approach, remembering that validity, in particular, concerns the degree to which an account is accurate or truthful: 'Validity is not a commodity that can be purchased with techniques ... Rather, validity is, like integrity, character and quality, to be assessed relative to purposes and circumstances' (Brinberg and McGrath, 1985: 13).

Concerns about legitimation and representation are also the main reason qualitative researchers use 'thick description' (Ponterotto, 2006) as an essential component of qualitative research. Such thick description is enhanced by the contextual detail provided by a detailed explanation of the research approach. In addition, by presenting findings in sufficient contextual detail we can evaluate the extent to which the conclusions drawn are transferable to other times, settings, situations and people. In positivist research, it is triangulation that provides similar rigour.

I consider there are a number of arguments in favour of using a 'ready-made' research approach:

1. It provides consistency across disciplines – other researchers know what we are talking about.
2. It makes the research process more coherent, which is useful for new researchers – ontology, epistemology, data collection and analysis are often prescribed or hinted at in the approach.

3. Expectations of examiners and readers are managed.
4. Although the word 'qualitative' does imply certain things, there is a richness conveyed if the research is described as, say, phenomenological, case study, action research or grounded theory – it says more about the philosophy and epistemology than is possible for each individual student to explain.

Using a recognised, ready-made research approach is, in fact, a shorthand way of identifying a set of practices and behaviours which are characteristic of a particular research design. If as readers we know what the research approach is, then we know what research is appropriate to the execution of that approach and therefore what to expect from the study. Insofar as each approach involves specific expectations, the structure of those expectations is determined, more or less, by the approach and researchers do not have to set it up for themselves, only modify or explicate as appropriate.

Arguments against a ready-made approach might include the fact that bespoke approaches could challenge students, particularly doctoral students, to think more carefully about the demands of the research. Thus, they may be able to create better fit with a specifically tailored approach, or combination of approaches.

Participant selection and access

One of the practical aspects of research that researchers frequently find challenging is gaining access to the right kind of participants. Participants either need to be part of a representative sample to produce valid quantitative data, or they need to be theoretically sampled to ensure that they meet criteria that will enable the collection of useful qualitative data.

Two of the most common issues faced by researchers when trying to gain access are illustrated by queries from two of my own (anonymised) students (Box 3.3).

Box 3.3   Examples of access issues

Niall

I will be using LinkedIn groups as a source for participants. These groups have large membership numbers, but I am not sure how exactly to engage interest in my research and get willing participants. I am also not familiar with the LinkedIn research etiquette as such, for instance do I first introduce myself to the group 'administrator' and ask permission to invite participants? Also, how do I ensure the participants are who they say they are in order to meet my sample criteria?

(Continued)

> **Phoebe**
>
> What I am really focused on right now is my strategy to recruit participants, namely recruiting and managing gatekeepers since I will not have direct access to participants.

Niall has two issues: one relates to approaching gatekeepers, in this case a group administrator on LinkedIn, and the other to ensuring participants meet his criteria. Gatekeepers should be sent a participant information sheet, which is usually developed as part of the procedural ethics process. This information can be accompanied by a shorter email that explains what the gatekeeper is being asked to do. Phoebe's issue is similar in that she will not have direct access to the participants. Thus, the quality of the information provided to gatekeepers in the participant information can make all the difference to the success of the recruitment.

Access to participants can be negotiated in a variety of ways depending on the type of participant required. It may be obtained through formal decision makers (HR departments or other gatekeepers), through professional networks (LinkedIn, professional bodies, unions, etc.) or it may be through personal contact with colleagues or acquaintances. In any event it is useful to adopt multiple methods for accessing participants.

The issue of ensuring that participants meet the criteria is sometimes tricky, but participants are normally self-selecting based on the information provided in a well-constructed participant information sheet. For this reason, it is vital that the information is as complete and explanatory as possible.

Ethics

Linked to the challenges of access to participants is the need for an ethical approach to the research design. As Iphofen (2009) points out, all research intrudes on participants' lives to a greater or lesser extent and so it is very important that the research is what he calls a 'justifiable intervention'. That is, the research should be worth the sacrifice of time that the participants are being asked to make: there should be some societal benefit that makes their contributions worthwhile.

Because of this fundamental requirement, all universities have research ethics procedures which must be adhered to. Some other institutions, such as the (UK) National Health Service also have rigorous ethical requirements. These procedural ethics are concerned with safeguarding participants by:

1. Making sure that researchers guarantee participants are well informed about the purpose and process of the research they are being asked to participate in. It is vital that participants understand any risks they may face as a result of taking part, but also that they

understand any benefits there might be and so a participant information sheet will be essential.

2. Ensuring participants are free to make independent decisions about
    whether to take part, or continue to take part, without fear of any
    negative consequences. Consequently, all participants should also
    sign a consent form that makes this explicit.

Once the challenges of navigating institutional procedural ethics processes
have been addressed, then researchers face the reality of practical ethical
issues. Qualitative data collection methods such as interviewing or focus
groups can stir emotions. In most cases this is not risky, but it could be in
extreme cases. Consequently, researchers may need to plan ahead and provide
some kind of referral services for participants. Students are always advised to
stop data collection whenever they are in doubt and to ask supervisors for
guidance.

Another practical challenge concerns confidentiality and safety of data.
Researchers need to ensure that field notes and transcripts do not contain
personal identifiers and they need to find ways of keeping the raw and pro-
cessed data locked and password protected on their computer or laptop. Such
data should only be shared with those who are part of the supervision team and
who have received ethics training. Similarly, anonymising data when writing
up findings is crucial.

Some of the ethical challenges that students face during the procedural
ethics process are:

1. Identifying who are the research participants in the study in order to
    ensure each has the necessary information. For instance, if team
    coaching is being observed in an organisation, there are likely to be
    three different types of participant: the organisation, the team
    coaches, and the members of the teams themselves.
2. Identifying potential risks to participants. The risks may come from
    emotional arousal, or they may come from others involved in the
    study. For example, if a researcher was interviewing staff members
    in an organisation where there are a lot of staffing problems and high
    staff turnover, the HR manager may be interested in knowing the
    results of the interviews. The researcher's challenge then is to bal-
    ance the manager's need for information against violation of partici-
    pants' confidentiality.
3. Making sure the data collection methods are appropriate for their
    purpose. For example, focus groups are typically best used for topics
    that are less sensitive, where loss of confidentiality is not a substan-
    tial risk. Diaries can be useful for capturing thoughts, but also allow
    participants to self-censor, so that they are not at risk of inadvertently
    sharing sensitive material.

All these challenges suggest the need for transparency when describing the
research process:

By revealing and discussing our own judgement calls, we further the building of a moral order underpinning the primary goals of social research activity. (Iphofen, 2009: 183)

Coaches often think that because they adhere to the standards of ethical practice set out by their professional coaching body, they will automatically be working ethically as a researcher. However, as Iphofen identifies, professional codes of ethics are for professional protection, whereas research ethics 'aim to "educate" in order to assist the individual researcher's own moral choice' (2009: 175). Thus, the scope of ethical awareness for a researcher is necessarily wider than that of the professional coach, encompassing wider cultural aspects and organisational sensitivities that may not be a concern for the practising coach.

Undertaking ethical training as part of the research training provided by a university is therefore most important. Such training will include discussion of the value of having clearly articulated participant information, which includes explaining how research participants can contribute to a copy of the completed thesis or an executive summary.

Summary

This chapter has focused on the design of a research project and in particular the challenges facing students as they tackle the different stages of the design process: writing a research proposal, identifying aims and objectives, literature searching, deciding on the research approach, confronting research ethics and access to participants.

In the chapter, I argued that a well-conceived research proposal should justify the need for the study and explain the research question. It should also provide a map for the subsequent literature search. The research approach, I suggested, will become more obvious as the design takes shape and will also link to ontological and epistemological decisions. Ethical challenges also need to be addressed, both at the procedural stage and at a more practical level during the field research. Access issues were also discussed and the recommendation made that, once sampling criteria have been set, multiple ways of approaching participants be considered.

In Part II, the challenges of identifying and adopting some commonly used research approaches are discussed in more detail.

References

Bauwens, T., Kennes, P. and Bauwens, A. (2013). 'Paradigms: Waving the flag or flagging the wave'. In K. Beyens, J. Christiaens and B. Claes (eds), *The Pains of Doing Criminological Research*. Brussels: VUB Press, pp. 23–37.

Booth, A. (2006). 'Brimful of STARLITE: Toward standards for reporting literature searches'. *Journal of the Medical Library Association* 94 (4): 421–9.

Brinberg, D. and McGrath, J.E. (1985). *Validity and the Research Process*. Newbury Park, CA: Sage Publications.

Coghlan, D. and Brannick, T. (2014). *Doing Action Research in Your Own Organization*. London: Sage Publications.

Cox, E., Bachkirova, T. and Clutterbuck, D. (eds) (2018). *The Complete Handbook of Coaching* (3rd edition). London: Sage Publications.

Creswell, J.W. (2013). *Qualitative Inquiry and Research Design: Choosing among Five Approaches* (3rd edition). London: Sage Publications.

Creswell, J.W. and Plano Clark, V.L. (2017). *Designing and Conducting Mixed Methods Research*. London: Sage Publications.

Denzin, N.K. and Lincoln, Y.S. (eds) (2005). *The SAGE Handbook of Qualitative Research* (3rd edition). Thousand Oaks, CA: Sage Publications.

Iphofen, R. (2009). *Ethical Decision-Making in Social Research: A Practical Guide*. Basingstoke: Palgrave Macmillan.

Karboul, A. (2014). 'Experiencing coaching for the first time: First coaching sessions from the executive client's perspective'. Doctoral thesis, Oxford Brookes University.

Lincoln, Y. and Guba, E. (1985). *Naturalistic Inquiry*. Thousand Oaks, CA: Sage Publications.

Montuori, A. (2005). 'Literature review as creative inquiry: Reframing scholarship as a creative process'. *Journal of Transformative Education* 3 (4): 374–93.

Ponterotto, J.G. (2006). 'Brief note on the origins, evolution, and meaning of the qualitative research concept thick description'. *The Qualitative Report* 11 (3): 538–49. Available at: https://nsuworks.nova.edu/tqr/vol11/iss3/6.

Smith, J.A., Flowers, P. and Larkin, M. (2009). *Interpretative Phenomenological Analysis: Theory, Method and Research*. London: Sage Publications.

Stake, R. (2008). 'Qualitative case studies'. In N.K. Denzin and Y.S. Lincoln (eds), *Strategies of Qualitative Inquiry*. Thousand Oaks, CA: Sage Publications, pp. 119–49.

Yin, R.K. (2003). *Case Study Research: Design and Methods* (2nd edition). Thousand Oaks, CA: Sage Publications.

PART II

RESEARCH STRATEGIES

4
Grounded theory

Teresa Carmichael and Natalie Cunningham

Introduction

The interest in using the grounded theory method in the field of coaching is growing, as evidenced by a flurry of recent doctoral dissertations and theses (Abravanel, 2018; Hollis, 2013; Seitz, 2009; Sheppard, 2016). The place of theory in research endeavours is core to the academy, as theory is necessary to interpret data: 'without theory, it is impossible to make meaningful sense of empirically-generated data' (Handfield and Melnyk, 1998: 21).

Coaching has a multi-disciplinary history and has relied on the theoretical underpinnings from a number of fields to inform different aspects of practice, for example drawing on Carl Rogers' (2012) theory of positive self-regard to inform the coaching relationship and space. Coaching research is maturing, but the field of coaching needs to develop more coaching-specific theory in order to continue to mature. Grounded theory is an ideal method to build a much-needed theoretical underpinning of the field. Before exploring the nature of grounded theory and its use in coaching research, we first need to examine what theories actually are.

A consolidation from various definitions and discussions of theory (Anfara Jr and Mertz, 2015; Apramian et al., 2017; Charmaz, 2014; Garrison, 1988; Glaser and Strauss, 1967; Jaccard and Jacoby, 2010; Spradley, 2016; Weber, 2003) suggests that a good theory has the following characteristics:

- The purpose of a theory is to explain and/or predict a phenomenon.
- Theories are abstractions.
- Theories are parsimonious.
- Theories have utility.
- Theories are internally logically consistent.
- The assumptions on which the theory rests must be articulated.
- The building blocks of theory are concepts and constructs which are derived directly or indirectly from empirical data.
- The relationship between each concept and construct is made explicit (causation is not the only possible relationship).
- Each theory has a clearly defined boundary within which it applies.
- Theories assist in understanding and guiding practice.
- Theories may or may not be generalisable in themselves, but they should be empirically testable or verifiable.

These criteria should be useful as a checklist for grounded theory method researchers in the field of coaching to establish that their theory-building will, in fact, result in something that can be classified as a theory. However, theories are not descriptions (however conceptual), models, or empirical generalisations, and grounded theory coaching researchers presenting any of these as grounded theory would be incorrect. Glaser is particularly critical of descriptions masquerading as theory as the claimed result of the grounded theory method by some researchers (Glaser, 2016a).

Although there are three main approaches to grounded theory (see Box 4.1), this chapter focuses on Glaser's classic grounded theory (Glaser and Strauss, 1967, 1998, 2017) and Charmaz's constructivist grounded theory (2000, 2014, 2017).

Box 4.1   Key concept – Three main approaches to grounded theory method

Amongst a literature that abounds with different interpretations of grounded theory, there are three main schools of thought, labelled by Apramian et al. (2017) as Glaserian (classic grounded theory), Straussian, and Charmazian (constructivist grounded theory). Glaser and Strauss (1967) discovered the method, then Strauss shifted his views and teamed up with Juliet Corbin (Strauss and Corbin, 1998). Subsequently, Kathy Charmaz (2000, 2014) developed her constructivist approach to grounded theory.

This chapter outlines the distinctive features of grounded theory, which are supported by examples from students who are currently using grounded theory in their research or by one of the co-authors of the chapter who completed her PhD using grounded theory.

We have used pseudonyms for the current student work as it has not been published yet. We refer to two students using pseudonyms: Mohammed, who used a classic grounded theory approach to investigate the role of coaching in assisting hospital doctors to cope with managerialism interference in their professional roles, and Nosi, who is using classic grounded theory to develop a new theory about transfer of learning among millennials. The third student is Natalie (co-author of this chapter), who used constructivist grounded theory to propose a new theory of the coaching process from the coachee's perspective.

The most parsimonious definition of grounded theory comes from Bryant and Charmaz (2007) in describing it as theoretical research grounded in data (see Box 4.2 for alternative definitions). However, the term grounded theory itself leads to confusion because it refers to both the research process and the end result. For clarity, following Bryant and Charmaz (2010), we will use the terms grounded theory method for the rigorous and systematic method for gathering and analysing empirical field data and grounded theory for the actual theory or theoretical propositions that arise from using the method.

Box 4.2   Key concept – Defining grounded theory

Classic grounded theory (GT) is simply a set of integrated conceptual hypotheses systematically generated to produce an inductive theory about a substantive area. Classic GT is also a highly structured but eminently flexible methodology. Its data collection and analysis procedures are explicit and the pacing of these procedures is, at once, simultaneous, sequential, subsequent, scheduled and serendipitous, 'forming an integrated methodological "whole" that enables the emergence of conceptual theory as distinct from the thematic analysis characteristic of QDA research' (Glaser and Holton, 2004: 3).

Grounded theory is 'Theoretical research grounded in data' (Bryant and Charmaz, 2010).

Grounded theory is the discovery of theory from data (Glaser and Strauss, 1967).

Having defined grounded theory, researchers would benefit from knowing when using the method is appropriate; we provide insights from our three student examples.

Box 4.3   Doing research – When to use the grounded theory method

Mostly, the grounded theory strategy is positioned for developing theory in fields where existing theories are not well-developed, such as in the coaching field.

There is an alternative view that even when existing theory is strong, it may not apply to the context in which a study is taking place, for example, in the case of one student, Nosi.

(Continued)

Nosi is conducting classic grounded theory into learning transfer through coaching because, as she put it, 'there is a strong theory base in this area, but frankly it doesn't apply in our South African context, and it doesn't work in practice. I want to start from scratch with what *African* people are saying'.

Grounded theory method is also appropriate when a researcher wants to move beyond describing something to developing a conceptual account of behaviours or experiences, for example, Mohammed, who chose classic grounded theory method for his study into coaching and coping with managerialism in a hospital setting. He explained that: 'I knew that the topic that I wanted to investigate required a methodology that allowed the respondents to speak freely about their concerns and how they managed to get by. The method steered me away from description and allowed me to develop a conceptual account of what was happening in their professional lives.'

Natalie (co-author) adopted a constructivist grounded theory approach because of her extensive experience in the coaching industry that could not be bracketed out of her study since it was so integral to her being. Needing to be mindful of her role as researcher, it was important to be conscious of potential biases which she kept track of through detailed memos.

Distinctive features of grounded theory method

Because of the distinct characteristics of the two main grounded theory methods, it is useful to examine the features they have in common and those differentiating them. There are some common features that apply to classic grounded theory as well as to constructivist grounded theory; there are also characteristics that are unique to each type of grounded theory. Table 4.1 describes these characteristics, listing five common factors and then describing a number of differentiating principles.

Table 4.1 The characteristics of classic and constructivist grounded theory

	Classic grounded theory (Glaser)	**Constructivist grounded theory (Charmaz)**	**Sources**
Common principle 1: sampling	The first participant is chosen purposively, then the rest using theoretical sampling achieved through simultaneous data collection and analysis		Hoare et al., 2012, Hood, 2010
Common principle 2: constant comparison	Constant comparison of data to emergent theoretical categories		Hood, 2010, Glaser, 2002
	Constant comparison of data to previous data and each transcript to previous transcripts		
Common principle 3: theoretical saturation	Theory development is via theoretical saturation of categories rather than substantial generalisable findings		Hoare et al., 2012, Hood, 2010

	Classic grounded theory (Glaser)	Constructivist grounded theory (Charmaz)	Sources
Common principle 4: memoing	Memoing and reflexivity are essential to the grounded theory method		Charmaz, 2014, Hoare et al., 2012, Hood, 2010, Rieger, 2018
Common principle 5: theory is grounded in the data, not the literature	Theory is developed purely from the data, not from pre-existing literature or *a priori* concepts and constructs; *all* data contributes to the theory and carries equal weight to all other data, including the outliers, exceptions and variations		Apramian et al., 2017, Charmaz, 2014, Glaser and Strauss, 1967, 1998, 2017, Hoare et al., 2012
Assumptions about theory	An abstraction that leads to context-free theoretical generalisation	An abstraction of concepts and their interrelationships from multiple voices within a context; the theory is provisional until verified	Apramian et al., 2017, Charmaz, 2014, Glaser and Strauss, 1967, 1998, 2017
What counts as grounded theory	Theory is discovered – by the researcher	Theory is constructed – during researcher / participant conversations	Charmaz, 2014, Glaser and Strauss, 1967, 1998, 2017, Holton and Walsh, 2017
Coding process	Open, selective, then theoretical coding	Initial, gerund, then focused coding	Rieger, 2018
Role and place of the literature	Literature excluded up front. Theoretically sensitising literature may be consulted during analysis but emergence of theory must not be forced	Literature may be consulted at a high conceptual level and integrated with reflexive memo-writing during analysis	Charmaz, 2014, Glaser, 1978, 2002, Hoare et al., 2012, Rieger, 2018
Positionality of the researcher	An objective observer Etic positionality Positivistic assumptions	An involved participant Emic positionality Interpretivist and constructivist assumptions	Charmaz, 2014, Glaser and Strauss, 1967, 1998, 2017, Morris et al., 1999, Rieger, 2018, Tinker and Armstrong, 2008
Previous researcher knowledge	Bracketed out	Part of the process	Glaser, 2016b, Glaser and Strauss, 1967, Konecki, 2018

(Continued)

Table 4.1   (Continued)

	Classic grounded theory (Glaser)	Constructivist grounded theory (Charmaz)	Sources
Research approach	Qualitative and/or quantitative	Qualitative	Khazanchi and Munkvold, 2014
What qualifies as data	'All is data'	Focus on qualitative; interviews, documents, behaviours, narratives, visual	Glaser, 1998 (quote, p. 8), Charmaz, 2014
Contextuality of the theory	Context-free; 'abstract of time, place and people'; generalises to the core variable, concern or process; emphasis on causation	Context-bound; generalises to the context; theorised relationships between concepts – seldom causation	Charmaz, 2014, Glaser, 2014, Glaser, 2016a, Rieger, 2018

When describing the approach to be used in a particular study, it is easy to get confused by the volume of methodological literature in the grounded theory space, since the different versions of the method have developed both sequentially and in parallel. Researchers need to be very clear on the distinguishing features and temporal characteristics of their selected method.

Box 4.4   Doing research – Writing up the grounded theory methodology

Natalie was overwhelmed initially by the contradictory statements regarding the nature of and processes in grounded theory. However, by carefully tracing the history of each type from 1967 until the present, she was able to appreciate where the differences were rooted (paradigmatically and methodologically), how they evolved and, therefore, how to describe them systematically and logically.

Practical issues

Ontology and worldview in choosing the specific grounded theory method

One of the key areas for researchers to understand at the beginning of their research journey, especially before their selection of methodology, is their ontology (beliefs about the nature of reality), epistemologies (how they come to know what they know), and worldviews (Denzin and Lincoln, 2000). This will inform their choice of grounded theory method.

In choosing whether to go with classic grounded theory or constructivist grounded theory, coaching scholars can be guided by reflecting on their own role as a researcher. Glaser's (Glaser and Strauss, 1967, 1998, 2017) more linear approach would likely be preferred by an objective researcher, whereas a student wanting to explore individual experiences and meaning with alternative explanations would be more comfortable with Charmaz's (2014) postmodern domain of constructivist grounded theory which evolved in response to a social reality that is multiple, processual and constructed.

The researcher's position is thus an inherent part of the reality of the research, and researchers are encouraged to articulate their worldview near the beginning of their study.

Box 4.5   Doing research – Awareness of your own worldview

Natalie confirmed that 'believing that the world consists of multiple realities, with multiple explanations for phenomena makes me a postmodernist. This philosophical orientation was influenced strongly by my 20 years of work experience in the coaching arena. In this line of work, it is clear that people see their world from different perspectives and that their experiences influence the language that they use to describe their world. For example, an adult who was bullied as a child might have the word "bully" in his vocabulary, which he may use in corporate contexts to describe an intimidating manager. In contrast, someone who has not had this experience might describe the manager as narcissistic, and interact differently with her. Perspectives influence beliefs which influence behaviour.'

Role and positionality of the researcher

The role of the researcher as an insider vs being an outsider has been highlighted in cross-cultural studies; Pike (1967) uses the term 'emic' to refer to the insider status and 'etic' for the outsider status (Morris et al., 1999; Peterson and Pike, 2002). Classic grounded theory takes more of an objective, outsider view and constructivist grounded theory favours a subjective insider stance.

These positionalities fundamentally determine the nature of the study. We may learn from ethnographic and cross-cultural studies (Shah, 2004) in planning for grounded theory data collection. The researcher should develop an acute level of self-awareness and other-awareness (Tinker and Armstrong, 2008) when using the grounded theory method. This is to avoid making assumptions that the world of the researched is necessarily the same as the world of the researcher (Zoogah, 2008), and that there is automatically a common understanding of the concepts being investigated and the words and language used (Morey and Luthans, 1984; Polkinghorne, 2005) in the interactions between the two parties.

Given the private and confidential nature of the coaching interaction, coaching researchers need to be more aware than most to maintain confidentiality (Cox et al., 2014) while still articulating the codes and categories that emerge from the data. Because classic grounded theory is concerned with de-contextualising the emergent theory, and constructivist grounded theory is fully contextual, coaching researchers need to choose their approach carefully.

Charmaz (2014) indicates how intensive interviewing provides the research participants with space and human connection in which reflection can lead to new meaning-making which in turn could lead to rich data that supports analytical insights. The level of self-awareness of one's own biases and assumptions as well as sensitivity to the research participants' biases can be addressed through sensitive, non-judgemental yet empathic interviewing.

The place of the literature and theoretical sensitivity

Coaching researchers should be aware that there are two important aspects to writing up the literature in a grounded theory study, and they apply equally to classic and constructivist grounded theory. The first relates to the position of the literature review in the study, and the second relates to the temporality of idea development in grounded theory. The field of coaching is still relatively theoretically sparse, so it is probably easier for coaching researchers to approach their research with minds uncontaminated by previous studies than in other disciplines.

The place of the literature review is clear-cut in classic grounded theory; the literature should not be consulted until the theory emerges (Glaser, 1978). When it does emerge, the literature is consulted only to see if there are any published references to the theory that is emerging from the data; the emergent theory drives the process forward. In the final write up, the emergent theory is at the centre and any pre-existing theoretical ideas are linked to it, not vice versa as in conventional qualitative analysis where the findings from a study are embedded into existing literature.

Box 4.6   Key concept – The place of the literature in grounded theory research

A grounded theory is grounded in and emerges from the *data*, not the literature; so the critical thing about the literature in a grounded theory study is that, wherever and however it is used, it does not interfere with, direct, guide or force the discovery (Glaser and Strauss, 1967), development or construction (Charmaz, 2014) of the resultant theory.

The concept of theoretical sensitivity has been subject to much debate. For Glaser (1978) it is about being theoretically competent to recognise theoretical concepts emerging from the data, but without *imposing* preconceived concepts on the data. Kelle (2007, 2010) points out that emergence and theoretical sensitivity are at odds with one another, seeming to pull in different directions and are almost mutually exclusive. Glaser does acknowledge that this is a difficult concept to grasp and implement. Hoare et al. (2012) take a lighter approach to theoretical sensitivity, and simply describe that it can be acquired by consulting the literature during the analytical process, drawing on one's previous experience, and practising reflexivity during memo writing.

Charmaz's (2014) constructivist approach to theoretical sensitivity and the place of the literature is intensely reflexive and iterative, requiring careful consideration of numerous different voices on the emergent theory (Hoare et al., 2012; Rieger, 2018), and following several different theoretical paths, often doubling back, more or less at the same time. Charmaz is happy for the literature to be consulted during the research 'but only as a point of departure' (2014: 30). Her process of theoretical coding with gerunds (-ing words formed by verbs functioning as nouns whereby, for example, 'to analyse' becomes 'analysing') assists the researcher to move from a static analytical place to a dynamic analytical place in following processes and movement (Carmichael and Cunningham, 2017; Hoare et al., 2012).

What qualifies as data

In defining what counts as data there is a difference between classic grounded theory and constructivist grounded theory. The much-quoted statement from Glaser (1967), that 'all is data' captures the view of data in classic grounded theory. The interpretive approach of constructivist grounded theory prefers the gathering of qualitative data such as interviews, documents, company records, and creative and/visual representations; the purpose is to extract the richest possible data from the best possible sources, so 'all is data' still applies, but it is qualitative data.

Box 4.7   Doing research – What qualifies as data

Mohammed was delighted with the data gathering and conceptualising process: 'Barney Glaser's statement that "all is data" meant that everything in the research area could be captured as data, and that classic grounded theory procedures would test it for relevance. Data is never right or wrong. Whatever participants said or did, even if the intention was to misrepresent what was happening, was recorded. The grounded theory took the data in the field and created abstract concepts to generate a theory grounded in data.'

Mohammed also shared, 'when I got there, the literature was treated as data for constant comparison purposes'.

Following the principle of getting the best possible data, coaching researchers might, for example, use their pilot data, use their own experiences, interview as many people as necessary, do repeat interviews if necessary, or use other sources of data if they will enrich the emerging theoretical ideas. Researchers should avoid judging a segment of data or discarding it as not fitting an emergent theory, but rather immerse themselves in it and see what comes up to give the creation of the knowledge the best possible chance.

Given the orientation of values within a capabilities model, the value of coaching is often seen as a co-creation process (Bachkirova, 2017; Cunningham, 2017; Stelter, 2016), so it is not a far leap to say that the values described in Charmaz's intensive interviewing and those of coaching are aligned. Constructivist grounded theory researchers will see the theoretical constructs arising from respondent conversations as the data emerge just as coaches will see the needs and insights of their client arising during coaching conversations. Constructivist grounded theory is therefore compatible with the ethos held in the coaching space.

Gathering data

> ### Box 4.8   Doing research – Sensitive, empathic interviewing
>
> Mohammed explained how he had to get the participants to relax 'in order that they speak so that their main concern and its routine resolution could be identified. Many of them were afraid to put their professional security at risk. They have nowhere else to go. They do not want to be identified as participants.'
>
> Many of those doing coaching research are coaches themselves, as was Natalie; this is advantageous because coaches are excellent listeners, which is also a key interviewing skill. Natalie explained how: 'as a coach, I have fine-tuned some competencies such as very active, engaged listening, asking questions in a non-judgmental way, and building trust with the client. It was important to recognise that this skill is useful in interviewing.'
>
> One of Natalie's PhD respondents illustrates appreciation of the non-judgemental and supportive approach of their coach as a precursor to asking a challenging question.
>
> > Executive 10: 'She listens without bias or judgement; there is something around the physical space, her whole way of being, her style is very empathic, it is gentle, but that enables her to ask the difficult questions in an entirely appropriate and supportive way.'

Connectivity between researcher and researched can be enhanced by accounting for the cultural dimensions of individualism and collectivism (Dorfman et al., 2012). Hofstede (1980, 2009) describes the way that many Western cultures are more individualistic and many Eastern, Latin American and African cultures are more collectivistic. Thus, a Western researcher might be inclined to take an efficient approach to an interview and get directly down to the business of data collection. This would not necessarily be appreciated by a more collectivist respondent who would want to establish a relationship of trust before divulging his/her private views and experiences to a stranger. Similarly, the individualistic researcher should spend not inconsiderable time establishing trust and moving at least some of the way from outsider status to insider status to improve the quality and richness of the data. Likewise, a collectivistic researcher may mildly irritate an individualistic respondent by 'wasting time with idle chit-chat' at the beginning of an interview. However, one should still not make unverified assumptions about regional similarities; countries in Protestant Europe, Catholic Europe and Orthodox Europe have quite different individualism/collectivism profiles (Inglehart, 2018).

A common error is made when objectivist-orientated researchers take an overly structured, standardised, predetermined and quantitative approach to their study. This approach does not resonate when the nature of the study (grounded theory method) is inherently subjective, unstructured, individually-focused, seeks meaning, symbolism and interpretations, and the approach is qualitative (Morey and Luthans, 1984). As Natalie pointed out, 'coaching researchers must be careful not to be trapped into asking closed-ended questions when trying to gather unstructured data; they need to constantly seek alternative views and multi-faceted aspects of the interview data'.

In our experience the much-published separation of qualitative and quantitative types of research is problematic, partly because the very nature of objectivism is to be binary. Moreover, objectivism (the scientific method) has been around a great deal longer than subjectivism, which takes a more nuanced, many-shades-of-grey approach that is comfortable with both/and, multiple realities, ambiguity and paradox. The coaching researcher needs to be open to probing for and identifying these nuances as described by Polkinghorne (2005: 137): 'the production of interview data requires awareness of the complexity of self-reports and the relation between experience and language expression ... requiring practised skill and time'.

Box 4.9   Doing research – The unstructured interview

Interview guides should use open-ended questions so as not to force *a priori* categories onto the respondent in the data gathering or the analysis processes. Terri Carmichael observed that it is very difficult for grounded theory method researchers to bracket out their prior knowledge, but if they take reflexivity seriously, they can identify when they are imposing pre-existing categories and self-correct. She feels that there is no place for semi-structured

(Continued)

interviews in the grounded theory method. A good place to start with a grounded theory interview is something along the lines of 'please tell me the story of how you ...' and probe for more detail from there. Only towards the end of the process, can one ask specifically about concepts as they emerge from the analytical process.

Concurrent data gathering and data analysis: theoretical sampling

Box 4.10   Key concept – Theoretical sampling

Synchronous data collection and analysis is a main tenet of the grounded theory method (Glaser et al., 2013); the first interview is analysed virtually immediately to identify emerging concepts and conceptual relationships, which then inform the selection of the next data source, and so on, with continuous adaptation by the researcher to maintain the relevance of the emerging theory to the data (Bryant and Charmaz, 2010).

Concurrent data analysis and gathering further influences how the research design process emerges and can influence factors such as sample size, the next sources of data collection and interview style. In this way, the researcher continuously adapts the data collection process to ensure the relevance of the data to the emerging theory. Theoretical sampling ensures that data collection is aimed at theory generation by utilising the ideas developed during the initial phases of analysis to determine the characteristics of subsequent participants and the focus of data collection (Charmaz, 2014). Thus, the cycle of sampling, data collection and analysis in grounded theory continues until no new dimensions of the categories emerge (Breckenridge and Jones, 2009). This is known as theoretical saturation and the point at which sampling and data collection end (Bowen, 2006).

Memos and reflexivity

Box 4.11   Key concept – Writing reflective memos

Memos are analytical notes written by the researcher as they read, process and analyse their data; they are used to question, compare and clarify different aspects of the data to inform theoretical sampling (Corbin and Strauss, 2015), and to note specific theoretical insights about the data.

Although memo writing is described as an intermediate step between data collection and writing drafts of the paper (Charmaz, 2014), in many cases, memos become the actual drafts of the paper. Memos result from reflexivity (Pillow, 2003), and capture thoughts, positionality, comparisons, crystallisation of questions, and make the work concrete and manageable. Part of the purpose of memos is to develop an awareness of the researcher's own prejudices and to be open to data that expose their biases and preconceived ideas (McGhee et al., 2007).

Box 4.12 Doing research – The importance of memos

Natalie wrote in her journal after each interview; 'interviews were transcribed and the analysis began with my reading each transcript and writing memos, which captured my reaction to and insights about each transcript. This informed my next interview, and the pattern of using memos as part of the concurrent analysis was established. I would compare interview one to interview two and then write a memo; sometimes these were only a line or two, at other times a page or two. These memos were an integral part of the analysis and theory development.'

Mohammed reinforced this approach: 'in classic grounded theory the researcher stays close to the data and allows it to cook slowly. In that time during the data collection and analysis processes intuitions and hunches might suggest ways to negotiate the gaps between data collection and analysis. The writing of memos is non-negotiable. It is a discipline that has to be adopted right from the start. The researcher should know that the grounded theory comes from the arrangement and rearrangement of piles of memos.'

As a research supervisor, Terri observed that many students reflect and write memos on their own, yet feels that reflexivity does not have to be an 'alone' activity. She has experienced the co-creation of knowledge that happens in the reflexive space during supervisory conversations in the same way that Charmaz (2017) describes knowledge co-creation between researcher and participant during their conversations. Terri finds that writing and thinking are wholly integrated and mutually constitutive, convinced that we do not do either of them very well without the other, and assumes that this is what Finlay (2002) refers to as reflexive writing.

Although an integral part of the analytical and theory-building process, reflexivity is particularly encouraged in coaching researchers using either grounded theory method, as it is one of the cornerstones of the approach. Benefits of reflexivity to researchers include:

• Identification of the influence that their positionality plays in their study (Berger, 2015; Orange, 2016). Students of coaching are taught that self-awareness is critical to their success, and their positionality in relation to their data collection will reinforce this awareness.

- Positioning the influence of their prior experiences and assumptions on their research (Orange, 2016); coaching researchers need to bracket out prior assumptions to prevent interpretive contamination.
- Awareness of the ethical aspects of their work (Berger, 2015; Orange, 2016) is critical to the practice of the coaching profession.
- Reflexively gaining personal and professional insights through introspection (Finlay, 2002, 2012) will lead to deep theoretical insights from their research.
- Collaboration through reflective dialogue to reach a collective understanding (Finlay, 2002, 2012) can lead to insights that may not come on one's own.
- Intersubjectivity awareness in which the researcher explores meaning within the relationships between themselves, their respondents and their supervisor (Finlay, 2002, 2012).
- Social constructions of power relationships may emerge from experiential accounts (Finlay, 2002, 2012; Jackson, 2011); coaching students would benefit in the same way that Natalie did from an equal status approach to their respondents as well as future clients.
- Challenging and deconstructing their own rhetoric so that multiple voices may be heard. The ambiguity of language and meaning-making through language is reflected in what Finlay (2002, 2012) calls ironic deconstruction, or the witty interpretation of one's own thoughts.
- A sense of researcher identity and voice (Cunningham and Carmichael, 2018) inspires self-confidence.

Coding the data

> ## Box 4.13   Key concept – Coding the data
>
> A code in qualitative enquiry is most often a word or short phrase that symbolically assigns a summative, salient, essence-capturing and/or evocative attribute for a portion of language-based or visual data. (Saldaña, 2016: 4)

Systematic coding procedures of at least two steps of preliminary and higher-order coding are the link between collecting data, interpreting the data and building a theory (Charmaz, 2008). The progressive development of abstract theories is facilitated by the constant comparative method which involves cycles of comparing data with data, data with codes and categories, and categories with categories (Starks and Brown Trinidad, 2007).

Box 4.14   Doing research – Comparative coding

Natalie recounts her coding process as follows: the first interview generated 56 codes, and there were no new codes after eight interviews. However, participant eight was an experienced, trained coach as well as being an executive, and her contribution added 24 new codes. After this substantial input, she re-analysed all the previous transcripts to seek whether her insights had been overlooked in the analysis. Subsequently, each time a new code emerged, all the previous transcripts were re-evaluated to see if some evidence had been missed, and also if any insights *about* the new code could be identified. This exercise appears to extend previously published ideas of constant comparison, which seem to have mainly taken place in a forward direction only (Carmichael and Cunningham, 2017).

Developing the theory

The building blocks of theory are concepts (Anfara Jr and Mertz, 2015; Jaccard and Jacoby, 2010), which are abstract labels given to raw data during the coding process (Corbin and Strauss, 2015). From there, Anfara Jr and Mertz (2015: 16) provide the following description of theory-building from empirical data:

> Working from the most concrete level of sensations and experience, concepts are words that we assign to events. Concepts enable us to distinguish one event or sensation from another. Often these concepts will cluster and form a higher-order unit known as a construct. Moving to the next level of abstraction, we encounter propositions. Propositions are expressions of relationships among several constructs. Because propositions are new inventions, they must be carefully defined and explained. Because one proposition is usually insufficient to explain a new insight about an aspect of reality, researchers use a set of propositions that are logically related. It is this relationship among propositions that constitutes theory.

The creation of concepts based on concrete experiences (presenting as data), then the clustering of the concepts into constructs, followed by framing the constructs into propositions and thence into theory is illustrated in Figure 4.1.

An oft-neglected aspect of theory-building is that of the *relationships* between the concepts and constructs (Spradley, 2016); some coaching students simply provide diagrammatic representations of theories with boxes and connectors or arrows. However, they almost never label the connectors, yet these represent the relationships between the concepts and are fundamental to the emergent theory. Although Glaser (1978) is happy with seeking causality in classic grounded theory, causality is by no means the only type of relationship between concepts and constructs; other possibilities for these relationships include parts of a whole, correlations, sequences, steps in a process, or attribution (Parfitt, 1996; Spradley, 2016); concept mapping is also a useful tool for

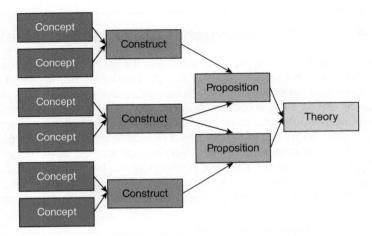

Figure 4.1 The building blocks of theory based on Anfara Jr and Mertz

Source: Adapted from Anfara Jr, V.A. and Mertz, N.T. (2015). 'Setting the stage'. In V.A. Anfara Jr and N.T. Mertz (eds), *Theoretical Frameworks in Qualitative Research*. Thousand Oaks, CA: Sage Publications, pp. 1–20.

identifying relationships between concepts (Davies, 2011; Jackson and Trochim, 2002). For example, the concepts of trust and trustworthiness may both emerge during the analysis of a coaching interview transcript; these two concepts could have a process relationship as in, 'being trustworthy is a step towards building trust'. Coding can be done manually or with qualitative data analysis software such as Atlas.ti; Friese (2014) provides an excellent text explaining in detail how to code using the software.

Integrating the literature

The final analytical step is to review the pertinent literature to identify how and where the developed theory compares with pre-existing knowledge (Strauss and Corbin, 1998). The emergence principle in classic grounded theory is against problematising the literature as a starting point for research. This does not mean that literature is ignored in classic grounded theory, but that we should wait until the main concern and the core category emerge before starting to consult the literature (Glaser, 1978; Walsh et al., 2015). In this way, the data is not being forced to fit into existing categories. This is in contrast to the views of constructivist grounded theorists (Charmaz, 2014; Thornberg, 2012), who believe that a high-level literature review can be done first if one's stance is critical, reflective and grounded in reflexivity.

Evaluation

The place of the grounded theory method in coaching research is exciting because of the poorly developed theoretical base in the field; opportunities abound for students to make their mark in the literature. However, completing the research for dissertation or thesis purposes is not alone sufficient to make an impact; the research must be published in the scholarly coaching literature.

Grounded theory is usefully applied to discovering insights into new concepts, contexts and issues – directly from those intimately involved in those issues. Additionally, because using the grounded theory method allows researchers to 'zero-base' theory development, there are opportunities to explore existing concepts with fresh eyes, unencumbered by pre-existing boundaries put in place by years of previous research in a particular direction.

Although a common criticism of the grounded theory approach is that it is not generalisable, this need not deter researchers. Glaser's approach can be more easily generalised because of the underlying assumptions and approaches detailed in Table 4.1, but one should also bear in mind that the purpose of qualitative research is theory or hypothesis *generation*, not testing. This means that the theories offered as the endpoint of grounded theory studies can easily enough be tested in a future study; the theories do not need to be generalisable in themselves, but they should be testable.

Further reading

Bennett, J.L. (2006). 'An agenda for coaching-related research: A challenge for researchers'. *Consulting Psychology Journal: Practice and Research* 58: 240–9.

Cox, E., Bachkirova, T. and Clutterbuck, D. (2014). 'Theoretical traditions and coaching genres: Mapping the territory'. *Advances in Developing Human Resources* 16: 139–60.

Passmore, J. and Fillery-Travis, A. (2011). 'A critical review of executive coaching research: A decade of progress and what's to come'. *Coaching: An International Journal of Theory, Research and Practice* 4: 70–88.

Walsh, I., Holton, J.A., Bailyn, L., Fernandez, W., Levina, N. and Glaser, B. (2015). What grounded theory is … a critically reflective conversation among scholars. *Organizational Research Methods* 18: 581–99.

Discussion questions

1. What is similar and different between a phenomenological method and the grounded theory approach within the coaching context?
2. Coaching is both an academic and professional discipline; how may coaching researchers leverage both orientations in their grounded theory study?
3. What are the challenges (either in the field or with the methodology) that you have come across while doing your coaching research using either grounded theory method? Articulate solutions to the challenges you have experienced.

References

Abravanel, M. (2018). 'Coaching presence: A grounded theory from the coach's perspective'. *PhD thesis, Concordia University, Montreal, Canada*. Available at: https://spectrum.library.concordia.ca/984432/ (accessed 15 November 2018).

Anfara Jr, V.A. and Mertz, N.T. (2015). 'Setting the stage'. In V.A. Anfara Jr and N.T. Mertz (eds), *Theoretical Frameworks in Qualitative Research*. Thousand Oaks, CA: Sage Publications, pp. 1–20.

Apramian, T., Cristancho, S., Watling, C. and Lingard, L. (2017). '(Re)grounding grounded theory: A close reading of theory in four schools'. *Qualitative Research* 17: 359–76.

Bachkirova, T. (2017). 'Developing a knowledge base of coaching: Questions to explore'. In T. Bachkirova, G. Spence and D. Drake (eds), *The SAGE Handbook of Coaching*. Thousand Oaks, CA: Sage Publications, pp. 23–41.

Berger, R. (2015). 'Now I see it, now I don't: Researcher's position and reflexivity in qualitative research'. *Qualitative Research* 15: 219–34.

Bowen, G.A. (2006). 'Grounded theory and sensitizing concepts'. *International Journal of Qualitative Methods* 5: 12–23.

Breckenridge, J. and Jones, D. (2009). 'Demystifying theoretical sampling in grounded theory research'. *The Grounded Theory Review* 8: 113–26.

Bryant, A. and Charmaz, K. (2007). 'Grounded theory research: Methods and practices'. In A. Bryant and K. Charmaz (eds) *The SAGE Handbook of Grounded Theory*. Thousand Oaks, CA: Sage Publications, pp. 1–29.

Bryant, A. and Charmaz, K. (eds) (2010). *The SAGE Handbook of Grounded Theory*. Thousand Oaks, CA: Sage Publications.

Carmichael, T. and Cunningham, N. (2017). 'Theoretical data collection and data analysis with gerunds in a constructivist grounded theory study'. *Electronic Journal of Business Research Methods* 15: 59–73.

Charmaz, K. (2000). 'Grounded theory: Objectivist and constructivist methods'. In N. Denzin and Y. Lincoln (eds), *Handbook of Qualitative Research*. London: Sage Publications, pp. 509–35.

Charmaz, K. (2008). 'Grounded theory as an emergent method'. In S. N. Hesse-Biber and P. Leavy (eds), *Handbook of emergent methods*. London: Guilford Press, pp. 155–72.

Charmaz, K. (2014). *Constructing Grounded Theory: A Practical Guide through Qualitative Analysis* (2nd edition). London: Sage Publications.

Charmaz, K. (2017). 'The power of constructivist grounded theory for critical inquiry'. *Qualitative Inquiry* 23: 34–45.

Corbin, J. and Strauss, A. (2015). *Basics of Qualitative Research: Techniques and Procedures for Developing Grounded Theory* (4th edition). Thousand Oaks, CA: Sage Publications.

Cox, E., Bachkirova, T. and Clutterbuck, D.A. (eds) (2014). *The Complete Handbook of Coaching* (2nd edition). London: Sage Publications.

Cunningham, N. (2017). 'A theory of the coaching process based on the lived experience of coached executives in South Africa'. PhD thesis, University of the Witwatersrand, South Africa.

Cunningham, N. and Carmichael, T. (2018). 'Finding my intuitive researcher's voice through reflexivity: An autoethnographic study'. *The Electronic Journal of Business Research Methods* 16: 55–65.

Davies, M. (2011). 'Concept mapping, mind mapping and argument mapping: What are the differences and do they matter?' *Higher Education* 62: 279–301.

Denzin, N. and Lincoln, Y. (eds) (2000). *Handbook of Qualitative Research*. Thousand Oaks, CA: Sage Publications.

Dorfman, P., Javidan, M., Hanges, P., Dastmalchian, A. and House, R. (2012). 'Globe: A twenty year journey into the intriguing world of culture and leadership'. *Journal of World Business* 47: 504–18.

Finlay, L. (2002). 'Negotiating the swamp: The opportunity and challenge of reflexivity in research practice'. *Qualitative Research* 2: 209–30.

Finlay, L. (2012). 'Five lenses for the reflexive interviewer'. In J.F. Gubrium, J.A. Holstein, A.B. Marvasti and K.D. McKinney (eds), *The SAGE Handbook of Interview Research: The Complexity of the Craft*. Thousand Oaks, CA: Sage Publications, pp. 317–32.

Friese, S. (2014). *Qualitative Data Analysis with Atlas.Ti*. London: Sage Publications.

Garrison, J.W. (1988). 'The impossibility of atheoretical educational science'. *The Journal of Educational Thought (JET)/Revue de la Pensée Educative* 22: 21–6.

Glaser, B. (1978). *Theoretical Sensitivity: Advances in the Methodology of Grounded Theory*. Mill Valley, CA: Sociology Press.

Glaser, B. (1998). *Doing Grounded Theory: Issues and Discussions*. Mill Valley, CA: Sociology Press.

Glaser, B. (2002). 'Conceptualization: On theory and theorizing using grounded theory'. *International Journal of Qualitative Methods* 1: 23–38.

Glaser, B. (2014). 'Applying grounded theory'. *The Grounded Theory Review* 13: 46–50.

Glaser, B. (2016a). 'Grounded description: No no'. *The Grounded Theory Review* 15: 3–7.

Glaser, B. (2016b). *The Grounded Theory Perspective: Its Origins and Growth*. Mill Valley, CA: Sociology Press.

Glaser, B.G. and Holton, J. (2004). 'Remodeling grounded theory'. *Forum: Qualitative Sozialforschung/Forum: Qualitative Social Research* 5(2): 1–22.

Glaser, B. and Holton, J. (2007). 'Remodelling grounded theory'. *Historical Social Research/Historische Sozialforschung* 19: 47–68.

Glaser, B. and Strauss, A.L. (1967, 1998, 2017). *The Discovery of Grounded Theory*. Berne: Huber.

Glaser, B., Bailyn, L., Fernandez, W., Holton, J.A. and Levina, N. (2013). 'What grounded theory is …'. *Academy of Management Proceedings*. https://doi.org/10.5465/ambpp.2013.11290symposium.

Handfield, R.B. and Melnyk, S.A. (1998). 'The scientific theory-building process: A primer using the case of TQM'. *Journal of Operations Management* 16: 321–39.

Hoare, K.J., Mills, J. and Francis, K. (2012). 'Dancing with data: An example of acquiring theoretical sensitivity in a grounded theory study'. *International Journal of Nursing Practice* 18: 240–5.

Hofstede, G. (1980). *Culture's Consequences: National Differences in Thinking and Organizing*. Beverly Hills, CA: Sage Publications.

Hofstede, G. (2009). *'Geert Hofstede' [Online]*. Available at: http://cl.rikkyo.ac.jp/zenkari/2009/2009/05/13/Geert_Hofstede.doc (accessed 22 December 2009).

Hollis, J.M. (2013). 'A grounded theory examination of coaching and mentoring: Human agency expressed in the one-with-one development endeavor'. EdD thesis, Southeastern Baptist Theological Seminary. Available at: www.proquest.com/en-US/products/dissertations/individuals.shtml (accessed 12 November 2018).

Holton, J.A. and Walsh, I. (2017). *Classic Grounded Theory: Applications with Qualitative & Quantitative Data*. London: Sage Publications.

Hood, J. (2010). 'Orthodoxy vs. power: The defining traits of grounded theory'. In A. Bryant and K. Charmaz (eds), *The SAGE Handbook of Grounded Theory*. Thousand Oaks, CA: Sage Publications, pp. 151–64.

Inglehart, R. (2018). *Cultural Evolution: People's Motivations are Changing, and Reshaping the World*. Cambridge: Cambridge University Press.

Jaccard, J. and Jacoby, J. (2010). *Theory Construction and Model-Building Skills: A Practical Guide for Social Scientists*. New York: Guilford Press.

Jackson, K.M. and Trochim, W.M. (2002). 'Concept mapping as an alternative approach for the analysis of open-ended survey responses'. *Organizational Research Methods* 5: 307–36.

Jackson, T. (2011). 'From cultural values to cross-cultural interfaces: Hofstede goes to Africa'. *Journal of Organizational Change Management* 24: 532–58.

Kelle, U. (2007). '"Emergence" vs. "forcing" of empirical data? A crucial problem of "grounded theory" reconsidered'. *Historical Social Research/Historische Sozialforschung* 19: 133–56.

Kelle, U. (2010). 'The development of categories: Different approaches in grounded theory'. In A. Bryant and K. Charmaz (eds), *The SAGE Handbook of Grounded Theory*. Thousand Oaks, CA: Sage Publications, pp. 191–213.

Khazanchi, D. and Munkvold, B.E. (2014). 'The rhetoric and relevance of IS research paradigms: Conceptual foundations and empirical evidence'. Paper presented at the 36th Annual Hawaii International Conference on System Sciences. Hawaii, USA.

Konecki, K.T. (2018). 'Classic grounded theory—the latest version: Interpretation of classic grounded theory as a meta-theory for research'. *Symbolic Interaction* 41: 547–64.

McGhee, G., Marland, G.R. and Atkinson, J. (2007). 'Grounded theory research: Literature reviewing and reflexivity'. *Journal of Advanced Nursing* 60: 334–42.

Morey, N.C. and Luthans, F. (1984). 'An emic perspective and ethnoscience methods for organizational research'. *Academy of Management Review* 9: 27–36.

Morris, M.W., Leung, K., Ames, D. and Lickel, B. (1999). 'Views from inside and outside: Integrating emic and etic insights about culture and justice judgment'. *Academy of Management Review* 24: 781–96.

Orange, A. (2016). 'Encouraging reflective practices in doctoral students through research journals'. *The Qualitative Report* 21: 2176–90.

Parfitt, B.A. (1996). 'Using Spradley: An ethnosemantic approach to research'. *Journal of Advanced Nursing* 24: 341–9.

Peterson, M.F. and Pike, K.L. (2002). 'Emics and etics for organizational studies: A lesson in contrast from linguistics'. *International Journal of Cross Cultural Management* 2: 5–19.

Pike, K.L. (1967). *Language in Relation to a Unified Theory of the Structure of Human Behavior*. Paris: Mouton.

Pillow, W. (2003). 'Confession, catharsis, or cure? Rethinking the uses of reflexivity as methodological power in qualitative research'. *International Journal of Qualitative Studies in Education* 16: 175–96.

Polkinghorne, D.E. (2005). 'Language and meaning: Data collection in qualitative research'. *Journal of Counseling Psychology* 52: 137–45.

Rieger, K.L. (2018). 'Discriminating among grounded theory approaches'. *Nursing Inquiry* 26: e12261.

Rogers, C. (2012). *Client Centred Therapy* (ed. L. Carmichael). London: Hachette.

Saldaña, J. (2016). *The Coding Manual for Qualitative Researchers*. Thousand Oaks, CA: Sage Publications.

Seitz, K.A. (2009). 'A grounded theory investigation of the relationship between positive psychology coaching and thriving'. PhD thesis, Capella University. Available at: https://search.proquest.com/openview/629e213332651435d33a4d63ba1c37c9/1?pq-origsite=gscholar&cbl=18750&diss=y (accessed 12 November 2018).

Shah, S. (2004). 'The researcher/interviewer in intercultural context: A social intruder!' *British Educational Research Journal* 30: 549–75.

Sheppard, L. (2016). 'How coaching supervisees help and hinder their supervision: A grounded theory study'. Doctor of Coaching and Mentoring thesis, Oxford Brookes University, Oxford. Available at: https://ethos.bl.uk/OrderDetails.do?uin=uk.bl.ethos.741036 (accessed 12 November 2018).

Spradley, J.P. (2016). *The Ethnographic Interview*. Long Grove, IL: Waveland Press.

Starks, H. and Brown Trinidad, S. (2007). 'Choose your method: A comparison of phenomenology, discourse analysis, and grounded theory'. *Qualitative Health Research* 17: 1372–80.

Stelter, R. (2016). 'The coach as a fellow human companion'. In L. van Zyl, M.W. Stander and A. Odendaal (eds), *Coaching Psychology: Meta-Theoretical Perspectives and Applications in Multicultural Contexts*. Switzerland: Springer, pp. 47–66.

Strauss, A. and Corbin, J. (1998). *Basics of Qualitative Research: Techniques and Procedures for Developing Grounded Theory*. Thousand Oaks, CA: Sage Publications.

Thornberg, R. (2012). 'Informed grounded theory'. *Scandinavian Journal of Educational Research* 56: 243–59.

Tinker, C. and Armstrong, N. (2008). 'From the outside looking in: How an awareness of difference can benefit the qualitative research process'. *The Qualitative Report* 13: 53–60.

Walsh, I., Holton, J.A., Bailyn, L., Fernandez, W., Levina, N. and Glaser, B. (2015). 'What grounded theory is … A critically reflective conversation among scholars'. *Organizational Research Methods*, 18(4): 581–99.

Weber, R. (2003). 'Editor's comments: The reflexive researcher'. *MIS Quarterly* 27: v–xiv.

Zoogah, D.B. (2008). 'African business research: A review of studies published in the *Journal of African Business* and a framework for enhancing future studies'. *Journal of African Business* 9: 219–55.

5
Phenomenological approaches

Tatiana Bachkirova, Alison Rose and Roger Noon

Introduction

In the developing discipline of coaching, researchers are spoilt for choice in terms of the focus of projects: the field is full of under-researched phenomena which are ripe for exploration. Researchers can choose many topics of interest, use different methodologies and aim to generate different kinds of knowledge and, at first glance, the research student may perceive phenomenology as just one amongst many other approaches. We, however, would like to make a case for a special role of phenomenology in coaching research. First of all, along with Spinelli (1989), we could see phenomenology as a rewarding starting point for *any* research. Even when the ambition of the researchers is to develop a generalisable account of events and processes, to design an experiment or to test a particular theory, they may need to start from understandings and descriptions of the phenomenon in question, which are drawn from exploratory studies or observations.

Second, we believe that phenomenology has a particular affinity with the coaching process. Coaching is about human action and interaction and the important features of what is happening in coaching are available for understanding

mainly from the first-person perspective – which may be best understood through
methods of inquiry that focus on people's own experiences. Direct observation of
the coaching process offers a limited perspective on what is going on in coaching
and even observations in many ways are experiences affected by the perceptual
frames of the observers. Therefore, phenomenology, being interested in the world
as experienced by human beings, with all the complexity involved in real life
situations and with all the nuances of the contexts in which they occur, is inevitably in close relationship with the core of coaching. Furthermore, it might be
said that the methods employed by coaches and phenomenological researchers
are also not too far apart. Coaches pay close attention to the subjective experiences of clients and the meaning they make of these experiences are the main
source of information for supporting clients. At the same time, coaches keep in
mind how tinted such perceptions can be because of their clients' and their own
frames of reference. Phenomenologists also are engaged in inquiries that see experiences as essential, but using various means of 'clearing the lens' for deeper
understanding of the phenomenon.

The theoretical origin and main principles of this approach to research can
be attributed to phenomenology as a branch of philosophy (Gallagher and
Zahavi, 2008).

Box 5.1   Key concept

Although not a single homogeneous body of thought, this philosophical perspective, as argued by Kvale (1996: 38–9) upholds in most instances 'a focus on
the life world, an openness to the experiences of the subject, [and] a primacy
of precise description'.

Two variations in phenomenological philosophy are often described in the
research literature. Husserlian phenomenology (that is, after Edmund
Husserl, German philosopher, 1859–1938), is associated with attempts to
'bracket' – to put aside – foreknowledge, and to uncover the essential nature
of what is experienced through unprejudiced reflection on its manifestation
in individual instances. Some voices, though, for example Zahavi (2019),
critique this interpretation of the main Husserlian ideas. Heideggerian phenomenology (that is, after Martin Heidegger, former student of Husserl's,
1889–1976), largely rejects the possibility of bracketing and the notion of the
essential on the grounds that our understanding of phenomena is invariably
bound up in our interpretation of them – we are 'thrown into [a] pre-existing
world of people and objects, language and culture and cannot be meaningfully detached from it' (Smith et al., 2009: 17). This critical difference
between an approach which attempts to describe the essential nature of
what is given in experience and one which attempts to interpret it meaningfully will govern the researcher's choice of methodology within the wider
phenomenological field. French phenomenologists Sartre and Merleau-Ponty

were also important for the development of phenomenology as philosophy. For example, Merleau-Ponty's contribution, highly relevant to recent developments in coaching research and theory, is concerned with giving due importance to both the body and the mind. Vagle reports Merleau-Ponty's position that 'the body lives the world well before the mind can reason or make sense of what is being lived' (Vagle, 2018: 10).

Variations in the philosophy of phenomenology give rise to phenomenological approaches to research also being plural (Vagle, 2018). Husserlian phenomenology is seen as represented in the 'pure' phenomenological psychology method or descriptive phenomenology (Giorgi and Giorgi, 2013). Other approaches, associated more closely with Heideggerian phenomenology, include the well-known interpretative phenomenological analysis (IPA) (Smith et al., 2009) and heuristic research (Moustakas, 1994) methodologies and the lesser known conceptual encounter (de Rivera, 1981). Alongside important similarities in each of these methodologies there are nuances that differentiate each of them, indicating specific strengths and limitations for different questions and directions of coaching research. In Table 5.1 this variety in methodologies and their roles and purposes is presented in as close a way as possible to the descriptions given by their main proponents.

In the rest of this chapter we explore the distinctive features and how some important aspects of phenomenological research play out in the context of coaching research. Then we use, as examples, the experiences of two doctoral researchers using IPA and conceptual encounter in their projects to share their challenges and learning.

Distinctive features of phenomenological research

We believe that those who wish to use a phenomenological approach for researching coaching would benefit from considering the following five aspects. Each of these aspects will be described together with discussion points from critics of phenomenological approaches to research (for example, Paley, 2018; Willig, 2006).

1. The view of viable knowledge and the role of the researcher.
2. The type of questions suitable for this research.
3. The focus of the inquiry, role of language and sampling issues.
4. Description versus explication and the role of theory in phenomenology.
5. Variations of phenomenological methodologies.

The view of viable knowledge and the role of the researcher

To provide a rationale for a methodological approach to a study, researchers describe what kind of knowledge they hope to produce and what philosophical assumptions about knowledge underpin their choices. This is not a straightforward task if their chosen methodology is phenomenology, which does not fit neatly into either the realist or relativist camps. To start with, phenomenologists

Table 5.1 Comparison of typical phenomenological research methodologies

	Phenomenological psychology method	Interpretative phenomenological analysis	Heuristic research	Conceptual encounter
Theoretical underpinning/associations	Transcendental phenomenology, Idiography	Idiography, Phenomenology, Hermeneutics, Symbolic Interactionism	Phenomenology, Idiography, Humanism, Constructivism	Phenomenological psychology, Humanism, Idiography, Interactionism
Main proponents	Giorgi and Giorgi (2013)	Smith et al. (2009)	Moustakas (1994)	de Rivera (1981)
Dimensions of differences				
Role of the researcher	Bracketing foreknowledge, comparing accounts, establishing a general structure of the phenomenon	Micro-analysing and interpreting with reflexivity the convergence and divergence in accounts to interpret the meaning of experiences	Researcher as an instrument for data collection, self-inquiry as well as the inquiry into the phenomenon	Gatekeeper of concept development, foreknowledge of researcher is included in the dialogue and analysis
Main purpose	The integrated picture (essence) of the phenomenon	A picture of similarity and variability of human experience	Personal change of the researcher and essence of the phenomenon	Elucidation of the structure that exists within psychological events
Role of theory	Theoretical assumptions bracketed Only description is offered	Theoretical propositions are explored and compared with existing literature alongside emerged themes at the final stage	Theoretical propositions are secondary to creating synthesis that could be seen as theory	Concept is gradually developed and can be seen as a theoretical proposition
Balance of text and visual means	Analysis of the observations or text	Analysis of text and own memos – other data collection methods are encouraged but not often used	Any means of data collection, creative approach to final synthesis	Concept can appear as a map or an 'elegant' model

do not deny the existence of the world (Gallagher and Zahavi, 2008; Husserl, 1931; Zahavi, 2019). However, they are against a naïve and dogmatic version of a scientific attitude that assumes that reality is 'mind-, experience-, and theory-independent' (Gallagher and Zavavi, 2008; Vagle, 2018) with inevitable consequences for their epistemological stance being constructivist. In this regard the ontological and epistemological positions of phenomenology are not always dissimilar to critical realism or pragmatism, in contrast to some postmodernist versions of the interpretivist paradigm.

To deal with the challenge of ontological realism and epistemological relativism, phenomenologists following Husserl's tradition introduce *epoche* or *phenomenological reduction*.

Box 5.2   Key concept – Epoche

Epoche or *phenomenological reduction* is a procedure that does not exclude reality from consideration but aims for 'suspending the judgment of the existence and pre-understanding of things outside of human mind, so that phenomena can be studied in their givenness to consciousness' (Vagle, 2018: 14).

It can be seen that for Husserl there is a distinct split between consciousness (subjectivity) and the world. Consciousness is not in the world, but transcendental to the world. It is separate from the world, and it is the separation which makes possible the *epoche* reduction. By contrast, Heidegger claimed we are not separate from the world – the world is only disclosed through being in the world. His term for this 'worldliness' and its disclosure through existence is *Dasein*.

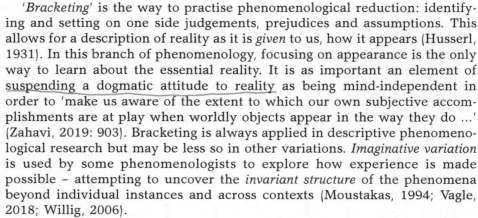

'*Bracketing*' is the way to practise phenomenological reduction: identifying and setting on one side judgements, prejudices and assumptions. This allows for a description of reality as it is *given* to us, how it appears (Husserl, 1931). In this branch of phenomenology, focusing on appearance is the only way to learn about the essential reality. It is as important an element of suspending a dogmatic attitude to reality as being mind-independent in order to 'make us aware of the extent to which our own subjective accomplishments are at play when worldly objects appear in the way they do ...' (Zahavi, 2019: 903). Bracketing is always applied in descriptive phenomenological research but may be less so in other variations. *Imaginative variation* is used by some phenomenologists to explore how experience is made possible – attempting to uncover the *invariant structure* of the phenomena beyond individual instances and across contexts (Moustakas, 1994; Vagle, 2018; Willig, 2006).

In this regard it is important to clarify a typical misunderstanding about the main intention of descriptive, Husserlian phenomenology. It is not about exploring the idiosyncratic experiences of individuals or nuances of their internal world, as coaches and therapists might in their practice. Rather, for

Husserlian phenomenologists the structures of experience uncovered in phenomenological inquiry may also prove to have an essential quality which transcends context and captures the 'true' nature of the world as it appears to us.

Box 5.3   Key concept

The underlying aim of phenomenology as a philosophy and research orientation is to capture the structures of experiences which can be intersubjectively accessible and therefore capable of being understood in relation to other experiences.

So, phenomenological researchers are not against the intention of science to extend our knowledge of the world. In fact, their aim is compatible with science. In focusing on the phenomenal world of the individual, without ignoring the constraints of the physical and social worlds (Harré, 1983; Willig, 2016), phenomenological researchers are extending knowledge from the first-person perspective with recognition that pure third-person science is impossible: as impossible as a view from nowhere (Gallagher and Zahavi, 2008).

The type of questions suitable for this research

The philosophical foundation of phenomenological inquiry has inevitable implications for what researchers choose as their focus of interest. Phenomenological study is typically considered when researchers are curious about questions that imply the need to engage with people's lived experiences. These experiences are usually about something that is important to researchers themselves, involving their sense-making about the experience, which may have implications as to how these researchers see themselves in relation to the objects of interest. Examples of such questions in relation to coaching could be:

- What is the experience of flow in coaching relationship?
- What is the experience of coaching those who are not ready for coaching?
- What it is like to coach for gravitas?
- What is the experience of working on the boundary between coaching and counselling?

It is clear that these types of questions imply the involvement of research participants who have had those experiences, with an aim to understand what is shared in them. The typical method of this research is interview, with a recent tendency to include sources other than language (for example, photographs, drawings, objects, etc.) in order to generate a richer analysis of feelings and embodied experiences (Cromby, 2015; Merleau-Ponty, 1968).

It could be said that 'the phenomenon calls for how it should be studied' (Vagle, 2018: 17); however, descriptive phenomenological research would be less likely to include measurement instruments and experiment. What is important in formulating a research question is that phenomenologists see the world as inseparable from individuals' mental orientations (for example, desires, emotions, drives), what is called *intentionality* (Moustakas, 1994; Willig, 2006). This means that when researchers plan to study something phenomenologically they will be studying both the phenomenon of interest and the wide-ranging intentional relations that appear in connection with it, for example confusion, respect, hope, etc. (Vagle, 2018).

Box 5.4   Doing research – Alison Rose

For me, the tenets of philosophical phenomenology resonated with how I understood coaching as a sense-making process, and a phenomenological approach to research therefore became effectively an extension of my reflective coaching practice.

The observation of the inseparability of individuals and the world is equally applicable to the researchers themselves. Even when trying to *bracket* their presuppositions and avoid inherent biases, researchers recognise the fallibility of acquired knowledge and engage in critical examination of their customary ways of relating to the world through the process of *reflexivity* (Spinelli, 1989; Vagle, 2018; Willig, 2006).

The focus of inquiry, role of language and sampling issues

Significant and valid critique of phenomenological research is concentrated on the issue of the unit of analysis which is associated with sampling, and the use of language in naming the phenomenon of interest. For example, Willig (2007) describes how in her research on the experiences of those involved in extreme sports she chose to bring together different sports which had not previously been seen as part of the same group. This could be seen as leading to an artificial integration of a range of possibly quite different activities in different contexts. A similar concern is expressed by Paley (2018) in his critique of a study by van Manen (1990) in which he argued that the phenomenon of children 'being left behind' included too dissimilar a range of experiences of the participants in unrelated contexts. Linking significantly different instances of this phenomenon without sufficient justification built a misleading picture of it, not helpful for real life understanding and for helping practices.

The issue of language presents another challenge and influences the task of selection of the participants. Phenomenology expects a rich and fresh description of the phenomenon, but not every potential participant can provide this, only those (probably rare) individuals who have a high level of awareness and

---

Box 5.5   Doing research

As Willig (2007: 216) suggests '... the researcher's choice of label for the phenomena of interest is not merely a descriptive act but a constitutive one'. The choice of the unit of analysis is therefore very important and requires careful consideration whether the project is about examination of a pre-existing phenomenon or creating a new category of meaning. It is important then to be clear what is meant by 'a phenomenon'. If a coaching researcher is planning a phenomenological inquiry they would be advised to make sure that it is about an experience which is recognisable to participants even if it can be experienced in one or another way. For example, the experience of coaching an uncommitted client may vary because of the reasons for non-commitment; however, the experience of being involved in such an assignment should 'ring the bell' for participant coaches and be meaningful for exploration.

sufficient vocabulary to express their experiences. In coaching research, this challenge is particularly important when clients are chosen as participants with an expectation to provide their perspective on the coaching process. However, in the normal course of events, clients are not expected to be familiar with the terminology used in describing elements of the coaching process. In addition, clients' attention is unsurprisingly occupied by the *content* of coaching engagement and not focused on the coaching process. It would be unwise in such research to rely on linguistically rich input from the clients, unless more creative methods of data collection are developed.

Quite an opposite challenge for phenomenological study might present itself when clients or, more often coaches, with sophisticated linguistic abilities are chosen as participants. They might tend to theorise by shifting the description of phenomena to an abstract level thus losing the raw and immediate nuances that are most important in phenomenology. Another aspect of this 'linguistic challenge' relates to coaches as participants who overuse so-called 'coaching speak' and are seemingly unable to separate their immediate and authentic feeling from accepted labels used in their craft. It is probably reasonable in this case to have a pre-interview with potential participants to gauge their suitability for the project, particularly if the time line for it is tight and the sample is small. Sample selection is therefore not random, but part of the researcher's active shaping of the research process and outcomes.

Description versus explication and the role of theory in phenomenology

One of the most significant debates in relation to phenomenology is concerned with description vs explication as an outcome of phenomenological research. In the early work of Husserl (1931) phenomenology was intended as a descriptive enterprise and, accordingly, the main purpose of phenomenological research has been seen as creating integrated *description* of the phenomena in question (Giorgi and Giorgi, 2003). This is, of course, of value in itself, because a worthwhile understanding of a phenomenon has to start from a faithful and rich description. However, this does not mean simply summarising the participants' accounts of experience. An expectation is to extract wider meaning, bring to light what is not obvious (Giorgi and Giorgi, 2003), to move from the content to the structure of the experience and from appearances to the conditions that bring them about (Willig, 2007). Even more than that, according to Zahavi (2019: 902), 'The descriptions in question are means rather than ends. To think otherwise is fundamentally to misconceive the philosophical character of phenomenology'. Some phenomenologists believe that it is possible to link identified themes conceptually and produce theoretical formulations that may explicate them (Vagle, 2018). This requires the further interpretative work that is, for example, more explicitly expected in phenomenological approaches such as IPA (Smith et al., 2009) and conceptual encounter (de Rivera, 1981).

Variations of phenomenological methodologies

The issues that phenomenological researchers face can be addressed in different ways, keeping at the same time an integrity of approach and consistency with the various branches of the philosophy. As we have seen, there are different versions of phenomenological approaches to research and Table 5.1 described how the most recognisable approaches are different in relation to some important dimensions. It is not surprising to see differences between the approaches, because they are influenced by variations in the theoretical perspectives behind them and the tasks they were aiming to accomplish. The proponents of these theories were also trying to address some of the challenges that we described in this chapter. Coaching researchers accordingly may choose these approaches because of the particular focus of their study or personal resonance with their principles.

To bring some of these approaches to life in the context of coaching research, in the following section we share specific experiences and challenges that might be relevant to researchers of coaching using IPA and conceptual encounter.

Practical examples of interpretative phenomenological analysis (IPA) and conceptual encounter in coaching research

Case study – Alison Rose

My research question was 'What are the experiences of coaching as part of high potential development programmes, from the perspective of participants and coaches?' IPA's emphasis on lived experience, first-hand accounts,

Critical explanation or interpretation of text.
(vs hermeneutics — which is about the principles
used to interpret) Phenomenological approaches **83**

particularity, and researcher–participant co-construction of meaning, suggested that it was well-suited for exploration of this question.

In working with this variant of the phenomenological method, the IPA researcher commits to deep interpretation and reflection on data from single cases, ultimately moving to higher order analysis and comparison between cases to form a tentative theoretical exegesis. Ultimately researcher and reader are expected to connect the findings of an IPA study to existing literature, so as to shed light on existing research (Smith et al., 2009). In light of recent criticism of IPA (Paley, 2018), it is worth noting that this should be the maximum extent of the claims of an IPA study. Existing theory is never the starting point, so the method is not appropriate for testing hypotheses. Each idiographic account is considered to add to our corpus of knowledge, but not to be subject to being tested by it. Generalisability is limited to within-study comparison of themes, and relies on the reader making links between the evidence presented, their own experience, and their knowledge of existing literature.

IPA is rooted in the Heideggerian branch of phenomenology, in hermeneutics and in idiography. Contrary to recent challenges about a disconnection between phenomenological philosophy and phenomenological research methods (Paley, 2018) these traditions are not just background. Given the involved role of the IPA researcher, anyone undertaking an IPA study needs to understand and commit to the ontological and epistemological claims of this system of thought. As Giorgi puts it in relation to phenomenology generally, they need to 'think and dwell' within these frameworks (Giorgi, 2017: 83).

While phenomenology provides the foundation of the approach, and idiography underpins its process, hermeneutics licenses the IPA researcher to attempt to unravel the meaning of experience, and therefore distinguishes IPA from more descriptive methods. Hermeneutic principles justify the IPA researcher in generating a reading of accounts which goes beyond witnessing and description. An IPA-based study allows for an iterative, but broadly chronological process in which the researcher moves through stages of bracketed witnessing, to a hermeneutically-involved, interpretative state of authorship. Interpretation is therefore not simply a faithful rendition of accounts – it is a shaping process which contributes to findings and does not just convey them. Smith et al. suggest that 'the analyst is implicated in facilitating and making sense' of the appearance of phenomena (Smith et al., 2009: 28). The word 'implicated' carries weight, as Willig points out, since it implies that analysis is dependent on the researcher's own conceptions and standpoint (Willig, 2006).

For my study, I collected data from twelve participants – six coaches and six clients – using recorded semi-structured interviews. I transcribed these interviews and the resulting transcripts were analysed through several iterations using a process of coding to achieve higher levels of abstraction. Ultimately this resulted in the identification of a number of super-ordinate themes, and then cross-case and cross-sample patterns. The process of data analysis is outlined in Figure 5.1.

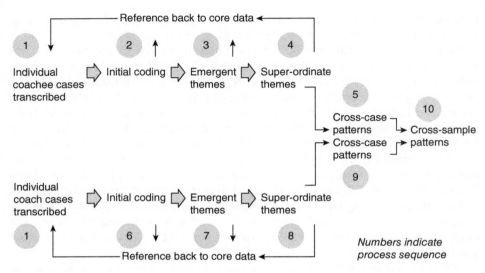

Figure 5.1 Challenges of IPA in researching coaching

Phenomenological research methodologies are not easy (a common misconception of those who judge the challenges and value of research by the size of the sample). Here are some aspects of my experience as a researcher that illustrate how challenging this methodology can be.

Firstly, on a practical level, using IPA in my study generated high volumes of data. My sample size was relatively large for an IPA and my research participants provided more than twelve hours of in-depth insight. There were many lenses through which their accounts might be understood. The practicalities of managing and analysing large amounts of data in an IPA project should not be underestimated and the data interpretation stage of research necessarily involves developing creative ways of ordering, visually capturing and mapping data, as well as multiple coding methods.

Secondly, as noted above, phenomenological methods call for participants to be able to articulate their experiences so as to convey their unique experience and the meaning made of it, and IPA is no exception. Over and above the challenge of identifying articulate and self-aware participants, I found that, in a business setting, it could be difficult to facilitate participants to move beyond a cognitively-oriented stance in which they *gave opinions* about their experiences. This meant that it was harder to get at the personal and emotional aspects which might uncover more of their phenomenological intentionality, and the risk was that accounts would be one-dimensional. Coaching researchers working with business-based topics will find that they not only have to carefully select participants for articulacy, but also to invest time to build their trust and to normalise 'deeper' level conversations.

A further challenge for the IPA researcher is that where there is interpretation, there must be reflexivity, especially in phenomenological methods, which are not well suited to mere assertion. However, in my view, IPA has not yet developed a sufficient corpus of studies to provide a roadmap for the researcher in terms of their own reflexive stance and approach. Reflexive capabilities are not even mentioned in Smith et al.'s list of the qualities required by IPA researchers (Smith et al., 2009). I found that I had to turn to other sources (e.g. Schon, in Etherington, 2004) for guidance on how and why to apply a reflexive lens to my analysis. Similarly, cross-checking and auditing of interpretation by third parties are only mentioned in passing by the main authorities. While his criticism is too sweeping, being based on only one study, Paley's identification of the risk of deficiencies in IPA researchers' interpretations is a fair challenge (Paley, 2018). Smith et al. acknowledge that transparency of method and plausibility of interpretation are required to generate a good IPA study (Smith, 2011), but in my view, the methodological disciplines which would help researchers to meet these standards, e.g. self-reflection, triangulation and seeking out alternative readings, are not given sufficient weight in the key texts to date. The IPA researcher, while never ceding their own responsibility as an interpreter, would be likely to benefit from feedback which could challenge or confirm their readings of material, and several research groups and online forums exist to facilitate this.

My biggest challenge as an IPA researcher, however, was in allowing myself to fully enter into the interpretative process. I found that, notwithstanding my conviction that my own thoughts, assumptions and pre-judgements (my fore-structures in Heideggerian terms) were inevitably elements of the process, I was nervous about 'imposing' order on the data, for example by identifying the criteria for what constitutes 'a theme'. The early stages of an IPA rely on an anchoring discipline of textual analysis, and themes emerge, apparently sui generis, from transcriptions. But from the super-ordinate theme stage onwards the IPA researcher has to commit with confidence to their own process of abstractive interpretation. Description gives out, density of data is only partly useful and there is no theoretical framework to rely on. Stepping fully into a condition of authorship was my biggest challenge, and successfully grappling with it was a turning point in my sense of myself as a researcher. From that point on, I felt able to work creatively with the methodology and was no longer constrained by it. In the end, and consistently with IPA's hermeneutic principles, themes at all levels emerged through my own engagement with the material – from the ways in which I noticed participants' accounts converging, diverging and constellating around an issue, from the ways in which material resonated with me and surprised me and from how it generated connecting patterns in my own sense-making across cases and samples.

Coaching researchers, particularly practitioners like myself who work in psychological modalities, are typically interested both in their clients' meaning-making and in their own role in the creation of the coaching relationship. Notwithstanding some limitations, with its phenomenological underpinnings and its requirement that the researcher be a co-creator of meaning, it is not hard to see why IPA is an attractive methodology in this field of research.

Case study – Roger Noon

Conceptual encounter (de Rivera, 1981) was selected as a suitable methodology to explore the research question: 'What is presence and how is it experienced by coaches and clients during the executive coaching conversation?' (Noon, 2018). The study was approached from a constructivist epistemological stance, which acknowledges multiple perspectives of reality, an appreciation that meaning is created through dialogue, and that an individual's interpretation of their reality can change (Guba and Lincoln, 1994). In common with other phenomenological methods, 'social reality has to be grounded in people's experiences of that social reality' (Crotty, 1998: 24). However, what is unique for conceptual encounter is that its procedure involves the researcher first developing an initial concept resulting from their experience and a review of the literature. This then 'encounters' a research partner's recalled experiences of the phenomenon during a series of semi-structured interviews. These meetings of the abstraction with the lived experience of successive research partners allow the concept to evolve.

The alignment of this approach to the phenomenological tradition may be summarised in two ways. As a feature of description (Husserlian school of phenomenology) the concept is grounded in the experience of the research partners. If there is no 'meeting' of an abstract construct with lived experience, there is no justification for its inclusion. As an accent of interpretation (Heideggerian school of phenomenology) the researcher is 'in' the research through a sensitising process, the development of an initial concept and due to the collaborative nature of the interviews. This means that the researcher acts as a gatekeeper of concept development, which necessarily involves interpretation.

The research question intentionally involved both the client and coach voice and a fundamental requirement from the outset was to design a procedure which ensured that both sides of the conversation were equally represented during data collection. This suggested performing two parallel 'conceptual encounters', one investigating the client's perspective and the other, the coach's. An outline of the procedure is shown in Figure 5.2. In step 1, I used a literature review and my personal experience as a practising coach to develop a concept which acted as a starting point for use in the interviews. This process served to sensitise me to the phenomenon and to the research question I had framed to explore it. Following the left-hand (client) path in the diagram, the first half of the first interview (step 2) focused on the research partner recounting a detailed narrative of their experience of presence. My stance during this stage was to set aside my initial ideas, suspend judgement and to draw out as rich a description of this experience as possible. In the second half of the interview, the initial concept was presented to the research partner and discussed in light of this description. As a result of this discussion and subsequent data analysis, the concept evolved and a modified map emerged (step 3). This transition version was used in the next interview.

This procedure was repeated for each of the six client interviews so that the map evolved each time in an iterative fashion, with each subsequent iteration incorporating the experiences of the previous research participants.

The conceptual encounter from the coach perspective followed the same approach (the right-hand side of Figure 5.2) with an overarching map emerging in step 4 that encompassed both perspectives.

Figure 5.2 The parallel conceptual encounter process

The sources of data were therefore client and coach research partners, me as the researcher, and the literature. Data collection occurred through the transcription of interviews, and by means of a reflexive researcher diary. The diary became an invaluable sense-making and experimental tool and a constant companion throughout the indwelling process. Data analysis was performed after each interview, allowing the concept to continuously evolve as the interviews progressed. It involved identifying common characteristics, qualities and patterns in the data that provided insight into the underlying structure of the phenomenon. This creative, immersive process and the integration that the researcher brings to its performance is a key differentiator for quality.

Subsequent to the conceptual encounters, a focus group was also convened (involving two clients and two coaches) to further explore the concept.

The rationale here was an intent to leverage the creative potential of group dynamics to generate 'interaction data' (Lambert and Loiselle, 2008). During the focus group, the Q-sort technique was employed (Stainton Rogers, 1995) which asked participants to force rank statements about presence which had emerged from the conceptual encounter approach. This enabled the output from conceptual encounters to be discussed in the group and levels of consensus to be explored. So the overall research design was something of a bricolage with conceptual encounters and a commitment to a phenomenological stance at its heart.

Challenges of researching using conceptual encounter

One of the challenges of researching coaching using conceptual encounter as a phenomenological approach is that there is a lack of clarity around procedure, especially concerning data analysis. Whilst this ambiguity can be unsettling, it also allows flexibility and customisation. The methodology as described by de Rivera (1981) is rich in the spirit of how it should be approached but relatively non-prescriptive in terms of procedural detail. So for instance, the parallel conceptual encounters approach described here was novel, and thematic analysis was selected as a flexible means of developing a conceptual structure.

A second challenge centres on the role of the researcher, who is a collaborative investigator of the lived experience of others whilst also being knowledgeable in the subject area and responsible for iterating a model of the phenomenon. The tension inherent in these differing roles can test one's ability to maintain a phenomenological stance throughout the research. At the outset, developing an initial concept will generate a set of assumptions which, however lightly held, will naturally influence how the researcher interprets the experience recounted by the partner or vice versa. A different initial concept may suggest a different set of assumptions and consequently it may evolve in a different direction. The researcher needs to be aware of these assumptions, their origins and practical implications. Reflexive practice is the primary means to achieve this.

The emphasis on collaborative meaning-making sits well with the interpretative phenomenological tradition. In the study into presence, an example of such co-creation was an instance during an interview when I spontaneously introduced a metaphor to illustrate my interpretation of an experience that the research partner was narrating. The partner then built on this, accentuated a particular aspect and extended it, again in a spontaneous manner. This experience of co-created meaning was common and shows how both partners move collaboratively back and forth between description and interpretation.

There are also implications that arise from the power dynamics between researcher and partners, which may affect how the partners see the concept 'fitting' their experience. The issue of researcher influence also arises during the development of the model and de Rivera (1981: 6) emphasises that there is considerable skill involved in intuiting 'an abstract form that succeeds in capturing the essential relationships involved in all of the concrete experiences'.

There is therefore significant power, trust and analytical expertise in the hands of the researcher to arrive at a final, elegant conceptualisation.

A further potentially significant consideration concerns language. This study was conducted in English, yet a minority of research partners did not speak English as their first language. This presented challenges when attempting to relate and interpret nuanced and complex experiences, again leaving the researcher with some important decisions to make.

Managing these challenges and therefore demonstrating credibility, largely depends on the experience, reflexivity and integrity of the researcher and the transparency of the audit trail throughout the research process. For these reasons, as a novice research-practitioner, I felt a level of intimidation when embarking on my study. A phenomenological stance asks the researcher to commit to its tenets in every moment. It is in itself a deep reflexive practice – a philosophy in action – and confidence comes from practice. Conceptual encounter's appeal to me was that this stance is reflected in my values as a coach. Its recognition that the researcher is involved as a collaborator and its emphasis on a dialectical construction of meaning is mirrored in many coaching processes. This affinity between the spirit of the research method and the coaching process has been addressed in the introduction to this chapter and was a reassuring touchstone throughout the research.

In summary, conceptual encounter uses collaborative meaning-making to develop new structures of experience within a phenomenological inquiry. The goal is to explicate structure rather than to explain how or why the phenomenon occurs. As a coach my motivation was to use the research to understand presence in the coaching process more deeply, to apply the learning in my own practice and to make it available to others.

Evaluation

Overall the value of phenomenological approaches to coaching research cannot be overestimated. They allow the researcher an intimate engagement with an object of interest with full appreciation of the nuances of the phenomenon in its natural context. They particularly appeal to coaches who see the reductionist and oversimplified messages from some quantitative studies as dry and removed from the realities of their practice. Phenomenological studies are designed for investigating the tacit aspects of meaningful but elusive experience for the accurate understanding of phenomena which are difficult to describe in words. As a result, new meanings and nuances are revealed which might otherwise have remained hidden and which contribute to the emergence of a richer descriptive language for what we wish to understand.

It is interesting therefore that one of the most serious critiques of phenomenology is that language precedes and therefore shapes experience and, in some way, prescribes what we can think and feel (Willig, 2006). According to this view, believing that language can express actual experiences may not be justified. However, use of language is inevitable in coaching and in researching coaching. Phenomenological research therefore makes an attempt to engage with the limitations that the use of language presents in an explicit and collaborative way and thus pave the way for other types of research. This is, for example, how O'Connell (2018: 56) describes her choice of method in the IPA study: 'In order to see what was happening, I wanted coaches to relive the experience of using intuition. At the same time, I was mindful that a lot of our decision-making and judgment happens outside of conscious control, so it didn't make sense to ask people to express their experience through abstract and formal language. Instead, I encouraged participants to describe their experience in terms of images, metaphors, and feelings.'

A superficial understanding of phenomenological approaches might suggest that they are an easy option. They require no theoretical 'proof'. They deal with the intangible and ambiguous. They license the researcher to freely interpret what is before them. The reality is that these apparent freedoms are precisely what make these methods far from easy. They demand of the phenomenological researcher that they exert both self- and methodological disciplines to a very high degree if the outcome is to be a rigorous, credible and persuasive research project.

Further reading

De Rivera, J. (1981). *Conceptual Encounter: A Method for the Exploration of Human Experience*. Washington, DC: University Press of America.

This text is out of print. However, extracts from it are available through Google Scholar. Edited by the originator of the approach it also contains very good examples of how these types of studies can be conducted.

Smith, J.A., Flowers, P. and Larkin, M. (2009). *Interpretative Phenomenological Analysis: Theory, Method and Research*. London: Sage Publications.

This book is written by the originators of the approach. It provides extensive coverage of the theoretical underpinning and detailed guidance to carrying out research projects. This is an obvious resource for anyone who wishes to utilise this approach.

Discussion questions

- Do you feel more comfortable thinking about yourself as the author of your research, as a co-researcher or as a witness to your research participants' experience? What are the implications of this choice for your research?
- Does your research question imply an intention to prove a hypothesis? If so, how does this align with the ontological and epistemological claims of phenomenological methods?
- How could describing experience be useful research?
- How useful is research if it is not generalisable?

References

Cromby, J. (2015). *Feeling Bodies: Embodying Psychology*. London: Palgrave.

Crotty, M. (1998). *The Foundations of Social Research: Meaning and Perspective in the Research Process*. Thousand Oaks, CA: Sage Publications.

De Rivera, J. (1981). *Conceptual Encounter: A Method for the Exploration of Human Experience*. Washington, DC: University Press of America.

Etherington, K. (2004). *Becoming a Reflexive Researcher: Using Our Selves in Research*. London: Jessica Kingsley.

Gallagher, S. and Zahavi, D. (2008). *The Phenomenological Mind: An Introduction to Philosophy of Mind and Cognitive Science*. London: Routledge.

Giorgi, A. (2017). 'A response to the attempted critique of the scientific phenomenological method'. *Journal of Phenomenological Psychology* 48 (1): 83–144.

Giorgi, A.P. and Giorgi, B.M. (2003). 'The descriptive phenomenological psychological method'. In P.M. Camic, J.E. Rhodes and L. Yardley (eds), *Qualitative Research in Psychology: Expanding Perspectives in Methodology and Design*. Washington, DC: American Psychological Association, pp. 243–73.

Giorgi, A. and Giorgi, B. (2013). 'Phenomenological psychology'. In C. Willig and W. Stainton-Rogers (eds), *The SAGE Handbook of Qualitative Research in Psychology*. London: Sage Publications, pp. 165–78.

Guba, E.G. and Lincoln, Y.S. (1994). 'Competing paradigms in qualitative research'. In N.K. Denzin and Y.S. Lincoln (eds), *Handbook of Qualitative Research*. London: Sage Publications, pp. 105–17.

Harré, R. (1983). *Introduction to the Logic of the Sciences* (2nd edition). London: Macmillan.

Husserl, E. (1931). *Ideas* (trans. W.R. Boyce Gibson). London: George Allen & Unwin.

Kvale, S. (1996). *InterViews: An Introduction to Qualitative Research Interviewing*. London: Sage Publications.

Lambert, S.D. and Loiselle, C.G. (2008). 'Combining individual interviews and focus groups to enhance data richness'. *Journal of Advanced Nursing* 62 (2): 228–37.

Merleau-Ponty, M. (1968). *The Visible and the Invisible*. Evanston, IL: Northwestern University Press.

Moustakas, C. (1994). *Phenomenological Research Methods*. London: Sage Publications.

Noon, R. (2018). 'Presence in executive coaching conversations: The C2 model'. *International Journal of Evidence Based Coaching and Mentoring* S12: 4–20.

O'Connell, C. (2018). 'Understanding intuition (part II)'. *Coaching at Work* (October): 56–7

Paley, J. (2018). *Phenomenology as Qualitative Research: A Critical Analysis of Meaning Attribution*. London: Routledge.

Smith, J.A. (2011). 'Evaluating the contribution of interpretative phenomenological analysis'. *Health Psychology Review* 5 (1): 9–27.

Smith, J.A., Flowers, P. and Larkin, M. (2009). *Interpretative Phenomenological Analysis: Theory, Method and Research*. London: Sage Publications.

Spinelli, E. (1989). *The Interpreted World: An Introduction to Phenomenological Psychology*. London: Sage Publications.

Stainton Rogers, R. (1995). 'Q methodology'. In J.A. Smith, R. Harré and I. Van Longenhove (eds), *Rethinking Methods in Psychology*. London: Sage Publications, pp. 178–93.

Vagle, M.D. (2018). *Crafting Phenomenological Research* (2nd edition). London: Routledge.

Van Manen, M. (1990). *Researching Lived Experience: Human Science for an Action Sensitive Pedagogy*. Albany, NY: State University of New York Press.

Willig, C. (2006). *Introducing Qualitative Research in Psychology*. Maidenhead: Open University Press.

Willig, C. (2007). 'Reflections on the use of a phenomenological method'. *Qualitative Research in Psychology* 4: 209–25.

Willig, C. (2016). 'Constructivism and "the real world": Can they co-exist?' *QMiP Bulletin* 21: 33–7.

Zahavi, D. (2019). 'Getting it quite wrong: Van Manen and Smith on phenomenology'. *Qualitative Health Research* 29 (6): 900–7.

6

Autoethnography

Juliette Koning and Liam Moore

Introduction

Autoethnography is a research approach in which the researcher uses personal experiences to examine cultural practices. In a coaching context this could mean seeking answers to questions such as: What does it mean to train to be a coach? What does it mean to be an internal coach in a multinational company? What does it mean to be a coach returning to work after a career break? Other methodologies could be used to address these questions. Where autoethnography differs, however, is in its ability to elucidate, through close examination, the mutual influence of the researcher's personal experience (as subject) and the research context. The questions above are often either posed by a researcher to a research participant or are addressed in a purely autobiographical manner, without also examining the cultural context in which the experiences take place. Autoethnography, uniquely, interweaves the two. Autoethnography has rarely been applied to coaching and we feel this presents a missed opportunity since it provides an effective way to close the gap between coaching research and practice. In particular, the use of autoethnography could help to give voice, compel response, and offer insight into the social and cultural structures that impact on coaching by examining personal experiences and practices within a broader context (e.g. that of coaching practice or of specific organisational settings in which coaching takes place). With the growing interest in using autoethnography in and for professional practice and in organisational research, we are of the opinion that autoethnography holds value for coaching research, too.

To determine what autoethnography has to offer coaching research, we will explore in this chapter what autoethnography is, how autoethnography may be applied to coaching research and to what end. In the first part of the chapter we show our sense-making of the literature on autoethnography and how it relates to other forms of ethnography. We address the distinctive features of autoethnography and the implications it has for the role of the researcher, relationships with participants, philosophical synergies, and which coaching questions might be meaningfully investigated with it. In the second part, to illustrate how and why autoethnography might be applied to coaching research, we offer Liam's reflections on using an autoethnographic approach in his coaching research project. Finally, we will evaluate the strengths and limitations of autoethnography for coaching research.

Distinctive features of autoethnography

The following reflects our sense-making of autoethnography. In keeping with that methodology, we decided to stay close to our explorative journey as we believe this can help others, both newcomers and those who are engaged with other ethnographic approaches, in a similar way. The steps in our journey consisted of first exploring the various ways in which autoethnography has been defined; only after reaching this understanding did we investigate its origins and how it relates to other ethnographic approaches. On the basis of these insights we were able to articulate key features of autoethnography and how these might inspire coaching research.

Defining autoethnography

Autoethnography is research 'that places the self within a social context' (Reed-Danahay, 1997: 9). It is often considered a combination or integration of ethnography, or the exploration of social and cultural meaning of a given group and autobiography, or writing about the self. Definitions from the last twenty years (see Table 6.1) all make reference to this mix of the personal and the cultural, and autoethnography is often defined by explicating its three constituent parts, namely 'auto', 'ethno' and 'graphy'. This combining of self, culture and writing makes up the unique character of autoethnography. The table also indicates that researchers tend to choose one of three ways to illustrate autoethnography: by emphasising the three core words (see Adams et al., 2017; Doloriert and Sambrook, 2012; Kempster and Iszatt-White, 2013), by highlighting the writing as being a self-reflexive, evocative, thick description of lived experiences (Ellis et al., 2011; Haynes, 2011; Winkler, 2018), and/or by stressing the 'in context' (Anderson, 2006; Chang, 2007; Holt, 2003; Humphreys, 2005; Kempster and Stewart, 2010; Reed-Danahay, 1997). In addition, Holman Jones et al. (2016) highlight the use of personal experiences to critique cultural experience.

Table 6.1 Definitions of autoethnography 1997–2018

Definition or description of autoethnography	Reference
Autoethnography combines elements from autobiographical research (i.e., to retroactively and selectively write about past experiences with specific focus on turning points that are perceived as having particular influence on the course of life) and ethnographic research (i.e., to study cultural practices).	Winkler (2018: 236)
Autoethnography is a research method that uses personal experience ('auto') to describe and interpret ('graphy') cultural texts, experiences, beliefs and practices ('ethno') … Understanding autoethnography requires working at the intersection of autobiography and ethnography.	Adams et al. (2017: 1, 2)
One characteristic that binds all autoethnographies is the use of personal experience to examine and/or critique cultural experience.	Holman Jones et al. (2016: 22)
Autoethnography moves from the breadth of the social lens that is the focus of ethnography to the narrative perspective of the situated individual. The auto is the self where discovery is centred; the ethno is the self shaped by her/his social milieu; and the graphy is the writing of self as the primary mechanism of revelation.	Kempster and Iszatt-White (2013: 320)
Autoethnography is a genre of qualitative, reflexive, autobiographical writing and research which uses the researcher as subject … Drawing from the ethnographic tradition of participant observation and immersion in experience, in order to understand and interpret a particular cultural system such as an organisation (cf. Van Maanen, 1988, 2006), autoethnography also examines a social and cultural context, but through the personal experience of the researcher.	Haynes (2011: 135)
When researchers write autoethnographies, they seek to produce aesthetic and evocative thick descriptions of personal and interpersonal experience. They accomplish this by first discerning patterns of cultural experience evidenced by field notes, interviews, and/or artifacts, and then describing these patterns using facets of storytelling (e.g., character and plot development), showing and telling, and alterations of authorial voice.	Ellis et al. (2011: 277)
Autoethnography does not merely require us to explore the interface between culture and self; it requires us to examine ourselves in this context.	Kempster and Stewart (2010: 211)
I argue that autoethnography should be ethnographical in its methodological orientation, cultural in its interpretive orientation, and autobiographical in its content orientation. This implies that self-reflective writings deficient in any one of these ingredients would fall short of 'auto-ethno-graphy.'	Chang (2007: 208)

(Continued)

Table 6.1 (Continued)

Definition or description of autoethnography	Reference
By virtue of the autoethnographer's dual role as a member in the social world under study and as a researcher of that world, autoethnography demands enhanced textual visibility of the researcher's self. Autoethnographers should illustrate analytic insights through recounting their own experiences and thoughts as well as those of others.	Anderson (2006: 384)
It is both a method and a text ... [and] can be done by either an anthropologist who is doing 'home' or 'native' ethnography or by a non-anthropologist/ethnographer. It can also be done by an autobiographer who places the story of his or her life within a story of the social context in which it occurs.	Humphreys (2005: 841)
Autoethnography is a genre of writing and research that connects the personal to the cultural, placing the self within a social context (Reed-Danahay, 1997).	Holt (2003: 18)
An autobiographical genre of writing and research that displays multiple layers of consciousness, connecting the personal to the cultural.	Ellis and Bochner (2000: 733)
In this volume, autoethnography is defined as a form of self-narrative that places the self within a social context.	Reed-Danahay (1997: 9)

Studying the ways in which autoethnography has been 'defined' over the years, not only offers better understanding, it also hints at the challenges a researcher will encounter, such as deciding what cultural or social 'context' is and how to examine it, or how to find voice for writing about the self in evocative ways. As Winkler (2018) addresses in detail, finding the 'right' balance between the personal and cultural is a real challenge for autoethnographers. An oft-heard critique, therefore, is that autoethnography is egotistical (Doloriert and Sambrook, 2012) and relies too much on the self as main data source (Holt, 2003). One way to circumvent such critique is to undertake continual checks as to how the personal story enables the researcher and the readers to understand culture, 'this helps me to zoom out of the auto to be able to see the ethno' (Winkler, 2018: 237). This and other challenges are addressed in Liam's story, which we present in the second part of this chapter. The article by Winkler (2018) is also very useful as a **key resource** for understanding how to overcome certain of these challenges.

Where does autoethnography come from?

Autoethnography is not a recent phenomenon; some date the use of the term to the early 1970s. For example, Heider (1975) used 'auto-ethnography' to describe cultural members giving account of their culture and Hayano (1979) referred to 'auto-ethnography' when writing about researchers who study their own people. However, researchers were not yet explicitly using personal experience as it is used today (Adams et al., 2017: 1); the 1980s are seen as laying the groundwork for the inclusion of personal experiences that now constitute a core feature of autoethnography. It was the time referred to as 'the crisis of confidence', particularly in objective social science research. At the same time, postmodernism questioned the idea of 'one grand narrative'. In anthropology, questions were asked about 'representing the other' and what was meant by ethnographic authority (Clifford, 1983). These developments led to a rethinking of the relationship between researcher and researched as well as between author and audience. Scholars started to realise that 'stories were complex, constitutive, meaningful phenomena that taught morals and ethics, introduced unique ways of thinking and feeling, and helped people make sense of themselves and others' (Ellis et al., 2011: 274). Autoethnography thus developed as a critique on objective knowledge of human behaviour and an appreciation of qualitative research, the uniqueness of people's experiences, the welfare of research participants, lived experiences, narratives, emotions and the body, positionality and reflexivity (Holman Jones et al., 2016: 25–6).

Autoethnography is considered a response to the traditional ethnographic approach in which fieldworkers risk ignoring their own outsider (etic) perspective and motivations. This was seen to be a result of assumptions generated in relation to their work within a culture, including those about the perceived 'truth' of the research participants' insider, or emic, perspective (Madden, 2010; Reed-Danahay, 1997). Nevertheless, ethnography is an important part of autoethnography and autoethnography is seen as part of the broader family of ethnographic approaches. Table 6.2 highlights some of the specific features of each, starting with ethnography, followed by organisational ethnography, autoethnography and organisational autoethnography. To highlight some of the core differences, in Table 6.2 we compare for each of the four: the core aim (what the specific approach aims to understand better), the role and position of research participants, the role of the researcher, what is the outcome (the what and how of the end product), and what specific coaching questions can be addressed with each of these ethnographic approaches. We also offer a few references as **core reading**.

Table 6.2 shows that while all ethnographies share a common interest in understanding culture, moving from ethnography to autoethnography involves a more intense examination of self; the researcher has become subject of the research. Whereas today's ethnography and organisational ethnography generally contain reflexive researcher accounts (that is, accounts of how the researcher impacts on the research) the researcher is not the subject of the research itself. This researcher-as-subject is a core feature of autoethnography and, as we briefly highlighted above, creates unique challenges for investigating and writing about oneself, and convincing the reader about its value. Liam's first-person account of conducting autoethnographic research (see below) sheds light on some of these concerns.

Table 6.2   Autoethnography amidst other ethnographies

	Ethnography	Organisational ethnography	Autoethnography	Organisational autoethnography
Aim	Understanding cultural understandings held by others	Understanding organisational life (or organisations and organising)	Exploring personal experiences to illustrate facets of cultural experience	Probe personal experiences of, with and within organisations
Research participants	Interactive engagement dialogical; main source of knowledge creation	Interactive, dialogical: how organisation members go about their daily working lives and how they make sense of their workplaces	Are part of the social and cultural context through which (or within which) the researcher examines him or herself	Are part of the organisational context through which (or within which) the researcher examines him or herself
Researcher	Is participant observer in situ (fieldwork, long period of time; living with and living like); conscious of own impact but generally more of an outsider	Is participant observer in situ (fieldwork, less long); conscious of own impact but generally more of outsider	Is subject of research, examines him or herself (use of memory); explore social processes from an insider perspective; can be combined with stories of others; researcher is an embodied participant	Is subject of research, examines him or herself (use of memory); understanding organisational processes from an insider perspective
Outcome	Thick description of a culture (written representation of a culture)	Showcase the complexities of the everyday in organisational life	Make characteristics of a culture familiar for insiders and outsiders	Insightful and emotionally-rich readings of organisational life
Coaching topics	Coaching in other cultures	Coaching and organisational culture; coaching in organisations	Being a coach, being coached, becoming a coach (identity related questions)	In-house coaches, exploring their own experiences
Core references	Van Maanen (1988); Eriksen (2015)	Ybema et al. (2009); Ciuk et al. (2018)	Doloriert and Sambrook (2009); Ellis et al. (2011); Winkler (2018)	Sambrook and Herrmann (2018)

Practical issues

Using autoethnography as a research approach requires some understanding of the intricacies of researching the self (in context) and reflecting on those around the self. It raises questions about voice, emotions, reflexivity, ethics and writing; we address these below.

The researcher researched

The autoethnographic researcher analyses and then reveals in autobiographic form that which is experienced within a cultural context permitting the researcher to be recognised as subjective, emotional, and influential within the research setting (Ellis et al., 2011). He/she is a social actor who both shapes and is, in part, shaped by the culture on which they report (Coffey, 1999). With its emphasis on answering 'questions of identity and selfhood, of voice and authenticity' (Reed-Danahay, 1997: 3), it demands a genuine interest in understanding, and giving voice to, the multiplicity of experiences, values and views that exist in that culture (Coffey, 1999; Duncan, 2004).

The extent to which the researcher is the sole participant in the research or part of a larger group that is studied can vary. Doloriert and Sambrook (2009: 29) propose a continuum, running 'from a more separate researcher-and-researched to that where the researcher-is-researched'. In the first example, the researcher shares the culture he/she is exploring; in the second example, the researcher is the core focus in the research; his or her lived experiences are the central narrative but reflected upon in context. In all instances however, 'the researcher features as intrinsic to the epistemology, her experiences, interpretations, and critical reflexivity (Cunliffe, 2004) are accepted as knowledge, linking her personal to her cultural and thus blurring the distinction between researcher and researched' (Doloriert and Sambrook, 2009: 30).

Autoethnography (on any point of such a continuum) is a suitable methodology for exploring a learning experience within a specific context, for example a university, or a practice, such as coaching, which involves a highly self-reflexive approach (Meekums, 2008). In the field, in higher education and in coaching, there is a level of convenience in 'writing about one's own professional environment, relationships, and culture' (Doloriert and Sambrook, 2009: 29). We can think of roles and relationships such as coach–coachee, supervisor–supervisee, work–personal and employee–manager. Coaching is at the same time considered to be a culturally sensitive practice that engages in exploration and giving of voice to individual identity (Rosinski and Abbott, 2006). Autoethnography and certain coaching modalities also share the use of narrative approaches (Drake, 2010; Law, 2007).

Autoethnographic practices

In such a 'personal' research approach, where lived experiences, narrative, reflexivity, researcher's voice and memory, relational ethics, dialogue with previously silenced others, and evocative writing are key features (see Box 6.1), the philosophical underpinning of research is to be found in qualitative, interpretive, and critical paradigms that house subjectivity, emotionality, and the researcher's influence on research. The focus is on meaning-making throughout and to share this via personal experiences. As addressed above, this has implications for the role of the researcher who is very much present through voice and experience and is, often, the only participant.

Box 6.1   Doing research

Using memory for much of our data Evocative Self-reflexivity	Winkler (2018: 238–9)
Purposefully commenting on culture or cultural practice Making contributions to existing research Embracing vulnerability with purpose Creating reciprocal relations with audiences to compel response	Holman Jones et al. (2016: 22)
Disrupting norms of research practice and representations Working from insider knowledge Manoeuvring through pain, confusion, anger and uncertainty Making life better Breaking silence (re)claiming voice and writing to right Making work accessible	Holman Jones et al. (2016: 32)
Layered accounts Challenging a single telling	Denshire (2014: 843)
Examining the self, our identity, emotions and experiences as relational and institutional stories affected by social and cultural structures	Haynes (2011: 136)
Recognise the innumerable ways personal experience influences the research process	Ellis et al. (2011: 274, 277)
Produce aesthetic and evocative thick descriptions of personal and interpersonal experience Relational ethics	Ellis et al. (2011: 281)
Researcher is visible, active, and reflexively engaged in the text	Anderson (2006: 383)
Challenging accepted views about silent authorship	Holt (2003: 19)

As shown in Box 6.1, doing autoethnographic research brings some unique and distinctive features, such as the use of memory as data, evocative writing about personal and interpersonal experiences, a high level of engagement and exposing vulnerabilities with the purpose of making life better or in order to understand specific cultural practices from the inside. Due to its highly personal and interpersonal character, autoethnography also raises some ethical issues and the question of how to tell the autoethnographic story.

Relational ethics and writing

With respect to the implications of autoethnography for those included in the narratives (who may be colleagues, partners, family members, research participants), there is a literature that addresses the ethics involved. A commonly used term to address such ethics is 'relational ethics'. As Ellis et al. (2011: 281) explain, using personal experiences implicates not only the autoethnographer but also those close to him or her. Such relational ethics are not unique to autoethnography of course, as most interpretivist research approaches would consider this part of their research as well (Cunliffe, 2004, 2008). They are naturally also constitutive of practice in professions such as coaching (compare for example, Global Code of Ethics, 2018). In a study where a coach reveals his or her experience of coaching executives for instance, clients are automatically implicated in the narratives. Some solutions are found in 'protective writing devices such as a nom de plume ... composite characterization ... and pseudonyms used in an effort to respect the privacy of those portrayed in an auto-ethnographic narrative' (Denshire, 2014: 840).

Whereas this falls under the expected ethical consideration of qualitative interpretivist research, autoethnography comes with additional ethical challenges. Two stand out. First the relational ethics of family, friends and work colleagues talked about in the narrative; and second, the autoethnographer's personal life that will be out in the open; 'you have to decide if you are ready to be outed or to put yourself out that way and consider the impact on personal identity' (Flemmon and Green, 2002 in Doloriert and Sambrook, 2012: 88). As revealed by Custer (2014: 11) autoethnography can be quite painful and overwhelming for the researcher due to the 'radical honesty required of the researcher'. Ways to work with these challenges are found in using forms of 'disguising' or 'modifying' such as 'fictionalisation', 'semifictionalised ethnography' and 'mindful slippage' (Doloriert and Sambrook, 2012: 89). As Winkler (2018: 244) rightly states, 'autoethnographers must decide how much they want to disclose about themselves and in this vein how honest they would like to be when creating and representing their life to others'. This is not to be considered as 'cheating' but must be seen in the tradition of interpretivisms and postmodernisms to which autoethnography can be said to 'belong', where the idea of 'a truth' is non-existent, it is about how people make sense of their lives.

In writing the autoethnography, a personal narrative style is often chosen; however, as suggested by Muncey (2005: 11), it can be further refined through the use of snapshots (photos), artefacts, and the use of metaphors in writing;

she points out that 'the use of metaphor enabled me to get to the core of the experience and write about it in a way that is both understandable and cathartic'. Writing an autoethnography requires creative explorations of how best to 'tell' one's story (Wall, 2008).

In the next part we present the narrative and lived-experience of the second author, Liam, which focuses on his wrestling with the idea of using autoethnography to support the research for his coaching and mentoring master's qualification. Placing a narrative in context is a key feature of autoethnography, and so Liam's account situates this decision-making process within a wider autobiographical frame that encompasses a 'before' and 'after'.

Liam's story: An autoethnographic vignette

Where it 'began'

In 2010 I decided upon a change of career. I had been working in the creative sector for 14 years before becoming interested in how to support learning and performance in the workplace. I took the opportunity of a restructure to move on and made a first tentative step into what is now an established career in learning and development but which at the time felt like a huge leap into the unknown. Motivated by a positive experience of being coached at work, I joined a coaching and mentoring master's programme. It turned out to be a profoundly developmental experience, and my dissertation research topic was influenced by questions with which I was wrestling as I entered this new professional world of coaching.

'Finding' ethnography

Having experienced generous and skilled coaching supervision during the first year of the course, I identified similar qualities in the person I approached to be my dissertation supervisor. That intuitive leap was the start of a collaboration that has seen us through my dissertation, publication of a research paper, and now the writing of this chapter. Juliette's background in ethnography offered a way for me to explore the questions I held about my evolving professional identity. What I learned during my research has influenced how I support coaching clients and underpinned my own professional growth from wannabe coach to in-house learning and development practitioner.

For my dissertation, I initially adopted a narrative methodology to explore the learning experience of individuals on a postgraduate coaching training programme. During early supervision conversations Juliette suggested autoethnography, itself a form of narrative methodology, as a means through which to bring in my own experience. Ultimately, autoethnography became more guiding philosophy than methodology. However, that early foray sowed the seed for our subsequent research, and autoethnography has provided an alternative lens through which to view my coaching and wider learning and development practice. For example, I am currently examining my own experience of the organisation in which I work to inform development of a workshop on leading in complex environments.

'Doing' coaching research

To answer the research question: 'What is the learning experience of individuals on a postgraduate coaching training programme?' I employed a narrative (and life-story) methodology (Riessman, 1993). Overcoming assumptions about the potential for achieving objectivity in my research, I recruited four fellow students on the coaching and mentoring programme. This factor, alongside the chosen professional context, lent itself to adopting an autoethnographic philosophy with me playing the role of cultural 'insider'. The research involved conducting semi-structured interviews of 60–90 minutes with each participant. Interview questions (tested and revised following a pilot interview) included: 'Could you start by telling me a bit about yourself' ... 'How did you come to coaching?' ... 'How would you describe the relationship you have with your studies?' I recorded the interviews and transcribed them myself verbatim, which provided an additional layer of analysis and of meaning-making (Riessman, 1993). I analysed the transcriptions, identifying key words and grouping these into themes. I then shaped a narrative for each participant using phrases that contained those key words and applied three main headings – motivations, challenges and outcomes – which seemed to fit with a narrative structure of beginning, middle and end.

I had intended to relate my own learning experience in the form of a narrative (an autoethnographic vignette) as part of the discussion. However, it proved to be too much of an undertaking on top of the work I had already carried out. Instead, I presented a short narrative section of my own as part of the conclusion. Doing so enabled me to recognise that while I would shortly be receiving a 'coaching piece of paper' as one of my participants put it, studying on the course represented a step towards professional credibility rather than an end in itself.

Autoethnography and coaching

My relationship with autoethnography continued later with publication of a research paper, discussed below. However, my early attempt at 'doing' autoethnography enabled me to understand one of its fundamental principles. Namely that, as a means of communicating and making sense of personal experience while relating this to the research setting, autoethnography establishes itself as 'both process and product' (Ellis et al., 2011). In this respect, autoethnography revealed itself to be a valuable theoretical perspective from which to view coaching practice.

In ethnographic terms, through their relationship with the client, the client's manager and their organisation, a coach immerses themselves in a new culture.

As a newcomer to that environment, it is critical for a coach not only to enable the client to make sense of their identity but to be able to recognise the nature of the coach's own experience of and influence on the coaching ('research') setting. As such, reflective practice (Schön, 1983), in which a coach writes about his or her experiences in order to learn from them, arguably benefits from being grounded in an understanding of autoethnography.

As an interpretive approach, narrative methodologies require the researcher to demonstrate reflexivity (Pillow, 2003). It has been argued that for autoethnographers the potential exists for research to suffer from insufficient reflexive rigour owing to 'self-indulgence' (Winkler, 2018) on the part of the author. Remaining alert to the influence of potential 'blind spots' on the outcome of their work is also a consideration for coaches. Therefore, in coaching supervision coaches engage with a professional 'other' in order to explore and critically evaluate (Carroll, 2007) their practice. My research highlighted the role of coaching supervision as a form of facilitated reflexivity, which also contributes to a coach's capacity for engaging reflexively while working with clients. In this way, autoethnography has helped me to recognise the (inter)subjective nature of human interaction and consequently to adopt a view of coaching as a systemic practice, a perspective that has found increasing popularity (for example, Lawrence and Moore, 2019). Moreover, autoethnography provides a valuable frame of reference in my current in-house Learning and Development Business Partner role in which I am required to shift between positions of cultural insider and outsider as I live my own and explore others' experience of organisational life.

What happened next

The focus of my master's research and its autoethnographic 'philosophy' enabled me to recognise that completing the course was one step on a path of evolving professional identity. Finishing the MA, the research and practice strands I had pursued together under the umbrella of the course now diverged. For example, although I maintained relationships with both my coaching practice and dissertation research supervisors, in a sign of professional growth these relationships took on a new shape and I began to forge a more independent path. In terms of my practice, I re-contracted with my coaching supervisor while I sought with limited success to establish a client-base working freelance as a coach. I experienced a similar shift in identity as a researcher. Invited by Juliette to seek publication for my master's research, I evolved from dissertation supervisee to primary author of a research paper (Moore and Koning, 2016). Here we adopted a more explicit use of autoethnography, employing autoethnographic vignettes (Humphreys, 2005) to illustrate the development of my professional identity during and after the course.

Autoethnographic vignettes consist of short, first-person accounts on the part of the author who attempts through these autobiographical snippets to explicate and to enrich research findings (Humphreys, 2005). The processes of self-examination and of positioning oneself in relation to the research setting that are involved in writing, editing and re-editing this content encourage reflexivity, and elucidate the mutual influence of author (ethnographer) and cultural context (Ellis and Bochner, 2000). From a practical perspective, I found writing the vignettes for our research (Moore and Koning, 2016) to be relatively straightforward since they were to a great extent a repackaging of autobiographical elements of my master's research (Moore, 2012). On reflection, the challenge I faced trying to write myself 'into' my dissertation in the first place involved overcoming a more generalised anxiety about how to get started – a problem I recognise now as perfectionism and which a student counsellor countered with the simple advice to 'just write!'

Conversely, I found myself untroubled by the process of bringing myself to my work in the kind of emotional depth that others might find uncomfortable. Here again, I see a connection between research methodology and coaching. Long practised as a coaching and counselling client I was able to articulate challenging life experiences with confidence and clarity. And importantly when it comes to the research context I am able (as evidenced by feedback from my line manager) to give account of myself and of others honestly and responsibly (Winkler, 2018).

For our subsequent paper (Moore and Koning, 2016), the challenge lay mostly in attempting to replicate those experiences faithfully, while also learning to appreciate the influence that time and new perspective will have on our attempts to make sense of and to represent those same experiences. This is a recognised issue in autoethnography, where memory and recollection are considered as core data (Chang, 2013). Indeed, Winkler (2018) states that memories are of equal value to written notes, recorded material, or other sources of data. That paper (Moore and Koning, 2016) explored the intersubjective nature of identity work and sense-making in complex scenarios. A key feature of the research was its proposal that factors such as fostering interpersonal relationships (real or virtual) and engaging reflexively in their work (for example through coaching supervision) enable coaches to mediate the experience of ambiguity that can slow or stall the development of a coherent professional identity. To support this view, we (as research co-authors) explored the evolving relationship between us, which entailed making sense of our identity (individually and collectively). The published research provided a further marker in the narrative of my professional journey.

Going it alone

When I started to look for in-house learning and development roles I had to let go of my aspired identity as a freelance coach and develop a new identity as a learning and development practitioner. As I applied for roles, my knowledge of autoethnography enabled me to see the value of establishing a narrative that spoke of and to the culture of which I was seeking to become a member. On the one hand, I created a social media presence (on for example LinkedIn, Twitter), building connections within and knowledge of that professional domain. And I regularly updated a professional profile (CV) by seeking the critical perspective of cultural 'insiders'. I reflexively reviewed my interactions on social media sites to understand how I was relating to members of that culture, and to shape over time a professional identity that felt authentic and credible. Thus my writing became 'both process and product' (Ellis et al., 2011). On the other hand, autoethnography gave me a language to employ in interviews when asked why I wanted to move from a freelance to an in-house role – namely that I preferred to work from the 'inside out'. Now, working for a large organisation, I reflect on the journey that I have made from student-practitioner of coaching to teacher of student-practitioners, applying autoethnographic principles to the production of coaching training to enable colleagues to understand how their identity as cultural insiders influences their own coaching practice.

Table 6.3 summarises key learnings from my research.

Table 6.3   Key learnings from Liam's research

Challenge	Reflection
Choosing a research question	Keep it simple; autoethnography is a useful tool to explore personal and cultural questions
Autoethnography is an inherently subjective methodology which can feel at odds with our perceptions of 'science'	Engage with research philosophy and be mindful of assumptions about achieving objectivity
Finishing autoethnographic writing can be challenging as experiences are often open-ended; it can feel like there is always something that can be added or improved	Be mindful of perfectionism and try to let go of the idea of achieving a clear ending
The nature of autobiography means we are not always the best judge of the quality of our work	Take your time and use short vignettes. Engage rigorously in reflexivity to hone your writing and enhance credibility
Writing oneself into research, particularly in emotional depth, can be challenging	Keep in touch with your personal 'comfort zone' – ask yourself 'what will I be happy for others to read about me?'
Working with memory and recollection	Appreciate the influence that time and new perspective will have on your attempts to make sense of and to represent experiences
Making the theoretical practical	Autoethnography provides a valuable way to understand how our identity as cultural insiders influences our coaching practice

Evaluation

Autoethnography is used across various disciplines but is also gaining interest among professional practice (Denshire, 2014). Autoethnographic counsellors for instance actively seek meaning-making by attempting 'to engage their clients on many levels, to recreate with them what it is in their stories that are important to them' (Custer, 2014: 10). With the synergies between research and practice in coaching, ask yourself, what are the issues and topics from the coaching field that could be suitably explored though autoethnographic research? Since the approach is hardly used in coaching research, it is interesting to think about how autoethnographic research can offer new and additional insights. Clearly there is much to learn from coaches and coachees writing about their careers and experiences with coaching by using, for example, autoethnographic vignettes. Humphreys (2005: 842) describes his autoethnographic vignettes as providing a way to 'construct a window through which the reader can view some of the pleasure and pain associated with an academic career change' aimed at creating 'emotional identification and understanding'. We can also see the value of autoethnography to internal coaches who wish to explore the mutual influence of organisational culture and coaching practice, for example, or simply as a means to explicate day-to-day challenges they share with colleagues who receive coaching support. Autoethnography opens the way to include the voice and lived-experiences of the researcher who in coaching research is very often part of (or is on his or her way to becoming part of) the coaching community. Using autoethnography to explore coaching practices from the inside seems to offer a way to further contribute to the evidence-based practice of coaching (Stober and Grant, 2006).

Autoethnography or an autoethnographic mindset can thus be an exciting and appropriate approach to doing coaching research. A commonly stated challenge is that the autoethnographic researcher must be comfortable with exploring and competent in expressing the self. Fortunately, as a form of reflective practice (Cox, 2013) in which practitioners engage in in-depth self-analysis as a matter of course, coaches may be more predisposed towards these behaviours than members of other professions. Due to the highly subjective nature of autoethnography, we anticipate hesitation from some quarters of the academic community where objectivist research still has a strong voice.

We have hinted at the use of memory as 'data' – something that would be hard to countenance in objectivist terms because of memory's unreliability. In this regard, Winkler (2018: 238) rejects the suggested use of 'entries from [one's] diary into the written account' arguing that this is likely merely to create the illusion of rigour that conforms to more positivist research philosophies and which would violate 'the ontological and epistemological assumptions of autoethnographic research'. In addition, a key strength of autoethnography is its ability to call to attention those 'experiences that are ignored, distorted or silenced because of the discomfort they cause'. Instead through autoethnography these instances, referred to in coaching as 'critical moments' (Day et al., 2008), can 'become known and understood' (Doloriert and Sambrook, 2012: 85), and contribute to more effective coaching practice.

Coaching is a profession that, if the extent of literature on the topic is an indication, increasingly looks to reflexivity as a means of supporting practitioner development and ethics. Perhaps what is required is, as Koning and Ooi (2013) propose, an even more rigorous approach to reflexivity that emphasises honest self-appraisal. Developing increasing familiarity with the nature of identity and of subjectivity, supported by approaches such as autoethnography within coaching research could well support this aim. We would like to conclude with a quote by Gabriel (1998) as used by Humphreys (2005: 855) in his article on his academic career presented through autoethnographic vignettes: 'ultimately the truth of the story lies not in its accuracy but its meaning'.

Further reading

Autoethnography across social sciences, communication studies in particular

Holman Jones, S., Adams, T.E. and Ellis, C. (eds) (2016 [2013]). *Handbook of Autoethnography*. Abingdon: Routledge.

Autoethnography within the fields of psychology and (mental) health

Short, N.P., Turner, L. and Grant, A. (eds) (2013). *Contemporary British Autoethnography*. Rotterdam: Sense Publishers.

Autoethnography as method

Chang, H. (2016 [2008]). *Autoethnography as Method*. Abingdon: Routledge.

Discussion questions

- Why is ethnography (all varieties) hardly used in coaching research? Discuss why and how you would resolve potential problems.
- How would you explain to others the value of autoethnographic 'data'? For example, how would you counter arguments that 'memories' are not data?
- Winkler (2018) talks about finding a balance in autoethnographic research between studying the self and studying culture. How would you try to find such a balance; what would be your approach or strategy?

References

Adams, T.E., Ellis, C. and Holman Jones, S. (2017). 'Autoethnography'. In J. Matthes (ed.), *The International Encyclopedia of Communication Research Methods*. Hoboken, NJ: Wiley-Blackwell, pp. 1–11.

Anderson, L. (2006). 'Analytic autoethnography'. *Journal of Contemporary Ethnography* 35: 373–95.

Caroll, M. (2007). 'Coaching psychology supervision: Luxury or necessity?' In S. Palmer and A. Whybrow (eds), *Handbook of Coaching Psychology: A Guide for Practitioners*. Abingdon: Routledge, pp. 431–48.

Chang, H. (2007). 'Autoethnography: Raising cultural consciousness of self and others'. In G. Walford (ed.), *Methodological Developments in Ethnography*. Bingley: Emerald Group Publishing, pp. 207–21.

Chang, H. (2013). 'Individual and collaborative autoethnography as a method: A social scientist's perspective'. In S. Holman Jones, T. Adams and C. Ellis (eds), *Handbook of Autoethnography*. Walnut Creek, CA: Left Coast Press, pp. 107–22.

Ciuk, S., Koning, J. and Kostera, M. (2018). 'Organizational ethnographies'. In C. Cassell, A. Cunliffe and G. Grandy (eds), *The SAGE Handbook of Qualitative Business and Management Research*. London: Sage Publications, pp. 270–85.

Clifford, J. (1983). 'On ethnographic authority'. *Representations* 1 (2): 118–46.

Coffey, A. (1999). *The Ethnographic Self: Fieldwork and the Representation of Identity*. London: Sage Publications.

Cox, E. (2013). *Coaching Understood*. London: Sage Publications.

Cunliffe, A.L. (2004). 'On becoming a critically reflexive practitioner'. *Journal of Management Education* 28 (4): 407–26.

Cunliffe, A.L. (2008). 'Orientations to social constructionism: Relationally responsive social constructionism and its implications for knowledge and learning'. *Management Learning* 39 (2): 123–39.

Custer, D. (2014). 'Autoethnography as a transformative research method'. *The Qualitative Report* 19 (37): 1–13.

Day, A., De Haan, E., Sills, C., Bertie, C. and Blass, E. (2008). 'Coaches' experiences of critical moments in the coaching'. *International Coaching Psychology Review* 3: 207–18.

Denshire, S. (2014). 'On auto-ethnography'. *Current Sociology* 62: 831–50.

Doloriert, C. and Sambrook, S. (2009). 'Ethical confessions of the "I" of autoethnography: The student's dilemma'. *Qualitative Research in Organizations and Management: An International Journal* 4 (1): 27–45.

Doloriert, C. and Sambrook, S. (2012). 'Organisational autoethnography'. *Journal of Organizational Ethnography* 1: 83–95.

Drake, D.B. (2010). 'Narrative coaching'. In E. Cox, T. Bachkirova and D. Clutterbuck (eds), *The Complete Handbook of Coaching*. London: Sage Publications, pp. 120–31.

Duncan, M. (2004). 'Autoethnography: Critical appreciation of an emerging art'. *International Journal of Qualitative Methods* 3 (4): 28–39.

Ellis, C., Adams, E. and Bochner, A.P. (2011). 'Autoethnography: An overview'. *Historical Social Research* 36 (4): 273–90. Also available online: *Forum: Qualitative Social Research* 12 (1): article 10: www.qualitative-research.net/index.php/fqs/article/viewArticle/1589/3095 (accessed 6 February 2019).

Ellis, C. and Bochner, A.P. (2000). 'Autoethnography, personal narrative, reflexivity: Researcher as subject'. In N.K. Denzin and Y.S. Lincoln (eds), *Handbook of Qualitative Research* (2nd edition). Thousand Oaks, CA: Sage Publications, pp. 733–68.

Eriksen, T.H. (2015). *Small Places, Large Issues: An Introduction to Social and Cultural Anthropology* (4th edition). London: Pluto Press.

Global Code of Ethics (2018). 'The Global Code of Ethics for Coaches, Mentors and Supervisors' [online]. Available at: www.emccouncil.org/quality/ethics/ (accessed 9 February 2019).

Hayano, D.M. (1979). 'Auto-ethnography: Paradigms, problems, and prospects'. *Human Organization* 38 (1): 99–104.

Haynes, K. (2011). 'Tensions in (re)presenting the self in reflexive autoethnographical research'. *Qualitative Research in Organizations and Management: An International Journal* 6: 134–49.

Heider, K.G. (1975). 'What do people do? Dani auto-ethnography'. *Journal of Anthropological Research* 31 (1): 3–17.

Holman Jones, S., Adams, T.E. and Ellis, C. (eds) (2016 [2013]). *Handbook of Autoethnography*. Abingdon: Routledge.

Holt, N.L. (2003). 'Representation, legitimation, and autoethnography: An autoethnographic writing story'. *International Journal of Qualitative Methods* 2: 18–28.

Humphreys, M. (2005). 'Getting personal: Reflexivity and autoethnographic vignettes'. *Qualitative Inquiry* 11 (6): 840–60.

Kempster, S. and Iszatt-White, M. (2013). 'Towards co-constructed coaching: Exploring the integration of coaching and co-constructed autoethnography in leadership development'. *Management Learning* 44: 319–36.

Kempster, S. and Stewart, J. (2010). 'Becoming a leader: A coproduced autoethnographic exploration of situated learning of leadership practice'. *Management Learning* 41: 205–19.

Koning, J. and Ooi, C.S. (2013). 'Awkward encounters and ethnography'. *Qualitative Research in Organizations and Management* 8 (1): 16–32.

Law, H. (2007). 'Narrative coaching and psychology of learning from multicultural perspectives'. In S. Palmer and A. Whybrow (eds), *Handbook of Coaching Psychology: A Guide for Practitioners*. Abingdon: Routledge, pp. 174–92.

Lawrence, P. and Moore, A. (2019). *Coaching in Three Dimensions: Meeting the Challenges of a Complex World*. Abingdon: Routledge.

Madden, R. (2010). *Being Ethnographic: A Guide to the Theory and Practice of Ethnography*. London: Sage Publications.

Meekums, B. (2008). 'Embodied narratives in becoming a counselling trainer: An autoethnographic study'. *British Journal of Guidance and Counselling* 36 (3): 287–301.

Moore, L. (2012). 'Rewriting the script: A narrative exploration of learning experience of individuals on a postgraduate coaching training programme'. MA thesis, Oxford Brookes University.

Moore, L. and Koning, J. (2016). 'Intersubjective identity work and sensemaking of adult learners on a postgraduate coaching course: Finding the balance in a world of dynamic complexity'. *Management Learning* 47 (1): 28–44.

Muncey, T. (2005). 'Doing autoethnography'. *International Journal of Qualitative Methods* 4 (1): 69–86.

Pillow, W. (2003). 'Confession, catharsis, or cure? Rethinking the uses of reflexivity as methodological power in qualitative research'. *Qualitative Studies in Education* 16 (2): 175–96.

Reed-Danahay, D.E. (1997). 'Introduction'. In D.E. Reed-Danahay (ed.), *Auto/ethnography: Rewriting the Self and the Social*. Oxford: Berg, pp. 1–20.

Riessman, C.K. (1993). *Narrative Analysis*. Qualitative Research Methods Series, 30. Newbury Park, CA: Sage Publications.

Rosinski, P. and Abbott, G.N. (2006). 'Coaching from a cultural perspective'. In D.R. Stober and A.M. Grant (eds), *Evidence-Based Coaching Handbook*. Hoboken, NJ: John Wiley & Sons, pp. 153–92.

Sambrook, S. and Herrmann, A.F. (2018). 'Organisational autoethnography: Possibilities, politics and pitfalls'. *Journal of Organizational Ethnography* 7 (3): 222–34.

Schön, D. (1983). *The Reflective Practitioner: How Professionals Think in Action*. New York: Basic Books.

Stober, D.R. and Grant A.M. (eds) (2006). *Evidence-Based Coaching Handbook: Putting Best Practices to Work for your Clients*. Hoboken, NJ: John Wiley & Sons.

Van Maanen, J. (1988). *Tales of the Field: On Writing Ethnography*. Chicago, IL: University of Chicago Press.

Van Maanen, J. (2006). 'Ethnography then and now'. *Qualitative Research in Organizations and Management: An International Journal* 1 (1): 13–21.

Wall, S. (2008). 'Easier said than done: Writing an autoethnography'. *International Journal of Qualitative Methods* 7 (1): 38–53.

Winkler, I. (2018). 'Doing autoethnography: Facing challenges, taking choices, accepting responsibilities'. *Qualitative Inquiry* 24 (4): 236–47.

Ybema, S., Yanow, D., Wels, H. and Kamsteeg, F.H. (eds) (2009). *Organizational Ethnography: Studying the Complexity of Everyday Life*. London: Sage Publications.

7

Quantitative and statistical approaches

Christine Davies and Annette Fillery-Travis

Introduction

The role of quantitative research in coaching has traditionally been rather limited (Clutterbuck, 2013), perhaps because the primary aim of most researchers in the field has been to understand the interactions between individuals as influenced by their perceptions and motivations. Quantitative approaches may also be considered inappropriate to describe the complexities of coaching relationships. However, there are many contexts in which researchers in coaching may wish or need to use a quantitative approach, and/ or gain numerical evidence (Fillery-Travis and Passmore, 2011). Typically, these have related to the measurement of impact, effect, or return on investment (ROI). Often, there is the further objective of generalisability, that is, deducing general principles that apply across a wide range of individuals and contexts. This chapter provides an overview of the main quantitative approaches to research in coaching, along with pointers to sources of more detailed information (see 'Further reading' at the end of the chapter). It also gives an insight into the real issues that researchers encounter when undertaking quantitative research in coaching, and suggests ways of moving forward.

Comment boxes are included to highlight specific issues that researchers in coaching may encounter when undertaking quantitative research.

Distinctive features of quantitative research

When we as research supervisors ask practitioners and students why they want to do quantitative research the reply is often less to do with methodological consideration and more to do with the perceptions of validity and 'correctness' or 'truth'. Quantitative research can be identified as providing higher levels of evidence than its qualitative alternative although this is a contentious point (Corrie, 2010). It is indeed well suited to the generation of universal or generalisable findings that allow prediction of events and outcomes, and particularly useful for the demonstration of effectiveness and optimisation of practice. However, quantitative research is not foolproof, and can provide misleading results when based on an incorrect premise or where there is an error in interpretation or analysis. It is also not applicable to every research question. For example, it is almost impossible to use if the phenomena of interest to us are the dilemmas, values, choices and relationships within practice unless it is present within a mixed-method design. It can also fail to take into account the nature of practice where innovations and improvisations are common and the outputs of quantitative methods, for example findings of theoretical significance, may be less informative than the pursuit of knowledge that is richly described and of direct practical application.

When considering whether to use quantitative methods the researcher must start at the beginning of the design process and consider how well it answers the question posed. Does the use of quantitative methods give the research integrity and coherence? Is it an effective strategy for this particular research question? Will the interpretation of data provide the basis for the output of strong evidence?

Box 7.1   Key concept – Strong evidence

Grant's (2017: 65) definition of evidence does not privilege one type of research approach over another but takes the more sophisticated view that different research designs have utility for addressing different research questions:

> Strong evidence can be understood as information and evidence from well-designed and peer-reviewed studies where the methodology is eminently suitable for the research questions being addressed and the results have been replicated in a range of populations where appropriate.

This is the heart of the quandary that researchers face when considering whether to use quantitative methods or not: What is their research question and what approach would be the most appropriate to address it? To explore this in more detail we need to look specifically at how researchers develop their research questions. This is by no means a trivial or straightforward task as the question must be specific, concise, and well defined, and by constructing it well the research question will lead directly to the most appropriate research approach. As suggested in Chapter 3 of this volume, it is the hub and anchor of all the activity within the research. It informs what methodology is appropriate and what data should be collected. The researcher will actively return to the research question during the research to check whether they are on the right track and therefore if it is ill-defined it can lead the research off track and lead to a confused outcome.

For practitioners particularly, the research question is not one developed through a disinterested curiosity but one that must lie at the heart of their practice. The researcher and the practitioner are two modes of working which cannot be completely separated. The beliefs, values, experience and knowledge about practice will influence how the practitioner views events, their role within them as well as the questions they have chosen to ask about their practice. As researching practitioners are effectively putting their theoretical underpinning and practice forward for scrutiny this makes the process of research, in whatever paradigm or methodology they choose, a deeply personal experience and one where reflexivity becomes an important consideration as illustrated in one practitioner's experience in Box 7.2.

Box 7.2 Doing research – Doctoral student 1

I worked in IT for years, and unlike many of my coaching colleagues, I like numbers, and so I always thought I would do quantitative research. But I soon released that the questions I was asking couldn't be answered that way. I've had to try very hard to learn how to use qualitative approaches like phenomenology.

The account in Box 7.2 suggests that it is important to start the research process with a clear question, and then to work out the correct methodological approach and design. At first sight this may seem at odds with the positivistic tradition which has dominated quantitative research for so long as researchers strove for detached indifference to their research. An academic or professional researcher will be interested in the development of knowledge per se and will look to validate their work through analysis and peer review. In contrast a practitioner researcher will be interested in research as an improvement strategy for their practice where validity is sought through acceptance by clients and peers as well as practical applicability.

This difference in approach requires the practitioner to reflect upon their practice and positions their research within it.

Researchers who are contemplating a quantitative methodology may lean towards an objectivist ontology, and positivist epistemology. This would almost certainly be the case if they have a strong belief in the value of numbers, and approach their research armed with a hypothesis, and needful of empirical data. However, many researchers within the field of coaching could be said to hold a pragmatic paradigm. This indicates that quantitative methodology provides an avenue to answer some or part of the research question(s) posed, but is not necessarily at the heart of the research, and qualitative methodology may also play an important role (Guba and Lincoln, 1994). This would also be true of the critical realist paradigm, and practitioner researchers may often find that their paradigm has a 'critical' element in the sense that they approach research hoping to make changes (Fillery-Travis and Lane, 2008). In the context of coaching, this implies that the research undertaken will improve practice in some way, and lead to better client outcomes. (See also Chapters 2 and 10 for the discussion of pragmatic approaches.)

Quantitative research designs

As mentioned above, the nature of the research design, and the methodological approaches employed, should always reflect the research question posed. Quantitative approaches are good at describing and making inferences about data, but they cannot explain. So, a researcher who wants to understand a situation needs to take a qualitative path. It is possible, however, for the research design to incorporate both quantitative and qualitative elements, as indicated in the list of designs below.

Box 7.3 Key concepts – Exploratory and confirmatory designs

Quantitative methodological approaches tend to be either exploratory or confirmatory (Atieno, 2009). Exploratory designs involve discovering and describing, and could address research questions such as 'What is coaching like in this organisation?' or 'What is the ROI resulting from a particular coaching practice in this organisation?' The quantitative approach to answering such questions tends to involve descriptive statistics, and data analysis might produce outputs such as bar charts (e.g. % different coaching practices), and means (e.g. ROI). It may also be appropriate to develop models based on the data obtained (Palmer, 2008).

Confirmatory designs, by contrast, are deductive in nature, and generally begin with a research question which is tied to a hypothesis. For example, the

(Continued)

question 'Will coaching change the job satisfaction of a sample of individuals?' is likely to be linked to the researcher's underlying belief that it will indeed change job satisfaction. This is often a reflection on ontology/epistemology, and is usually specific to a positivist paradigm. Put in more precise research terminology, there would be a null hypothesis (H_0) stating that coaching would make no difference to job satisfaction, and an alternate hypothesis (H_1) stating that it would make a significant difference. The methodological design in this instance is likely to involve a measurement of job satisfaction of the same individuals before and after coaching.

Despite the paucity of quantitative research in coaching, four main quantitative research designs have been utilised to date:

1. *Mixed method*: a design with both quantitative and qualitative elements which is often exploratory. Typically, the design consists of a survey distributed across an organisation followed by a small number of interviews. However, in Gray et al. (2011), a series of case studies interviews was followed by a survey.
2. *Case study*: this is dealt with in detail in Chapter 8, but it is worth noting here that some of the methods used in a case study design may have quantitative elements; for example, Andreanoff (2016) used a case study design, focusing on one organisation, in which there were quasi-experimental elements.
3. *Quasi-experiment*: in this confirmatory design, there are at least two groups which are compared in some way. Often, one or more groups experience an intervention such as a particular coaching practice (these are the 'experimental' group(s)), whilst one group does not (this is the 'control' group). This is not a true experimental design because not all variables can be controlled, and the researcher has to be on the lookout for 'confounding' variables which may have as much, or more, effect than the intervention. A good illustration of this is the 'Hawthorne effect' (Wickström and Bendix, 2000). Variations on this design include comparison of groups with different coaching approaches, including uncoached (for example, Losch et al., 2016, looking at the effect of coaching on procrastination behaviours), or performance before and after coaching (for example, Hunt, 2010, who examined self-efficacy in female entrepreneurs).
4. *Action research*: this type of design is discussed in detail in Chapter 9, but note that quantitative elements may be incorporated into action research designs to obtain numerical evidence of the efficacy of one or more implementation steps. For example, Olivero et al. (1997) used numerical indices of managerial competency within an action research design, and Leonard-Cross (2010) employed a quasi-experimental method within an action research cycle.

Quantitative methods

Quantitative research often involves direct measurement, and in the world of coaching this could involve measures such as sales over a particular time period, or the number of skills gained after a training course. There may be a requirement for a measure of more complex concepts related to impact or ROI, and a variety of scales exist within the world of coaching to quantify concepts such as empowerment and accountability (Hagen and Peterson, 2014).

One of the most widely used tools involved in the implementation of quantitative research methods in coaching is the questionnaire (a survey involves the distribution of a large number of these). Questionnaires are frequently self-completion in nature, administered via hard copy or online. Response rates may be disappointingly low, especially if surveys are over-long or visually unappealing. Alternatively, questionnaires may be completed by an interviewer within a highly structured interview. This process can be time-consuming, but has the merit of ensuring that selected participants respond.

The questions in questionnaires need to be devised with care, bearing in mind that if the wrong question is asked, an opportunity to get the required information is missed. Questions may need to be framed in an indirect way, avoiding topics that participants might find uncomfortable or difficult to understand, and ensuring that wording is clear and unambiguous.

Questionnaire questions often aim to provide numerical values for concepts such as 'satisfaction' or 'confidence', and typically Likert scales will be used for this. For example, leadership potential could be gauged from 1 to 4 on a Likert scale. Clearly, such scales do not give absolute measures, just an index of them, and quantifying complex ideas in this empirical way may not always be appropriate.

Box 7.4   Key concept – Empiricism

Empiricism is an epistemology in which facts are thought to 'speak for themselves'. Its difficulty is that empiricists assume the world consists of facts; this is unrealistic. The real world is very complex (Olsen, 2004: 14).

The nature of quantitative data

From a positivist perspective, the best sorts of research data are 'scale' or 'interval/ratio' data. These are easily measurable numerical variables with absolute, known intervals (for example, the difference between 3 cm and 4 cm is 1 cm, which is exactly the same as the difference between 6 cm and 7 cm). Variables like this include length of service, sales income, profit, number of clients. However, the questionnaire questions based on Likert scales generate 'ordinal' or 'rank' data. These data reflect order, or relative magnitude, and do not give precise values (so, for example, we cannot be sure that the difference between 'not content' and 'quite content' is the same as between 'content' and 'very content'). A last type of data that may be involved in quantitative research is 'categorical', and includes categories such gender and job type. On an individual basis, such data are not quantitative at all, but summarising such data produces numbers (or 'frequencies') per category which can be analysed using quantitative approaches.

Quantitative data analysis

The approach to analysis depends on the research question and design, and also on the type of data generated. If research designs are exploratory, data analysis may focus on descriptive statistics, for example, mean, mode, range, standard deviation. Pictorial representations such as pie charts or bar charts may also be helpful to summarise data and show trends. However, this sort of analysis does not help deduce relationships or differences, and certainly does not indicate how significant they are. For this, inferential statistical tests are needed, and these will be particularly appropriate where research designs are confirmatory, and the objective is to test one or more hypotheses related to the research question. A range of common statistical tests is outlined in Table 7.1. These tests are 'parametric' in that they are based on an assumed set of population parameters, one of which is that the data follow a 'normal distribution' (i.e. a distribution that looks like a bell-shaped curve with most values in the centre, and fewer at the edges). These tests work best with scale data. Ordinal data, as produced from questionnaires, are best analysed using 'non-parametric' variants of these tests, as listed in Table 7.2.

Table 7.1 A list of common parametric statistical tests (for scale data)

Type of research question	Statistical test/method	Example
Is there an association between two categorical variables? (e.g. gender, job type)	Chi-squared test	Cunningham and Sagas (2003) used Chi-squared tests to compare duration of tenure of male and female sports coaches in the USA
Is there a relationship between two scale variables? (e.g. between age and sales revenue)	Correlation and/or regression	Hwang et al. (2013) used correlation coefficients to assess relationships between paired combinations of emotional intelligence, coaching efficacy, and leadership style
Is there a difference (in a scale variable) between two separate groups? (e.g. number of customers logged by managers in two different regions)	Independent t-test	Griffin et al. (2008) used independent t-tests to compare the outcomes of coached and non-coached groups

Type of research question	Statistical test/method	Example
Is there a difference (in a scale variable) in the same individuals at two different times/conditions? (e.g. leadership rating before and after coaching)	Paired t-test	Newnham-Kanas et al. (2008) compared variables including self-esteem pre and post one-on-one coaching using paired t-tests
Is there a difference (in a scale variable) between more than two groups? (e.g. ROI from groups coached in four different ways)	ANOVA ('Analysis of Variance')	Fried and Irwin (2016) compared stress levels in university students in three different categories, pre-, mid-, and post-coaching intervention, using a one-way ANOVA
Is there an underlying variable influencing other measured variables? (e.g. one or two key variables influencing a range of variables assessed in a survey)	Factor analysis	Newsom and Dent (2011) used exploratory factor analysis to determine the main factors assessed by the Executive Coaching Work Behaviour Survey

The statistical test(s) used depend on the research question and the nature of the data generated, and should be selected at the stage of research design. It should be noted that the Chi-squared test will handle data that are not normally distributed, and also deals with 'categorical' variables.

Table 7.2 Parametric statistical tests and their non-parametric equivalents

Parametric statistical test	Non-parametric equivalent
Independent t-test	Mann–Whitney test
Paired t-test	Wilcoxon
Analysis of variance (ANOVA)	Kruskal–Wallis test
Pearson correlation	Spearman correlation

See also: https://research.phoenix.edu/blog/selecting-right-statistical-analysis-tool-your-research

The process of carrying out a statistical test involves the calculation of a particular 'statistic' for the sample in question, and this is compared to a probability distribution – fortunately, both of these steps can be swiftly and painlessly carried out by software such as MS Excel or SPSS. A key output of a statistical test is a probability value, or 'p value': this relates to the probability of the null hypothesis being correct. A small p value contradicts the null hypothesis of a confirmatory research design, and reinforces the alternate hypothesis, in that it indicates that there is a significant difference. In the example question posed earlier, 'Will coaching change the job satisfaction of a sample of individuals?', if the p value obtained was less than 0.05 (or 5 per cent), this would indicate a significant effect of coaching on job satisfaction. It is important to note that statistical tests cannot prove cause and effect – they just imply that one variable has an effect on another.

Researchers may additionally need to report on values such as validity, reliability and effect size. Validity refers to whether a particular measure actually assesses what it is meant to assess. For example, is a questionnaire question on 'length of lunch-break' an appropriate measure of job satisfaction? Validity is also important with respect to coaching scales (Hagen and Peterson, 2014). Reliability, by contrast, gives an indication of the repeatability of results. This is often discussed in the context of questionnaires: for example, would the same person answer the same question the same way on two different occasions? Reliability can be gauged using a measure called 'Cronbach's Alpha', and this is discussed thoroughly by Field (2017). His book is also a good source for information on 'effect size', which may be required when looking at the relationship between specific scale variables. It can be thought of as another term for 'correlation', but there are other values that can indicate effect size, such as 'Cohen's d'.

Practical issues

It is not always easy to identify the exact knowledge you need (Knorr Cetina, 2001), or how to acquire it. It is not uncommon for doctoral researchers to take a considerable amount of time to find a research question that works for them, but until this is clear, it is not possible to decide on the best research design and methods, and the variables that need to be measured. This is certainly true of a complex topic such as coaching (Williams, 2014), and it is important not to oversimplify, and to be as specific as possible about the question that needs to be asked (Fillery-Travis and Lane, 2006), as suggested by one of our postgraduate students (Box 7.5).

Box 7.5   Doing research – Practical issue 1

I'd read loads of books, and I was really pleased that I was finding out more and more about my field. But in hindsight, my reading wasn't directed enough, and I was just muddying the waters in terms of working out what I was going to write in my research proposal. In the end, it boiled down to: 'What do I really need to know?' Once I'd sorted out my priorities, and realised what I needed for my coaching, I was a lot more focused about how to approach my literature review, and eventually my methods.

Another specific practical issue relates to the importance of selecting scales that are demonstrably valid and appropriate (Box 7.6).

Box 7.6   Doing research – Practical issue 2

I was working with a group of coaches, and we had set up a small research project focusing on leadership capabilities. We decided to interview ten managers in the company and chose Reed et al.'s (2011) scale to measure leadership potential. All went well until the seventh interview, which was with a senior accountant. He was adamant that the scale was inappropriate as a measure of leadership, and so we had to terminate his interview. This meant a loss of an individual from our sample, but the bigger issue was whether we should carry on using the Reed scale or find some other way to assess leadership.

Ethical issues

All research involving people should be planned carefully to ensure that any potential harm to participants, and researcher(s), is minimised, as discussed in Chapter 3. However, it is often thought that quantitative methods pose fewer ethical issues than more interpretive methods, and it is true that issues of anonymity and confidentiality are reduced by the use of tools such as online surveys. However, it is important to treat quantitative methods just like any others, and ensure, for example, that all participants consent to their participation, even if online. It is always best to obtain written consent if possible, though in the case of surveys administered online it is common practice to explain to participants (for example, via an initial web page) that their continued participation implies their consent.

Different coaching scenarios will have their own ethical issues in the context of quantitative research. Andreanoff (2016), for example, noted that in quasi-experimental designs, the selection of individuals for 'control' groups may pose issues, for such individuals may have been denied coaching interventions, or may have been waiting for coaching for some time.

Quantitative research approaches may have many of the same ethical concerns as qualitative studies: in Box 7.7 a researcher deals with issues of anonymity.

Box 7.7   Doing research – Ethical issue

I had decided to get my scores on attainment, goal-seeking, and motivation via short interviews. I wasn't looking for any narrative, only scores, so I didn't need to use an audio recorder, and I was feeling quite chuffed about that because I knew that people sometimes object to being recorded. But what I hadn't bargained on was the room I was allocated: it was a small meeting room with glass partitions, and everyone in the open plan office could see who was in there. There was no privacy, and I knew no one would agree to going in there. We ended up using the office of one of the associate directors.

Sampling issues

A common aim of quantitative research is to find the characteristics of a population, based on an investigated sample. So, for example, if it is found that a particular training course has raised the target-setting abilities of a sample of thirty employees, it might be assumed that the course would help all employees. If there is a need to generalise in this way, it is best to use a large, randomly-selected sample. Small samples, and/or samples selected via 'convenience sampling' (such as selecting those who are easy to find) or 'snowball sampling' (asking a participant to pass on a request to their colleagues/friends, and so on) may result in biased outcomes. It is possible to use sample size estimators (for example, www.surveymonkey.com/mp/sample-size-calculator/) to find the minimum sample size for the research task based on variables including the required confidence interval and acceptable margin of error. However, it may not be so easy in practice to obtain the recommended number and, as suggested in Box 7.8, it is not always easy to obtain an adequate sample size.

Box 7.8   Doing research – Sampling issue

I was using skills levels as an estimate of ROI, and I thought it would be best to use an online survey because it wouldn't take too much of my time, and I could get a big sample. I sent the survey link out to all management personnel, but after a week I still only had five responses. So then I sent out a reminder, and I had a few more, but eventually I had to ask the CEO to email them all; she wasn't very happy about that. I got the data I needed in the end, but for a smaller firm, short interviews might have been a lot better.

Data storage issues

If personal data need to be retained, then data storage may have implications for confidentiality, and this ethical issue is discussed in Chapter 3. It may be helpful to upload quantitative data to data archives held within an organisation or in the public domain, so that other researchers may benefit from opportunities to carry out secondary analysis, so long as such storage conforms to the General Data Protection Regulation (GDPR) based on the Data Protection Act 2018. The storage of personal data in quantitative research may be an issue for some researchers as reported by the doctoral student in Box 7.9.

Box 7.9   Doing research – Data storage issue

If you're doing pre and post studies on the same people, you have to be able to identify them. This wasn't a problem for the coach I was working with as they were all her clients, but I had to make sure to explain on my application for ethical approval exactly why I needed personal contact details.

Analysis issues

Insufficient data is frequently an issue in quantitative research, especially as statistical tests have limited validity and reliability if sample sizes are small. It is therefore important to make contingency plans well in advance to help ensure that adequate data can be acquired, or alternative strategies employed.

Another common problem is not being clear about the correct statistical test to use. As mentioned above, this issue should be addressed at the stage of research design. Researchers can encounter difficulties when their initial planning is weak. Fortunately, there was a work-around in the example in Box 7.10.

Box 7.10   Doing research – Analysis issue 1

We started up a coaching programme in an industry that was completely new to the concept, and one of the things we wanted to know about was the effect on coaches. At the end of the programme, we gave them some self-completion questionnaires with questions that focused on emotional intelligence. So that was fine for the end point, but we didn't have a baseline. Looking back, we should have planned for that, but it didn't occur to us at the time. As it happened, though, most of the coaches already had this information via feedback we'd given them on a different project. So we used this in a 'post hoc' way – it wasn't ideal, but it allowed us to do the 'before' and after' comparison that was needed.

One doctoral supervisor explained why a statistical test which is appropriate for the data type as well as the research question should be selected (see Box 7.11).

Box 7.11   Doing research – Analysis issue 2

One doctoral candidate of mine wanted to compare the same coaching programme in two different public sector organisations. He wanted to know about people's satisfaction with the programme, and how they felt it had affected their ability to meet their goals. He utilised a quantitative design with a survey as the main method, and collected a lot of data, all of which consisted of responses on a six-point Likert scale. Given that this is ordinal data, I recommended that he use a Mann–Whitney test instead of a t-test.

The longer case study from the HR context (Box 7.12) illustrates a mixed methodological design. It also indicates the potential value of factor analysis when analysing questionnaire data.

Box 7.12 Case study – The HR professional also studying for a doctorate in professional practice

I'm a senior executive in the HR department of a major financial services firm, and also a candidate for a professional doctorate. Five years ago, my firm experienced a takeover, and shortly afterwards we had to downsize. The Directors wanted to make the change as positive as possible so just after the change we decided to invest in development activities, so that remaining staff knew that they were appreciated, and knew we wanted them to stick with us. From the HR point of view, we particularly wanted to prepare managers for potential leadership roles, and we decided to use coaching as our main development approach.

I also wanted to get data for my research that would help us assess the effectiveness of coaching and help us work out which aspects of the coaching interventions were most valuable. The firm was also keen to find the ROI, since a two-year coaching programme with sixty managers was a major expense, and so I needed to collect 'before and after' data for things like individual sales figures, and % retention of sales team members. This set me off on a quantitative pathway, with a survey right at the end to get coachees' assessments of the programme in terms of variables such as trust and satisfaction. I felt it was also important to understand their responses, so I added a qualitative element involving a small number of interviews. Overall, therefore, my research design was mixed methodology.

Analysing ROI data was quite straightforward, basically a case of subtracting before and after per individual, and then averaging. Fortunately, the survey went well also, and we had a great response rate. Again, it was fairly easy to find the modal response per question, but I went a step further and used factor analysis to find the questions that seemed to be significantly meaningful. Factor analysis was new to me: it is a statistical process based on correlation that basically weighs up which factors have the greatest effect, and so can point to underlying factors that could be responsible for results obtained. I used SPSS for this, and undertook a process called 'Principal Component Analysis' which confirms whether potential factors are as important as we might think. I expected that 'confidence' and 'encouragement' would figure prominently, and that proved to be the case. I had to bear in mind, though, that even with sixty managers, my sample size wasn't very big, and the margin of error would have been more acceptable if my sample size had been in excess of 100. The outcomes of thematic analysis of interview transcripts tied in well with what I found from factor analysis, though obviously there were a lot more details and nuance.

Evaluation

Quantitative approaches can be of great benefit to research in coaching. Quantitative methods such as surveys can be relatively simple to implement, particularly when administered online, and quantitative analysis, despite its reputation, is usually far quicker and more straightforward than its qualitative counterpart. The numerical outcomes of quantitative analysis are relatively easy to judge and compare with others, and the large sample sizes involved tend to inspire confidence and can allow for generalisability. This means that clients and peers, particularly in the world of business, may be disproportionately impressed by quantitative research outputs.

However, whilst quantitative research can be very good at describing a situation, it does not provide reasons, and for those we have to turn to the 'richness' of qualitative research (Fillery-Travis and Cox, 2018). Also, generalised theories may oversimplify situations which are actually very complex (Olsen, 2004), and this is a particular hazard when it comes to the feelings and motivations of human beings. There are practical issues to bear in mind, also, such as the need for large sample sizes which may be difficult to achieve. There must also be careful consideration of possible confounding variables which can completely invalidate data which may have taken a great deal of time and effort to generate.

Overall, quantitative approaches have much to offer research in coaching, but they should be used thoughtfully, and in response to appropriate research questions. In many cases, a mixed methodological design will be the most useful approach and will help to ensure that the clarity of numbers is balanced by the explanatory power of words.

Further reading

Bluman, A. (2017). *Elementary Statistics: A Step By Step Approach*. New York: McGraw-Hill Education.

Clear explanations of a wide range of statistical techniques.

Bryman, A. (2015). *Social Research Methods* (5th edition). Oxford: Oxford University Press.

A good place to start for information on research design, and particularly good on surveys. Also discusses the use of SPSS.

Denscombe, M. (2017). *The Good Research Guide: For Small Scale Social Research Projects* (6th edition). Oxford: Oxford University Press.

Good overview of a wide range of research methods.

Field, A. (2017). *Discovering Statistics Using IBM SPSS Statistics* (5th edition). London: Sage Publications.

Invaluable for anyone intending to use SPSS for statistical tests.

Fillery-Travis, A. and Lane, D. (2008). 'How to develop your research interests'. In S. Palmer and R. Bor (eds), *The Practitioner's Handbook*. London: Sage Publications, pp. 176–92.

A chapter which provides a very readable introduction to research in coaching, and the importance of research paradigms.

Saunders, M., Lewis, P. and Thornhill, A. (2015). *Research Methods for Business Students* (7th edition). Harlow: Pearson.

Very good on options for analysis, especially descriptive analysis, with tips on using Excel and SPSS.

Discussion questions

- Have you examined the literature in your specific field of interest to see if any quantitative research already undertaken could help you with specific research tasks?
- Are you undertaking quantitative research for the right reasons, and not just because you, or your clients, are more likely to be influenced by positivist approaches than interpretive ones?
- What measures of ROI have you worked with to date? How could you use these in a way that would allow you to use inferential statistics?
- Which coaching models and frameworks do you make use of? Do they provide scope to collect data, and if not, could you adapt them?
- Do you have personal training needs in quantitative research? How best could these be met?

References

Andreanoff, J. (2016). 'Issues in conducting quantitative studies on the impact of coaching and mentoring in higher education'. *International Journal of Evidence Based Coaching and Mentoring, Special Issue* 10: 202–16.

Atieno, O.P. (2009). 'An analysis of the strengths and limitations of qualitative and quantitative research paradigms'. *Problems of Education in the 21st Century* 13: 13–18.

Clutterbuck, D. (2013). 'Where next with research in mentoring?' *International Journal of Mentoring and Coaching in Education* 2 (3). Available at: www.emeraldinsight.com/doi/full/10.1108/IJMCE-09-2013-0048 (accessed 6 January 2019).

Corrie, S. (2010). 'What is evidence?' In R. Woolfe, S. Strawbridge, B. Douglas and W. Dryden (eds), *Handbook of Counselling Psychology* (3rd edition). London: Sage Publications, pp. 44–61.

Cunningham, G. and Sagas, M. (2003). 'Occupational turnover intent among assistant coaches of women's teams: The role of organizational work experiences'. *Sex Roles* 49 (3): 185–90.

Field, A. (2017). *Discovering Statistics Using IBM SPSS Statistics* (5th edition). London: Sage Publications.

Fillery-Travis, A. and Cox, E. (2018). 'Researching coaching'. In E. Cox, T. Bachkirova and D. Clutterbuck (eds), *The Complete Handbook of Coaching* (3rd edition). London: Sage Publications, pp. 445–59.

Fillery-Travis, A. and Lane, D. (2006). 'Does coaching work or are we asking the wrong question?' *International Coaching Psychology Review* 1 (1): 24–36.

Fillery-Travis, A. and Lane, D. (2008). 'How to develop you research interests'. In S. Palmer and R. Bor (eds), *The Practitioner's Handbook*. London: Sage Publications, pp. 176–92.

Fillery-Travis, A. and Passmore, J. (2011). 'A critical review of executive coaching research: A decade of progress and what's to come'. *Coaching: An International Journal of Theory, Research and Practice* 4 (2): 70–88.

Fried, R.R. and Irwin, J.D. (2016). 'Calmly coping: A motivational interviewing via co-active life coaching (MI-VIA-CALC) pilot intervention for university students with perceived levels of high stress'. *International Journal of Evidence Based Coaching and Mentoring* 14 (1): 16–33.

Grant, A. (2017). 'Coaching as evidence-based practice'. In T. Bachkirova, G.B. Spence and D. Drake (eds), *The SAGE Handbook of Coaching*. London: SAGE Publications, pp. 62–84.

Gray, D.E., Ekinci, Y. and Goregaokar, H. (2011). 'Coaching SME managers: Business development or personal therapy? A mixed methods study'. *The International Journal of Human Resource Management* 22 (4): 863–82.

Griffin, B., Harding, D.W., Wilson, I.G. and Yeomans, N.D. (2008). 'Does practice make perfect? The effect of coaching and retesting on selection tests used for admission to an Australian medical school'. *The Medical Journal of Australia* 189 (5): 270–3.

Guba, E.G. and Lincoln, Y.S. (1994). 'Competing paradigms in qualitative research'. In N.K. Denzin and Y.S. Lincoln (eds), *Handbook of Qualitative Research*. London: Sage Publications, pp. 105–17.

Hagen, M.S. and Peterson, S.L. (2014). 'Coaching scales'. *Advances in Developing Human Resources* 16 (2): 222–41.

Hunt, C. (2010). 'A longitudinal study to explore and examine the potential and impact of an e-coaching programme on the learning and self-efficacy of female entrepreneurs in the north west of England'. PhD thesis, University of Manchester.

Hwang, S., Feltz, D.L. and Lee, J-D. (2013). 'Emotional intelligence in coaching: Mediation effect of coaching efficacy on the relationship between emotional intelligence and leadership style'. *International Journal of Sport and Exercise Psychology* 11: 292–306.

Knorr Cetina, K. (2001). 'Objectual practice'. In T.R. Schatzki, K. Knorr Cetina and E. Von Savigny (eds), *The Practice Turn in Contemporary Theory*. London: Routledge, pp. 184–97.

Leonard-Cross, E. (2010). 'Developmental coaching: Business benefit – fact or fad? An evaluative study to explore the impact of coaching in the workplace'. *International Coaching Psychology Review* 5 (1): 36–47.

Losch, S., Traut-Mattausch, E., Mühlberger, M.D. and Jonas, E. (2016). 'Comparing the effectiveness of individual coaching, self-coaching, and group training: How leadership makes the difference'. *Frontiers in Psychology* 7: 629. Available at: www.ncbi.nlm.nih.gov/pmc/articles/PMC4853380/ (accessed 15 January 2019).

Newnham-Kanas, C., Irwin, J.D. and Morrow, D. (2008). 'Co-active life coaching as a treatment for adults with obesity'. *International Journal of Evidence Based Coaching and Mentoring* 6 (2): 1–12.

Newsom, G. and Dent, E. (2011). 'A work behaviour analysis of executive coaches'. *International Journal of Evidence Based Coaching and Mentoring* 9 (2): 1–22.

Olivero, G., Bane, K.D. and Kopelman, R.E. (1997). 'Executive coaching as a transfer of training tool'. *Public Personnel Management* 26 (4): 461–9.

Olsen, W. (2004). 'Triangulation in social research: Qualitative and quantitative methods can really be mixed'. *Developments in Sociology* 20: 103–18.

Palmer, S. (2008). 'The PRACTICE model of coaching'. *Coaching Psychology International* 1 (1): 4–8.

Reed, L.L., Vidaver-Cohen, D. and Colwell, S.R. (2011). 'A new scale to measure executive servant leadership: Development, analysis, and implications for research'. *Journal of Business Ethics* 101: 415–34.

Wickström, G. and Bendix, T. (2000). 'The "Hawthorne effect": What did the original Hawthorne studies actually show?' *Scandinavian Journal of Work, Environment & Health* 26 (4): 363–7.

Williams, F. (2014). 'Decisions along the dissertation journey: Reflections of a coach-researcher'. *International Journal of Evidence Based Coaching and Mentoring* 8: 67–83.

8

Case study research

Andrea D. Ellinger and Rochell R. McWhorter

Introduction

This chapter introduces and describes case study research and qualitative case study research with the intent of clarifying some of the confusion that exists which relates to terminology, approaches that are used for engaging in this form of research, and what this type of research seeks to achieve. Common challenges and pitfalls associated with this mode of inquiry are discussed and some insights are provided about how to address several of these issues. Current examples of predominantly qualitative case study research are presented that illustrate the potential of case study research for richly understanding many facets of coaching to advance the state of the art in coaching research.

Case study research is intended to address specific types of questions, examine processes, and promote an understanding of a phenomenon in its real life context, all of which are relevant to researching coaching. However, despite the plethora of published articles that refer to case study research, there are many misconceptions, misunderstandings and criticisms associated with case study research. These often relate to what a case is, what a case study is, and what case study research is and is intended to do, along with a lack of precision and concerns about rigour that often accompany the reporting of case study research (Rule and John, 2015; Ulriksen and Dadalauri, 2016). In particular, as Yin (2018: xx) noted, 'case studies may still have a mixed reputation as a research method', particularly if non-research case studies have been confused with research case studies.

According to Gibbert et al. (2008: 1473), 'researchers have very different views on the case study method. Some researchers may see the case study method as an alternative to "mainstream" or positivist researcher methods and may be critical of an attempt to emulate the natural science model in data collection and analysis strategies'. In particular, Baskarada (2014) acknowledged that qualitative case study research is not well understood. However, as a form of empirical inquiry, case study research in general, and qualitative case study research specifically, are widely used in a number of disciplines. Case study research has been used in psychology, sociology, anthropology, economics, political science, education, healthcare, social work and nursing (Smith, 2018; Thomas, 2011; Yin, 2014, 2018). Within business and management, case study research has been used in the accounting, finance, strategy, operations management and supply chain and logistics disciplines and holds considerable promise for the field of coaching (Barratt et al., 2011; Ellram, 1996; McCutcheon and Meredith, 1993; Pagell and Wu, 2009; Wu and Choi, 2005).

To better understand its appropriateness and promise for conducting coaching research, we begin by examining several important terms that are often used interchangeably by providing necessary definitions to clarify confusion that exists in the literature. Doing so enables us to describe what a case is, what case study as a research method is, and qualitative case study research more specifically. We consider what case study research is designed to achieve and the different epistemological orientations associated with case study research. We also consider some of the practical issues that doctoral students and researchers often confront when engaging in case study research. These issues often relate to bounding the case, identifying appropriate research settings, considering data collection and analysis approaches, and writing up case study research. We then present some current examples of coaching case study research. We offer an evaluation of the strengths and weaknesses associated with case study research. Recommendations for additional reading for researchers interested in further developing their knowledge and skills in conducting case study research are provided along with discussion and application questions.

Distinctive features of case study research

Cronin (2014) acknowledged that defining case study research can be problematic because terms such as 'case study', 'case study method' and 'case method' are often used interchangeably, which results in confusion. Similarly, Carolan et al. (2016: 627) also suggested that 'nuanced definitions indicate that case study can be defined in terms of the case itself (the unit of study), the case study design (the process), and the case study (the product)'. Merriam

(1998) and others have also distinguished case study research from casework, case method, case history and case record. We begin by examining the concept of a case, case study, and case study research.

Box 8.1   Key concept – What is a case?

Gillham (2000: 1) defined a case as 'a unit of human activity embedded in the real world; which can only be studied or understood in context; which exists in the here and now; and, that merges in with its context so that precise boundaries are difficult to draw'. When more than one case is examined, the study is often referred to as collective case studies, cross-case, multicase, multiple case, multisite, or comparative case studies (Merriam, 1998).

Gillham (2000), among others such as Merriam (1998) and Ellram (1996), has indicated that a case can be an individual, a group, a programme, an event, a decision process, a policy, an intervention, an organisation, an institution, a community, a profession, an industry or type of operation, which are reflective of single cases, or can be multiple cases when a number of these types of cases are examined. In terms of defining what a case is, scholars have differentiated a case from a case record, which is commonly used as a form of record keeping in the medical and social work contexts. Such case records do not constitute case studies for case study research. Scholars have also suggested that case studies that are used for teaching purposes, often referred to as the case method, or what Yin (2018) referred to as *teaching-practice case studies*, or those that reflect *popular case studies* (Yin, 2018: xxi) often represent *non-research* case studies because explicit research procedures are often not used. These types of case studies 'exist outside of the domain of case study research' (Yin, 2018: xx).

The term, *case study* has been variously defined. Gillham (2000) defined a case study as one that investigates the case or cases to address a specific research question. According to Dul and Hak (2012: 4), a 'case study is a study in which (a) one case (single case study) or a small number of cases (comparative case study) in their real life context are selected, and (b) scores obtained from these cases are analyzed in a qualitative manner (visual inspection)'. They distinguish a case as 'an instance of an object of study' (2012: 4) and differentiate case study from other forms of research, such as experiments and survey research. They suggest that case study is a 'research strategy defined by the number of instances ($N = 1$ or $N =$ small) that is studied as well as the "qualitative" or non-statistical method of analysis of all kinds of (quantitative and qualitative) data' (2012: 6). For Dul and Hak (2012), the case study draws conclusions on the basis of qualitative analysis, whereas data collection and measurement in support of the case study may draw upon qualitative and quantitative techniques.

Within literature that describes case study research as a form of inquiry, the seminal work of three scholars is often referenced: Stake (1995), Merriam (1998), Yin (2012, 2014, 2018), along with a recent contribution by Yazan (2015) who presented a comparison of these three approaches. These researchers have offered foundational books and articles that describe their conceptions of what case study research is and offer recommendations about how it is done. In particular, Merriam (1998) and Stake (1995) are associated with qualitative case study research. In terms of defining case study research from the qualitative perspective, Stake (1995: xi) indicated that a case study 'is the study of the particularity and complexity of a single case'. While he recognises that quantitative case studies and instructional case studies exist, case study is 'a disciplined, qualitative mode of inquiry into the single case' (1995: xii). Similarly, Merriam (1998: 19) acknowledged that a qualitative case study design is employed to 'gain an in-depth understanding of the situation and meaning for those involved. The interest is in process rather than outcomes, in context rather than a specific variable, in discovery rather than confirmation.' According to Merriam (1998), qualitative case study research is distinguished by special features. These features are particularistic, descriptive, and heuristic, meaning that such studies are specifically focused, often provide thick, rich description about the phenomenon being studied, and enhance the researcher's understanding of the phenomenon. Qualitative case study research can be inductive or deductive to either build or test theory (Barratt et al., 2011). In their review of case studies in business research, Dul and Hak (2012) categorised such case study research as theory-building, theory-testing, and practice-oriented studies. Their review suggested that case study research was used primarily for 'illustration and exploration' (2012: 27).

Yin (2014: 16) defined the scope of case study research and its features as 'an empirical inquiry that investigates a contemporary phenomenon (the "case") in depth and within its real-world context, especially when the boundaries between the phenomenon and context may not be clearly evident'. Further, he acknowledged that 'a case study inquiry copes with the technically distinctive situation in which there will be many more variables of interest than data points, and as one result relies on multiple sources of evidence, with data needing to converge in a triangulation fashion, and as another result benefits from the prior development of theoretical propositions to guide data collection and analysis' (2014: 17).

More recently, Yin (2018: 16) defined case study research as 'an all-encompassing mode of inquiry, with its own logic of design, data collection techniques, and specific approaches to data analysis'. In his most current edition of *Case Study Research and Applications*, Yin (2018: xx) introduced a 'foundational trilogy' that describes case study research as 'the mode of inquiry', case studies as a 'method of inquiry or research method used in doing case study research', and a case or cases as the 'unit of inquiry in a case study' (2018: xx). Yazan (2015: 135) more fully examined Stake, Merriam and Yin's approaches to case study research and has considered their 'points of divergence, convergence, and complementarity'.

> ## Box 8.2 Key concept – The goal of case study research
>
> The goal of case study research is to holistically understand the case, or cases, in its real-world context, rather than 'independent of context' (Gibbert et al., 2008: 1466), without any manipulation of the phenomenon.

In summary, despite the plethora of definitions and distinctions that have been offered, researchers tend to agree that case study research is a valid approach to use when the topic is broad and complex, there is not a lot of available theory, and when context is important (Dul and Hak, 2012). Furthermore, data collection techniques and analysis techniques do not limit case study research. In other words, while some data collection methods, like interviews, observations and field notes, may be commonly associated with qualitative case study research, many other data collection strategies can be used to obtain multiple sources of data which is a hallmark of case study research. Case study research must also ensure rigour, but how such quality criteria are considered and applied may vary depending upon how issues associated with validity and reliability, or trustworthiness and authenticity, their qualitative counterparts, are articulated. Some apparent points of departure include whether case study research is a form or type of qualitative research, or distinct from it, and if qualitative analysis is the form of interpretation to arrive at conclusions. Yin (2018) suggested that determining whether case study research is subsumed under qualitative research may require further consideration. Thus, these aforementioned scholars' definitions of case study research reflect their varying philosophies, epistemologies and ontologies.

Distinctions between different theoretical stances

According to Yin (2018) and others, case study research can embrace different epistemological orientations such as realist, relativist or interpretivist perspectives (Table 8.1 presents some of these distinctions). The predominant orientation in Yin (2018: 16) is described as realist, meaning the 'existence of a single reality that is independent of any observer'. Yet, in contrast, those embracing a relativist or interpretivist orientation acknowledge the existence of multiple realities with multiple meanings with findings that are observer dependent. Employing a constructionist approach may enable the researcher to 'capture the perspectives of different participants and focusing on how their different perspectives illuminate your topic of study' (Yin 2018: 16).

Bryman and Bell (2015: 68) acknowledged that 'there is a tendency to associate case studies with qualitative research' because case study design often includes qualitative methods. However, they contend that both quantitative and qualitative approaches can be used. They further concede that

Table 8.1 Primary distinctions between theoretical stances in case study research

Theoretical stance	Description	Case study researchers	Case study research examples
Realist	The focus is on objectivity within methodology and design	Yin (2018)	Gray et al. (2011) Hamlin et al. (2007)
Relativist	There is no one absolute truth but is relatively situated in a context	Stake (1995, 2006)	Dupagne and Garrison (2006)
Interpretivist	Researcher 'assumes that reality is constructed intersubjectively through meanings and understandings developed socially and experientially' (Harrison et al., 2017: 10)	Merriam (1998)	Beattie (2006)

business research has been dominated by the epistemological tradition of positivism which has influenced the manner in which case studies have been done. Other researchers have indicated that case study research can be quantitative, qualitative and mixed-design, or used for evaluation purposes (Ellinger and McWhorter, 2016; Ellinger et al., 2005; McWhorter and Ellinger, 2018; Tetnowski, 2015; Yin, 2014, 2018). Many researchers have conceived of case study as a type of qualitative research (Creswell and Poth, 2017; Merriam, 1998; Stake, 1995) and have positioned case study 'at the conservative end of the qualitative research continuum in post-positivism' (White et al. 2009: 21). In contrast, at the other end of the spectrum, Willis (2007) cited in White et al. (2009) acknowledged that the case study approach is often used by critical and interpretivist researchers. Yin (2018: 16) contended that his book may offer helpful guidance for doing case study research, but may not offer 'comprehensive guidance on pursuing a relativist or constructivist approach'. Thus, for doctoral students and researchers who identify case study research as a form of inquiry that they may wish to pursue, important self-reflection about the nature of knowing and knowledge creation is necessary to determine which sources will be deemed most relevant given the different epistemologies and ontologies that guide case study research.

What does a case study achieve?

There are several different types of case studies that are undertaken to serve a variety of purposes and intentions that have been discussed in the literature.

In terms of qualitative case study research, Stake (1995, 2006, 2010) acknowledged that case studies may be intrinsic or instrumental. When the intent is to learn about a particular case, the case study is intrinsic. On the

> ### Box 8.3 Key concept – Case study and theory
>
> Case study research is often implemented to achieve rich description of a phenomenon, or to explore an under-developed phenomenon, or for purposes of explanation or assessment. Thus, case study research can be designed to build theory or to test it.

other hand, instrumental case studies help the researcher to accomplish something else and are instrumental in understanding something other than the case.

In terms of qualitative case study research in education, Merriam (1998) indicated that qualitative case studies may be descriptive, interpretive or evaluative. Descriptive case studies provide a detailed account and rich description of a phenomenon. Interpretive case studies also provide description, but the data gathered is used to 'develop conceptual categories or to illustrate, support, or challenge theoretical assumptions held prior to the data gathering' (Merriam, 1998: 38) with the intent of 'analyzing, interpreting, or theorizing about the phenomenon'. With regard to evaluative case studies, 'description, explanation, and judgment' (Merriam, 1998: 39) are the intent. Merriam further elaborated on different types of case studies in education that include: ethnographic, historical, psychological, and sociological case studies. The intentions of these types of qualitative case studies are to examine culture, the history of an event, to focus more exclusively on the individual, or to 'highlight the features or attributes of social life' (Merriam, 1998: 37) respectively.

For Yin (2014, 2018), case studies can be exploratory, explanatory, descriptive and evaluative. Exploratory case studies are used when limited research exists on a phenomenon and are used to help the researcher to explain how or why the phenomenon exists or to understand the sequencing of events. Explanatory case studies seek to 'understand and explain presumed causal links between events' (Tetnowski 2015: 40). Descriptive case studies seek to richly describe a phenomenon. Evaluative case studies are often used for assessment purposes. Thus, explanatory case studies may be used for theory-testing, and exploratory case studies may be used for theory-building.

Researchers in the business and management disciplines often use qualitative case studies 'primarily to develop new theories' thus reflecting an inductive approach, or have used them for their 'deductive, theory-testing purposes' (Barratt et al., 2011: 330–1). As Siggelkow (2007: 21) acknowledged, 'the goal of inductive theory generation features quite prominently in many case-based research papers' when limited theoretical knowledge exists on a particular phenomenon and the inductive approach enables theory to emerge from the data. Cases can also 'help sharpen existing theory by pointing to gaps and beginning to fill them' (Siggelkow, 2007: 21). Eisenhardt and Graebner (2007: 25) acknowledged that a 'major reason for the popularity and relevance of theory building from case studies is that it is one of the best (if not the best) of the bridges from rich qualitative evidence to mainstream deductive research'.

Practical issues

Challenges and pitfalls associated with the case study research

According to Yin (2014: xii), 'doing case study research remains one of the most challenging of all social science endeavors'. Most researchers agree that there are a number of issues that must thoughtfully be considered when engaging in case study research and qualitative case study research which include: the design of the case study research; the identification and selection of the case(s); the role of literature and theory; data collection approaches to be used, data analysis approaches to be used, how rigor will be achieved; and how the findings will be presented and reported. To this end, various step-wise processes have been articulated by many of these scholars. For example, Yin (2014, 2018) offered a six-step process that includes the following components: plan, design, prepare, collect, analyse, and share. He acknowledged that the process is linear but iterative. From a qualitative case study research perspective, Stake (1995) and Merriam (1998) have offered similar steps, and Baskarada (2014) amends Yin's (2009) nearly universally accepted six-stage case study process and enriches it by integrating additional guidelines from the wider methodological literature. More recently, within the healthcare context, Carolan et al. (2016) drew upon case study and mixed-method literature to develop their three sequential stage DESCARTE model that presents twelve guiding questions for researchers (**DES**ign of **CA**se Study **R**esearch in Heal**Th**car**E**). Additionally, Morgan et al. (2017) introduced the Case Study Observational Research Framework in response to concerns that observation has been underused in case study research. This model centrally situates observation data in the research design.

Despite the availability of these models and the step-wise process, stages, or components of these models, researchers from various fields and disciplines contend that there are several challenges associated with case study research and qualitative case study research. These include inconsistencies in articulating philosophical underpinnings associated with the approach, not describing the design logic, lack of 'detailed methodological description' (Carolan et al., 2016: 628) suggesting that researchers do not fully describe the various approaches for data collection and analysis, and their integration, and do not clearly articulate important issues associated with rigour (Carolan et al., 2016; da Mota Pedrosa et al., 2012; Gibbert and Ruigrock, 2010). In addition to these issues, our experiences in guiding qualitative case study research on coaching and other topics suggests that doctoral students and researchers often struggle with a number of issues. These include determining and bounding what the case is, making design choices that align epistemologies and ontologies with approaches to data collection and analysis, considering how to collect multiple sources of data, analysing large volumes of data and reporting the findings. We offer some insights with regard to these challenges relative to coaching research.

Articulating the philosophies of the researcher. Most researchers have some definitive perspectives about the nature of knowledge and knowing which help them to articulate their research philosophies and their role in conducting the research. Being aware of one's epistemological and ontological orientations provides some guidance for the selection of sources and references for engaging in case study research, or qualitative case study research and should be clearly articulated so that readers of the case study research understand the researcher's positioning. This is also important for promoting clarity and congruence with regard to design, analysis, interpretation and making judgements about the rigour and robustness of the research. Box 8.4 provides an example.

Box 8.4   Doing research

In an ongoing dissertation designed to explore managerial coaching dyads, Adele (2019) acknowledged that she sought to understand the social actors and their interactions within a social phenomenon, thus she adopted an epistemological position of interpretivism and an ontological orientation of constructionism and chose a qualitative case study research approach.

Determining the case and the design. Identifying the case, its boundedness, and the design of the case study research are often challenges that confront novice researchers. When determining what the case is, or what the main unit of analysis is, Yin (2014) indicated that the purpose of the research and the research question(s) guiding the case study research are often indicative of what the case is. The case is also going to be related to any theoretical propositions that may be of interest or theory that may inform the case. Yin (2018) provided a helpful figure that reflects a 2 × 2 matrix that describes holistic (single unit of analysis) and embedded (multiple units of analysis) on the left side vertical axis and single case designs and multiple case designs on the top of a horizontal axis resulting in four types of case study designs. These design types are '(Type 1) single-case (holistic) designs, (Type 2) single-case (embedded) designs, (Type 3) multiple-case (holistic) designs, and (Type 4) multiple-case (embedded) designs' (2018: 47). Further, Yin contends that 'every type of design will include the desire to analyze contextual conditions in relation to the "case," with the dotted lines between the two signaling the likely blurriness between the case and its context' (2018: 47). He also provides rationales for why a single case design might be appropriate and when more than one case, multiple-case study design may be warranted. If a single case is being used to examine the broad nature of an organisation or programme, for example, a holistic design may be optimal. If, however, there are embedded units that are going to be studied within the single case, then an embedded single case design is appropriate. The same is true for multiple case design that may be holistic, or which may have many embedded units of analysis. For example, if a researcher wanted to examine team coaching within an organisation, a single case embedded design might be appropriate as individuals are embedded in teams, and teams are embedded within the organisation. If, however, multiple organisations engaged in the practice of team coaching were to be studied, then a multiple case embedded design could be considered.

Data collection. Yin (2018) indicated that there are typically six sources of evidence that are found in case study research: documentation, archival records, interviews, direct observations, participant-observations, and physical artefacts. Those engaged in qualitative case study research typically draw upon interviews, observations and documents as the primary approaches for collecting data. Coaching research lends itself to the use of many data collection methods, not only those advocated by Yin and the typical approaches often used by qualitative researchers, such as visual methods, like photo-elicitation, or journaling, critical incidents, drawing, or metaphor. However, given the importance of obtaining multiple sources of data which is a defining characteristic of case study research (whether for the purposes of triangulation or enrichment, depending upon one's epistemological stance), researchers need to carefully consider the strengths and weaknesses associated with various data collection approaches as well as to keep the purpose of the study in mind to inform decision processes about what data collection strategies may optimally yield the data to enable the researcher to address the research questions. Managing large volumes of data can be difficult for seasoned researchers so novice researchers need to carefully consider data storage issues since some of these approaches will result in vast quantities of data that require computer storage space and ease of access. Utilising computer-assisted qualitative data analysis software may be useful for helping to manage the data in a digital repository for subsequent analysis.

Data analysis. With regard to data analysis approaches, Merriam and Tisdell (2016) acknowledged that data analysis for case study research and qualitative case study research is complex. They and other researchers have offered numerous possibilities for analysing case study research and qualitative case study research data. Yin (2018: 33) offered five analytical techniques – 'pattern matching, explanation building, time-series analysis, logic models, and cross-case synthesis' – and recommends that researchers develop an analytic strategy. From a qualitative case study research perspective, Merriam (1998) and others have suggested that narrative analysis, phenomenological analysis, interpretive phenomenological analysis, ethnographic analysis, constant comparison, content analysis and analytic induction are commonly used along with thematic analysis. Yet, the challenges often encountered relate to the adequate reporting of how such approaches were used. Carolan et al. (2016) proposed that three stances should be embraced by case study research researchers: philosophical, strategic and integrative. Their stances suggest that researcher's choice of data analysis should be congruent with their underpinning research philosophies and articulated orientations, should explicitly state the strategy used for data analysis, and should also articulate how they are integrating data analysis.

> ## Box 8.5   Doing research
>
> One of our students designed a phenomenological multiple case study embedded design so it was imperative that the appropriate strand of phenomenology be articulated, and the specific approaches to data analysis that resonated with that particular strand. Given the embedded nature of the multi-case design, it was also necessary to consider how to begin the approach for analysing a vast quantity of data from individual interviews and team interviews conducted with multiple teams within and across two organisations.

Presenting findings and writing up the case study research. According to Yin (2014), writing up case study research 'makes great demands on a case researcher' and suggested that novice case study researchers begin the writing phase by first reading a published research study relevant to their study, then review notes about data gathered and initial impressions, and talk to a colleague about the study to 'get the ideas in your mind flowing before you can expect to do any composing' (2014: 219). Once the researcher (or team of researchers) is ready to write, decisions about how findings are best presented will need to be made depending upon whether the case study research is a single case or multiple case design.

Merriam (1998: 220–45) offered a three-step approach for writing case studies: (1) *preparing to write* (determining audience, selecting a focus, outlining the report, beginning to write); (2) *content of a qualitative study report* (components of a qualitative research report, placement of component parts, description and analysis); and (3) *disseminating the study report*. Other advice for presenting findings and writing up the qualitative case study research is found in Ellinger and McWhorter (2016: 9), McWhorter and Ellinger (2018: 194–5) and Yin (2014: chapter 6).

> ## Box 8.6   Doing research
>
> When considering options for displaying her findings, Adele (2019) developed a number of tables to present themes and sub-themes along with figures that depicted the coaching processes derived in her study. She also provided thick, rich illustrative quotations to offer support for the themes and sub-themes in the narrative that she created to articulate her findings. In the other aforementioned study that involved individual and team interviews, mini-portraits (brief descriptions and research interpretations) of each team member and of the team were created, along with the development of process models for each team and composites of teams within each of the two organisations in the study. Summary tables were used to capture themes as well as comparative tables of themes for each organisation, along with sample quotations drawn from the data set to illustrate and support themes derived from the analysis.

In Boxes 8.7, 8.8 and 8.9, we offer three illustrations of recently published case study research. In addition to the foci of their coaching research, one strength of these studies is that each researcher offered insights about the philosophical orientation of the research they undertook. Relative to the aforementioned concerns that have been raised by various scholars, we note where some enhancements can be made in their case study research which relate to clearly presenting the research question(s) guiding the case study research, providing more insight about the case(s) itself and the design choices that were made. As noted, semi-structured interviews are the primary approaches to data collection that were used, and in some cases, multiple types of stakeholders were interviewed which gathers multiple sources of interview data, but as a multi-source mode of inquiry, researchers should consider other data sources that can be used which would be consistent with the aims of case study research. It would also be helpful to elaborate on how the data was analysed, and as scholars contend, it is critical to discuss issues related to rigour and robustness.

Box 8.7   Case study 1

Author

Bonneywell (2017) 'How a coaching intervention supports the development of female leaders in a global organization'.

Purpose

'This case study research is situated within GSK [a large multinational pharmaceutical organisation] and focuses specifically on how coaching can be used to address the issue of gender imbalance at middle and senior leadership levels' (Bonneywell, 2017: 57).

Type of case study

An ontological stance that is social constructionist was adopted. The unit of analysis for the study was the coaching stream of an Accelerating Difference (AD) programme. The epistemological stance was interpretivist. Bonneywell explains that 'the choice of case study was also reinforced by the context in which all the participants were situated, one organisation, GSK. The boundaries defined who to interview – the female leaders who were participants, coaches and steering team members of the AD initiative; the cohort to be studied – Cohort One (2013 – 2014)' (2017: 59).

Instrumental case study design

Data collection – Semi-structured interviews among multiple types of participants/stakeholders

Data analysis – Thematic analysis

(Continued)

To further enhance case study research, the researcher might consider other sources of data for purposes of further enhancing triangulation with sources of data drawn from other data collection approaches, and attention to issues associated with rigour are recommended.

Box 8.8   Case study 2

Author

Gill (2017) 'What is the perceived contribution of coaching to leaders transitioning to more senior roles in the NHS?'

Purpose

'This case study explores the contribution of coaching in addressing the adaptive challenges of senior leadership transitions from the perspective of leaders who have recently transitioned to more senior roles in the NHS' (Gill, 2017: 70).

Type of case study

A constructivist interpretivist paradigm was adopted, investigating a single organisation; seven participants.

> **Data collection** – Semi-structured interviews

> **Data analysis** – Thematic analysis

To enhance case study research, explicating the design and rationale for design, providing more insight on the selection of the participants, considering other sources of data for purposes of triangulation, and attention to issues associated with rigour are recommended.

Box 8.9   Case study 3

Author

Wotruba (2016) 'Leadership team coaching: A trust-based coaching relationship'.

Purpose

'This study explores the importance that leadership team coaching practitioners attach to the coaching relationship and as a consequence what that means for how they work with teams' (Wotruba, 2016: 98).

Type of case study

Qualitative single case study method approached from an interpretivist perspective.

Identification of coaches who had worked with leadership teams; six coaches participated.

Data collection – Semi-structured interviews and critical incident technique

Data analysis – Thematic analysis

To enhance case study research, explicating the rationale for the selection of a single case study design, providing more insight on the selection of the participants, providing more detail on the use of the two data collection approaches and providing more detail on the analysis performed, and attention to issues associated with rigour are recommended.

Evaluation

Houghton et al. (2017: 36) contend that a major strength of case study research is 'the opportunity to use multiple sources of evidence' which can result in case study research being a very powerful form of research that enables researchers to address how and why questions, to understand processes, and to richly describe phenomena in their unique settings. In fact, Gibbert et al. (2008: 1465) acknowledged that case study research is 'ideally suited to creating managerially relevant knowledge'. Furthermore, Gibbert and Ruigrok (2010: 711) contended that case studies 'have provided the management field with some of its most ground-breaking insights' because case studies can be used as tools for generating and testing theory. Yet, these same researchers and others have also acknowledged that case study research has been widely criticised in the literature as a result of a number of misunderstandings and misconceptions, and concerns have been raised with regard to rigour (Carolan et al., 2016; Ellram, 1996; Flyvbjerg, 2006).

Box 8.10   Key concept

Case study research is often criticised and critiqued for a variety of reasons relating to misunderstandings that have to do with theory, reliability and validity (Flyvbjerg, 2006; Gibbert and Ruigrok, 2010), for its perceived lack of generalisability and rigour (Carolan et al., 2016; da Mota Pedrosa et al., 2012), and as an approach that is considered to be easily employed by anyone (Ellram, 1996). These points have been refuted by many scholars who have articulated the strengths associated with this mode of inquiry and advocate for its use.

Flyvbjerg (2006: 221) acknowledged and described five misunderstandings about case study research which he suggested may be 'oversimplifications of the nature of such research'. According to Flyvbjerg, the first misunderstanding relates to the notion that context-independent knowledge is more valuable than context-dependent knowledge, and the second relates to the inability of case study to be generalised thus limiting its contribution. The third misunderstanding suggests that case study research is more appropriate for generating hypotheses as opposed to testing them and building theory. The fourth misunderstanding relates to the potential of subjective bias on the part of the researcher, and the fifth misunderstanding relates to the difficulty in summarising case studies given their potentially lengthy narrative. Flyvbjerg eloquently refuted all of these misunderstandings by reinforcing the value of context-dependent knowledge that it might be possible to generalise, depending upon the case, and that case study research can be used for exploratory and explanatory purposes, and thus can contribute to theory-testing and theory-building. He acknowledged that other research approaches may also be biased towards researchers' preconceived notions so the criticism may not only apply to case study research. He also questions whether summarising and generalisation are always desirable and, with others, contends that case study research often lends itself to the consideration of rival explanations. Flyvbjerg drew upon an insight of Kuhn (1987): 'that a discipline without a large number of thoroughly executed case studies is a discipline without systematic production of exemplars, and that a discipline without exemplars is an ineffective one' (Flyvbjerg, 2006: 242).

Some other misconceptions that have been identified relate to the notion that case study research is an ad hoc method that can be employed by anyone (Ellram, 1996). Quite to the contrary, Yin (2018) and others contend that case study research is a mode of inquiry that details specific processes and is time intensive and laborious, suggesting that there are specific skills that are needed by researchers to engage in case study research. Many of the mainstream concerns associated with case study research relate to the lack of rigour in conducting and reporting case study research (Carolan et al., 2016; da Mota Pedrosa et al., 2012). In addressing the issues associated with ensuring rigour, Gibbert and Ruigrok (2010) suggested that what to report and how to report may be a result of unresolved debates between positivists and interpretivists. These scholars and others provide several recommendations for how rigour can be achieved in published case study research. In particular, Gibbert and Ruigrok (2010) outlined three strategies that researchers should adopt that relate to researchers thoroughly addressing their methodological choices, more clearly articulating a comprehensive understanding of validity and reliability criteria (what other scholars may also refer to as trustworthiness and authenticity, and transferability, truth-value, and traceability). Others suggest that researchers improve their description and justifications for the unit of analysis, designs, selection of cases, and how analysis was done (da Mota Pedrosa et al., 2012). Lastly, with interviews being a dominant source of data, Runfola et al. (2017) indicated that more attention to describing the nature of the interviews, their length, and other critical information is needed to address concerns about rigour. Thus, researchers should be knowledgeable about quality criteria and guidelines for enhancing the reporting of high-quality case study research and qualitative case study research (Anderson, 2017; Barratt et al., 2011).

It is our fond hope that the promise of case study research, and qualitative case study research, as a mode of inquiry to enhance the knowledge and theory base of the field of coaching, encourages researchers to become more immersed in the literature on case study research and qualitative case study research and to cultivate the skills to design, carry out, report and publish high quality and impactful case study research that continues to advance the field of coaching.

Further reading

Dooley, L.M. (2002). 'Case study research and theory building'. *Advances in Developing Human Resources* 4 (3): 335–54.

Ellinger, A.D. and McWhorter, R.R. (2016). 'Qualitative case study research as empirical inquiry'. *International Journal of Adult Vocational Education and Technology* 7 (3): 1–13.

Ellinger, A.D., Watkins, K.E. and Marsick, V. (2005). 'Case study research'. In R.A. Swanson and E.F. Holton III (eds), *Research in Organizations: Foundational Principles, Processes and Methods of Inquiry*. San Francisco, CA: Berrett-Koehler Publishers, pp. 327–50.

Gehman, J., Glaser, V.L., Eisenhardt, K.M., Gioia, D., Langley, A. and Corley, K.G. (2018). 'Finding theory-method fit: A comparison of three qualitative approaches to theory building'. *Journal of Management Inquiry* 2 (3): 284–300.

McWhorter, R.R. and Ellinger, A.D. (2018). 'Qualitative case study research: An initial primer'. In V.C.X. Wang (ed.), *Handbook of Research on Innovative Techniques, Trends, and Analysis for Optimized Research Methods*. Hershey, PA: IGI Global, pp. 185–201.

Tight, M. (2017). *Understanding Case Study Research*. Thousand Oaks, CA: Sage Publications.

Yin, R.K. (2018). *Case Study Research: Design and Methods* (6th edition). Thousand Oaks, CA: Sage Publications.

Discussion questions

- How does case study research distinguish itself from other modes of inquiry?
- How do one's epistemological and ontological orientations influence the design and implementation of case study research?
- Are the common criticisms associated with case study research warranted?
- How can case study research be designed and implemented to optimise rigour and robustness?

Application questions

1. Given scholars' current calls for undertaking additional coaching research (see for example: Beattie et al., 2014; de Haan and Nieß, 2012; Ellinger et al., 2017; Grant et al., 2010; Hagen 2012; Lawrence 2017), how can case study research be specifically applied to address a particular call for research?
2. In addressing the specific call for research using the case study research approach in question 1, how will you determine and bound your case? What sources of data do you believe will be the most appropriate for addressing the research question(s) associated with your case study?
3. How will you analyse your data given the myriad sources that you may have at your disposal, and what approaches will be used present your findings?
4. How will you ensure that your case study meets the standards of rigour expected of case study research?

References

Adele, B. (2019). 'Examining managerial coaching dyads and the developmental learning outcomes of managers serving as coaches and the reverse coaching behaviors of their subordinate coachees'. Unpublished doctoral dissertation. Tyler, TX: The University of Texas at Tyler.

Anderson, V. (2017). 'Criteria for evaluating qualitative research'. *Human Resource Development Quarterly* 28 (2): 125–33.

Barratt, M., Choi, T.Y. and Li, M. (2011). 'Qualitative case studies in operations management: Trends, research outcomes, and future research implications'. *Journal of Operations Management* 29 (4): 329–42.

Baskarada, S. (2014). 'Qualitative case study guidelines'. *The Qualitative Report* 19: 1–18.

Beattie, R.S. (2006). 'Line managers and workplace learning: Learning from the voluntary sector'. *Human Resource Development International* 9 (1): 99–119.

Beattie, R.S., Kim, S., Hagen, M.S., Egan, T.M., Ellinger, A.D. and Hamlin, R.G. (2014). 'Managerial coaching: A review of the empirical literature and development of a model to guide future practice'. *Advances in Developing Human Resources* 16 (2): 184–201.

Bonneywell, S. (2017). 'How a coaching intervention supports the development of female leaders in a global organization'. *International Journal of Evidence Based Coaching and Mentoring* 11: 57–69.

Bryman, A. and Bell, E. (2015). *Business Research Methods* (4th edition). Oxford: Oxford University Press.

Carolan, C.M., Forbat, L. and Smith, A. (2016). 'Developing the DESCARTE model: The design of case study research in health care'. *Qualitative Health Research* 26 (5): 626–39.

Creswell, J.W. and Poth, C.N. (2017). *Qualitative Inquiry and Research Design*. Thousand Oaks, CA: Sage Publications.

Cronin, C. (2014). 'Using case study research as a rigorous form of inquiry'. *Nurse Researcher* 21 (5): 19–27.

da Mota Pedrosa, A., Naslund, D. and Jasmand, C. (2012). 'Logistics case study based research: Towards higher quality'. *International Journal of Physical Distribution and Logistics Management* 42 (3): 275–95.

de Haan, E. and Nieß, C. (2012). 'Critical moments in a coaching case study: Illustrations of a process research model'. *Consulting Psychology Journal* 64 (3): 198–224.

Dul, J. and Hak, T. (2012). *Case Study Methodology in Business Research*. Abingdon: Routledge.

Dupagne, M. and Garrison, M. (2006). 'The meaning and influence of convergence: A qualitative case study of newsroom work at the Tampa News Center'. *Journalism Studies* 7 (2): 237–55.

Eisenhardt, K.M. and Graebner, M.E. (2007). 'Theory building from cases: Opportunities and challenges'. *Academy of Management Journal* 50 (1): 25–32.

Ellinger, A.D., Hamlin, R.G. and Beattie, R.S. (2017). 'Coaching in the HRD context'. In T. Bachkirova, G. Spence and D. Drake (eds), *The SAGE Handbook of Coaching*. Thousand Oaks, CA: Sage Publications, pp. 470–85.

Ellinger, A.D. and McWhorter, R.R. (2016). 'Qualitative case study research as empirical inquiry'. *International Journal of Adult Vocational Education and Technology* 7 (3): 1–13.

Ellinger, A.D., Watkins, K.E. and Marsick, V. (2005). 'Case study research'. In R.A. Swanson and E.F. Holton III (eds), *Research in Organizations: Foundational Principles, Processes and Methods of Inquiry*. San Francisco, CA: Berrett-Koehler Publishers, pp. 327–50.

Ellram, L.M. (1996). 'The use of the case study method in logistics research'. *Journal of Business Logistics* 17 (2): 93–138.

Flyvbjerg, B. (2006). 'Five misunderstandings about case-study research'. *Qualitative Inquiry* 12 (2): 219–45.

Gibbert, M. and Ruigrok, W. (2010). 'The "what" and "how" of case study rigor: Three strategies based on published work'. *Organization Research Methods* 13 (4): 710–37.

Gibbert, M., Ruigrok, W. and Wicki, B. (2008). 'Research notes and commentaries: What passes as a rigorous case study?' *Strategic Management Journal* 29: 1465–74.

Gill, A. (2017). 'What is the perceived contribution of coaching to leaders transitioning to more senior roles in the NHS?' *International Journal of Evidence Based Coaching and Mentoring* 11: 70–83.

Gillham, B. (2000). *Case Study Research Methods*. London: Continuum.

Grant, A.M., Passmore, J., Cavanagh, M.J. and Parker, H. (2010). 'The state of play in coaching today: A comprehensive review of the field'. *International Review of Industrial and Organizational Psychology* 25: 125–67.

Gray, D., Ekinci, Y. and Goregaokar, H. (2011). 'A five-dimensional model of attributes: Some precursors of executive coach selection'. *International Journal of Selection and Assessment* 19(4): 415–28.

Hagen, M. (2012). 'Managerial coaching: A review of the literature'. *Performance Improvement Quarterly* 24 (4): 17–39.

Hamlin, R.G., Beattie, R.S. and Ellinger, A.D. (2007). 'What do effective managerial leaders really do? Using qualitative methodological pluralism and analytical triangulation to explore everyday "managerial effectiveness" and "managerial coaching effectiveness"'. *International Journal Management Concepts and Philosophy* 2 (3): 255–76.

Harrison, H., Birks, M., Franklin, R., et al. (2017). 'Case study research: Foundations and methodological orientations'. *Forum: Qualitative Sozialforschung/Forum: Qualitative Social Research* 18 (1).

Houghton, C., Casey, D. and Smyth, S. (2017). 'Selection, collection and analysis as sources of evidence in case study research'. *Nurse Researcher* 20 (4): 12–17.

Kuhn, T. (1987). 'What are scientific revolutions?' In L. Krüger G. Gigerenzer and M.S. Morgan (eds), *The Probabilistic Revolution, Vol. 2: Ideas in the Sciences*. Boston, MA: MIT Press, pp. 7–22.

Lawrence, P. (2017). 'Managerial coaching: A literature review'. *International Journal of Evidence Based Coaching and Mentoring* 15 (2): 43–69.

McCutcheon, D.M. and Meredith, J.R. (1993). 'Conducting case study research in operations management'. *Journal of Operations Management* 11: 239–56.

McWhorter, R.R. and Ellinger, A.D. (2018). 'Qualitative case study research: An initial primer'. In V.C.X. Wang (ed.), *Handbook of Research on Innovative Techniques, Trends, and Analysis for Optimized Research Methods*. Hershey, PA: IGI Global, pp. 185–201.

Merriam, S.B. (1998). *Qualitative Research and Case Study Applications in Education* (2nd edition). San Francisco, CA: Jossey-Bass.

Merriam, S.B. and Tisdell, E.J. (2016). *Qualitative Research: A Guide to Design and Implementation* (4th edition). San Francisco, CA: Jossey-Bass.

Morgan, S.J., Pullon, S.R.H., Macdonald, L.M., McKinlay, E.M. and Gray, B.V. (2017). 'Case study observational research: A framework for conducting case study research where observation data are the focus'. *Qualitative Health Research* 27 (7): 1060–8.

Pagell, M. and Wu, Z. (2009). 'Building a more complete theory of sustainable supply chain management using case studies of 10 exemplars'. *Journal of Supply Chain Management* 45 (2): 37–56.

Rule, P. and John, V.M. (2015). 'A necessary dialogue: Theory in case study research'. *International Journal of Qualitative Methods* 14 (4): 1–11.

Runfola, A., Perna, A., Baraldi, E. and Gregori, G.L. (2017). 'The use of qualitative case studies in top business and management journals: A quantitative analysis of recent patterns'. *European Management Journal* 35: 116–27.

Siggelkow, N. (2007). 'Persuasion with case studies'. *Academy of Management Review* 50 (1): 20–4.

Smith, P.R. (2018). 'Collecting evidence when conducting a case study'. *The Qualitative Report* 23 (5): 1043–8.

Stake, R.E. (1995). *The Art of Case Study Research*. Thousand Oaks, CA: Sage Publications.

Stake, R.E. (2006). *Multiple Case Study Analysis*. New York: Guilford Press.

Stake, R.E. (2010). *Qualitative Research: Studying How Things Work*. New York: Guilford Press.

Tetnowski, J. (2015). 'Qualitative case study research design'. *Perspectives on Fluency and Fluency Disorders* 25: 39–45.

Thomas, G. (2011). 'A typology for the cast study in social science following a review of definition, discourse, and structure'. *Qualitative Inquiry* 17 (6): 511–21.

Ulriksen, M.S. and Dadalauri, N. (2016). 'Single case studies and theory-testing: The knots and dots of the process tracing method'. *International Journal of Social Research Methodology* 19 (2): 223–39.

White, J., Drew, S. and Hay, T. (2009). 'Ethnography versus case study'. *Qualitative Research Journal* 9 (1): 18–27.

Willis, J.W. (2007). *Foundations of Qualitative Research: Interpretive and Critical Approaches*. Thousand Oaks, CA: Sage Publications.

Wotruba, S. (2016). 'Leadership team coaching: A trust-based coaching relationship'. *International Journal of Evidence Based Coaching and Mentoring* 10: 98–109.

Wu, Z. and Choi, T.Y. (2005). 'Supplier–supplier relationships in the buyer–supplier triad: Building theories from eight case studies'. *Journal of Operations Management* 24 (1): 27–52.

Yazan, B. (2015). 'Three approaches to case study methods in education: Yin, Merriam, and Stake'. *The Qualitative Report* 20 (2): 134–52.

Yin, R.K. (2009). *Case Study Research: Design and Methods* (4th edition). Thousand Oaks, CA: Sage Publications.

Yin, R.K. (2012). *Applications of Case Study Research* (3rd edition). Thousand Oaks, CA: Sage Publications.

Yin, R.K. (2014). *Case Study Research: Design and Methods* (5th edition). Thousand Oaks, CA: Sage Publications.

Yin, R.K. (2018). *Case Study Research: Design and Methods* (6th edition). Thousand Oaks, CA: Sage Publications.

Acknowledgements

The authors would like to thank Tynia Porter and Brooklyn White for their assistance in searching for literature for this chapter. They were students at The University of Texas at Tyler at the initiation of this writing project. The authors would also like to recognise the co-editors, commissioning editor, and external reviewers for their helpful feedback on previous versions of this chapter.

9

Action research

Elaine Cox, Hany Shoukry and Janice Cook

Introduction

In this chapter, we explore action research as a strategy for developing evidence-based practice in the coaching context. Traditional research approaches may be unable to answer some questions about the professional practice of coaching: the confidential nature of the coaching relationship requires a research approach that takes account of the intimate and experiential nature of the interaction. One such approach is action research, where it is possible to conduct research in real time and, as will be discussed in this chapter, there is a close affinity with coaching through the relationship with the experiential learning cycle (Kolb, 1984). Action research offers the unique opportunity to generate both experiential and empirical knowledge, while improving and developing the practice, and possibly driving change in the researcher, participants and the context of the research. It frequently combines the roles of being a researcher, practitioner, co-learner, and possibly activist.

Using students' action research studies as examples, we discuss the usefulness of action research as a methodology for exploring coaching problems. In the course of the chapter we draw out four commonly used 'modes' of action research that have emerged from our supervision of coaching students' research over the last fifteen years. By introducing this four-part typology and providing examples of each in use, we shed light on the challenges of the different drivers and purposes of action research in relation to coaching. We also examine the differing participant and researcher involvement and expectations of each mode.

Whilst we see action research as an appropriate methodology to explore the coaching interaction, we also detect some uncertainty surrounding action research itself. For example, Lai Fong Chui (quoted in Reason and Bradbury, 2008: 696) has argued that:

> action research is an umbrella term for a variety of practical and intellectual efforts for change. Its seemingly broad outlook, fluid boundaries and inter-disciplinarity provide both opportunities and danger for future development.

So, in addition to demonstrating the use of action research to shed light on coaching, in this chapter we also highlight new thinking in relation to the boundaries within action research that may alleviate confusion. Our aim is to clarify action research for coaching researchers, and illuminate a discourse that could presently be seen as difficult or obfuscated by the specific interests of researchers from different disciplinary traditions.

The chapter has three main parts. The first is a brief overview of the distinctive features of action research. We then introduce four inferred modes of action research which we illustrate with actual examples from students. The final part draws together the strengths and limitations of action research for the study of coaching and emphasises areas for further research.

Distinctive features of the strategy

Recently, Zuber-Skerritt (2015: 5–6) highlighted some of the forms of action research that she had observed, such as action learning, educational action research, collaborative action research, critical participatory action research, action science and appreciative inquiry. All of these forms of action research can be seen as having aspects in common. For example, all have a 'forward looking orientation' (Reason and Bradbury, 2008: 696); they draw on either a critical or pragmatic paradigm (Dziuban et al., 2016); they all involve learning through action; and, as Zuber-Skerritt (1992) described, they all involve four 'moments' which are repeated as cycles during the research process: planning, action, reflection and subsequent conceptualisation (Box 9.1)

Box 9.1   Key concept – The action research cycle

1. A specific problem is identified. The 'hypothesis' or model is developed and the course of the action planned.
2. The hypothesis or model is tested via an action or intervention of some kind.
3. Data are collected and reflected upon. Observations are made.
4. Data are analysed, evaluated and conceptualised.

In most action research the researcher either 'tests' a theory or attempts to solve a problem in the real world, in an experiential research design. The link with Kolb and Kolb's (2008) experiential learning cycle is evident: planning, action, reflection and conceptualisation are broadly aligned with Active Experimentation, Concrete Experience, Reflective Observation and Abstract Conceptualisation respectively (Figure 9.1). This cyclical process is common across all the variants of action research and is something that distinguishes action research from other forms of research. Heron and Reason (2006) further stress the function of the repeat cycling process as enhancing the validity of the findings and, as Brannick and Coghlan point out: 'action research focuses on research in action rather than research about action' (2007: 65).

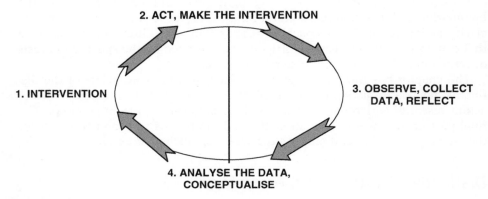

Figure 9.1   Mapping a single action research cycle

The role of the researcher and the participants

Gibbon has explained how, in *traditional* research, the roles of researcher and participants within the research process are quite distinct:

> The researcher defines the questions for the research and determines how data collection is to proceed. Both the research problem and the methodological tools are predetermined. The informants provide information but are seldom involved in the collection or analysis of data. (Gibbon, 2002: 547)

However, in action research, although the researcher usually keeps an 'outsider' perspective, there is greater collaboration by participants in the research process (Kemmis, 2012). There is much agreement in the action research literature that active participation and collaboration by respondents is a key facet.

It is important to highlight that often the terminology and definitions used in action research render it confusing. For example, as long ago as 1988, Kemmis and McTaggart asserted that it is not action research unless it is 'collaborative', but this is not a universally used term in the world of action research: Whitehead and McNiff (2006), and others (for example McIntyre, 2008), describe this type of action research as 'participatory action research'. As a student, Cook (2011) experienced this as a semantic distinction as both the words 'collaborative' and 'participatory' require some form of 'researching together', but nevertheless it can cause unnecessary confusion.

Box 9.2   Doing research

In action research, as in other research approaches, the researcher is the person seeking to collect information and analyse it to produce new knowledge. However, based on our observations, we would suggest five further potential roles that the action researcher sometimes choses to fulfil:

1. **Research facilitator** – in some cases, the research question is decided by the community and the 'researcher' is mainly facilitating rather than pre-determining what is the problem and how it will be investigated.
2. **Practice designer/developer** – in most cases, the researcher or the community will design an approach to solve a problem; this often requires specific technical and contextual knowledge of the problem that is not required in many other methodologies.
3. **Group designer/facilitator** – action research is often carried out in a group setting and the dynamics of designing and facilitating the group have significant implications for the validity and outcomes of the research.
4. **Participant** – in many situations, the researcher is also generating experiential knowledge and is involved in the iterative cycles of the experience.
5. **Change agent** – action research does not take place outside its real context. Intentionally or inadvertently it may cause a change in the context and the members of the community being researched, so researchers need to be aware of their role as change agents.

The purpose of action research

Action research appears to have a range of purposes or drivers, depending on the context within which the research is being carried out, the research questions being pursued and the philosophical stance of the researcher. Different purposes have been identified by different action research commentators and include improving and developing understanding of practice, facilitating cultural, social and political change, generating and testing theory, facilitating professional learning and reflective practice, and helping people to empower themselves (Titchen, 2015).

In our research with postgraduate students, a number of distinct purposes or 'modes' of action research have become apparent, each suited for researching a different type of question and with a different purpose and outcome:

1. **Inquiry Action Research** aims to create changes/improvements in the researcher's own understanding of the problem. When the researcher is engaged in praxis, as an individual, the focus is on the individual, who, through reflection and action in the world, learns new ways of seeing the world, and changes skills and behaviours to deal with personal challenge. Inquiry Action Research needs the lowest engagement with the community (only as a backdrop to gathering understanding) and is primarily driven by the researcher.

2. **Evolutionary Action Research** aims to create changes/improvements to a model or theory, for example when the action researcher is seeking to develop external knowledge about the world (theory) or models and coaching practices. This is still an individual pursuit in the sense that the researcher is the one asking the research question and is seeking technical knowledge, but Evolutionary Action Research is normally collaborative between coach and coachees or a number of coaches.

3. **Collective Action Research** aims to create changes/improvements in group understanding and practices – within an existing system. When action researchers approach a community as both researchers and practitioners, they have a shared interest in helping the community to gain understanding and develop solutions and practices that are relevant to their specific contexts. They are seeking practical knowledge that is generated from the collective wisdom of their partnership. Our students have confirmed that Collective Action Research needs to be extremely collaborative, pragmatic and contextual.

4. **Transformative Action Research** aims to create changes/improvements not just within the system but to the system itself. If the action researcher approaches the community as a 'praxisioner', the interest is in helping the community to understand and transform the system and structures within which it operates. Transformative Action Research requires a critical and emancipatory stance. Student experiences suggest it needs more than collaboration: it needs a significant focus on embedding empowerment and criticality within the group. It is heavily contextual and grounded in action. Transformative Action Research also implies the development of new theory, through re-theorisation of existing phenomena.

The four modes are summarised in Table 9.1 and their purpose, implementation and outcomes discussed in the practical issues section that follows:

Practical issues

In the sections that follow we describe how although each of the four modes follows the process of action research described above, each can be seen to involve participants and researchers in different ways and each presents its own dilemmas for researchers. The four modes are illustrated by examples from published coaching related action research studies conducted by master's and doctoral level students.

Table 9.1 Main differences and challenges of action research modes used by students

Mode	Purposes	Participant Involvement	Researcher Role	Outcome
Inquiry Action Research	Improvement in understanding leading to development of new practices that may be both personally transforming and technically useful from a practitioner point of view	Participation by others where appropriate, acting as key informants	Researching as an 'insider' to gather information to enhance own understanding	Personal and professional learning mainly for the researcher's own professional improvement
Evolutionary Action Research	Evolution of a theory/practice or change model that will be of benefit to other coaches and their clients	Cooperation from participants towards the research outcome, but they remain representative of a target audience	Usually researching as an outsider to evolve a model or theory	Enhancement of theory or model resulting in change for practice/clients
Collective Action Research	Helping a community to develop understandings and solutions that are relevant to them. The principal researcher may take some of the learnings and transform them into new theory and practice (evolutionary), but the primary driver is for the community to solve its own challenges	Collaboration between a collective group of individuals with an active shared interest in the research outcome	Part of a group, working and researching as an insider alongside the 'co-researchers' in a social context	Changes within existing system for the benefit of the collective and/or their clients/other stakeholders
Transformative Action Research	Change or transformation of the system for the benefit of clients and communities. The transformative and emancipatory aspect is linked to a re-theorisation of the system	Total commitment to a shared social goal/contribution and to criticality and empowerment to be embedded in each step of the research, models and actions	Researching as an insider and working with participants to achieve a shared social transformation	System, communities and clients/other stakeholders are transformed. As in Inquiry Action Research, the researcher engaging in this mode will go through a personal journey of change

Inquiry action research

As a mode of action research 'inquiry action research' is specifically concerned with enhancing practitioner learning and/or an improvement in understanding of a problem to inform individual practice.

Our starting point for understanding this mode is Cochran-Smith and Donnell's (2006) explanation of the popularity of practitioner inquiry for professional development and how this has increased significantly in the education field. These authors identify the proliferation of words used to indicate the systematic exploration of educational problems. They point out how:

> research, inquiry, scholarship, or study has been combined with a term referring to the identity of the agent involved in the inquiry process such as teacher, practitioner, teacher educator, participant, or self, or combined with one or more modifying words or phrases such as action, collaborative, narrative, pedagogical, participatory, on practice, autobiographical, reflexive, of teaching, and critical. (Cochran-Smith and Donnell, 2006: 1)

This, Cochran-Smith and Donnell argue, has resulted in a multitude of permutations such as 'critical action research, collaborative teacher inquiry, critical narrative inquiry, teacher research on practice, the scholarship of teaching, and teacher educator self-study' (2006: 1). So even in the well-established field of educational research, action research suffers from lack of definition.

Torbert's (2004: 1) definition of 'action inquiry' is one example of the kind of self-study and research on practice that this mode epitomises:

> a lifelong process of transformational learning that individuals, teams, and whole organizations can undertake if they wish to become:
>
> - increasingly capable of listening into the present moment from which the future emerges;
> - increasingly alert to the dangers and opportunities of the present moment; and
> - increasingly capable of performing in effective, transformational, and sustainable ways.

Torbert also suggests that action inquiry can gradually become 'a moment-to-moment way of living whereby we attune ourselves through inquiry to acting in an increasingly timely and wise fashion for the overall development of the families, teams, and organizations in which we participate' (Torbert, 2004: 1–2). Thus Torbert is describing becoming a practitioner researcher, where 'first-person' action inquiry in the moment is the primary focus. The 'second-person' and 'third-person', that is other participants and informants, play a role in this mode but only incidentally. Participants are used primarily to inform an individual inquiry. Torbert and Taylor (2008: 249–50) further argue that action inquiry 'brings together action and inquiry by using multiple qualities of attention' and 'suggests a more explicit awareness of one's own practice'.

> # Box 9.3   Case study
>
> As an example of inquiry action research we highlight research undertaken by Wood et al. (2015) using McNiff's (2013) model of conducting a 'practitioner self-study' to explore how students can be helped to reflect critically on their research process. Their paper discusses Wood's 'data set' comprising students' responses to questions designed to deepen reflective capability; transcriptions of action learning set meetings with students; students' monthly written reflections, plus a transcribed focus group meeting that gathered experiences of doing and sharing reflection (Wood et al., 2015: 82). The paper then describes how one of the authors, Wood, analysed the data using action learning as an analytical lens. It concludes with a reflection on Wood's own learning and the significance of this learning for developing capacity for enacting individual reflexivity.

In the coaching context there appear to be very few examples of published research that have applied practitioner or inquiry action research. This may be because the action learning involved is personal to the inquirer. What is often missing in this form of 'research' is the writing up of the outcome. As Zuber-Skerrit (2002: 146) noted, it is only when practitioners make the effort to 'commit their thoughts and findings to writing and public scrutiny [that] action learning becomes action research'. In a recent research study into coaching supervision, for example, Hodge (2014) referred to 'action research inquiry' in an attempt to find out what actually goes on in supervision from a practitioner perspective (2014: 20). This statement seemed to place the study in the 'inquiry action research' arena. However, Hodge (2014), positioning herself as a pragmatist, ultimately decided against using Torbert's (2001) action inquiry as a primary focus, perhaps because of the difficulty of writing purely personal and practical learning as outcomes for a doctoral research study. Where students need to show transferability of their findings, their focus only on practitioner learning is usually discouraged.

The purpose of inquiry action research, as we observe it, is improvement in understanding of a problem in order to inform practice, but generally with no theory or model being shared as part of the research process: its entire focus is on individual transformation and improvement of practice. In this mode, representative participants act only as key informants to assist the researcher in his/her personal and professional learning. There is a possibility of incidental learning for the participants but this is not the purpose. In a coaching context, the focus would be solely on the coach improving his/her learning and practice.

Evolutionary action research

Drawing on Habermas' writings, Kemmis et al. (2013) distinguished between three types of action research: technical, practical and emancipatory.

In identifying the evolutionary action research mode we are interested in the application of technical action research, which, according Carr and Kemmis (2003), aims for greater efficiency or effectiveness and takes an instrumental view of development. These authors explained how technical action research is involved in improving control over outcomes, while Cohen et al. (2013: 349) describe it as being typically undertaken by individual practitioners on a relatively short-term basis and aimed at making 'an existing situation more efficient and effective'.

We believe that in some coaching research this technical definition is useful, but would go a stage further and include in the definition the developmental or evolutionary aspects of model or client development. Gathering student experiences of action research has led us to draw out an action research mode where participants are involved as representatives of a target group but who are also keen to cooperate in the research itself – not as collaborators sharing the same interest in the research, but as participants interested in their own development. We call this mode evolutionary action research to capture the idea of evolution – the improvement of a coaching model or practice or the development of a cohort of practitioners or clients over time.

In all three examples of evolutionary action research, the purpose was to produce a theoretical model, ultimately for use by practitioners to develop their work with clients. All three student researchers used terminology drawn from traditional action research literature to position their work methodologically, but their focus was on the evolutionary development of a model of practice to solve a problem followed by the systematic reporting of findings to the wider professional field of coaching.

Box 9.4   Case study

In the first study, Cook, a doctoral student, recounts some difficulty in how to describe her action research. She notes it is collaborative, reflecting the collaborative relationship between the researcher and the participants in her coaching study. But she also observes that the study is: 'primarily technical in purpose in that it is focusing on changing my coaching practice, although one could argue that it is also practical because of its contribution to the wider coaching profession' (Cook, 2011: 42).

Cook's research focused initially on articulating her own model of coaching and then developed the model further for other coaching practitioners to use. Therefore her research did not exactly fit either the collaborative model (Pavlish and Pharris, 2012) or the technical model of Kemmis et al. (2013). We believe it fits our evolutionary action research mode. Cook continued this evolutionary action research with leaders into her post-doctoral research, further developing the transferability of her 'Coaching for Leaders' model (Cook, 2016).

One of the main challenges Cook experienced in her study was the need for clarity and transparency when working collaboratively. Her participant information clearly described the study as participatory but she notes how, in practice, it required commitment of the whole self and appeared to be a deeper involvement than just participation. Initially there was focus on participants' commitment to the research process but, ultimately, the study hinged on collaborative responsibility 'both within and outside the coaching experience' (Cook, 2011: 57).

Box 9.5   Case study

In our second example, Ives, a PhD candidate, described his research as following 'a traditional Lewinian approach to action research, emphasising development of theoretical knowledge rather than emancipatory and collaborative elements typical of more recent styles of action research' (Ives, 2011: 16). He also stated that in the design of the study there was a 'continuous effort to tailor the coaching model to best help the students achieve their self-set goals' (2011: 16).

In this example, which uses an explicit critical realist epistemology (Newton et al., 2011), an emergent theory that would expand the goal-focused coaching literature was contingent on the outcome of the action research. The challenge for Ives, bearing in mind that action research does not specify an analysis approach, was to find a way to analyse data that would allow theory development whilst respecting the practical outcomes of the study. Since Grounded Theory is 'bottom up' (Robson, 2002) and also has the potential to develop high-level theory this was used to identify patterns of behaviour and social mechanisms inherent in a goal-focused coaching approach.

There is clearly an alignment in Ives' study with the evolutionary action research mode: Ives' aim was to evolve a goal-focused, theoretically driven coaching model as an outsider researcher but with cooperation from a group of participants who represented the eventual target audience for the model.

Box 9.6   Case study

Similarly, in the third study, although McLaughlin (2012) described his action research as participatory because of the role of the co-researchers in the study, he also stated that it was important to 'understand the lived experience of co-researchers who were being exposed to the model and also have them involved in the iterative process of evolving the model' (McLaughlin, 2013: 128). McLaughlin set out to explore how a coaching model could be designed to help enhance bravery in organisational leaders, with the research objective stated as 'to design and implement a brave leadership coaching model and collect

(Continued)

data from six leaders, who would be coached using the model in order to critically review their experience during and after having been coached' (2013: 126). Therefore, this research could also be described as evolutionary because of the progressive developmental purpose and level of participant involvement: McLaughlin positioned himself as an outsider researcher developing a model with the cooperation of a group of representative participants. However, other action researchers may design studies that involve working as an insider researcher (Coghlan and Brannick, 2014) in their own organisation.

McLaughlin's main challenge was to find an analysis process that would help show whether bravery was actually being enhanced during the coaching intervention. Eventually a retroductive analysis approach was used to interrogate data in line with a critical realist epistemology (Zachariadis et al., 2013).

Collective action research

Collective action research is our term for the approach to action research that involves working closely with a group of participants as a team of 'co-researchers', to achieve a collective research goal. This type of action research is sometimes described by others as collaborative inquiry (Reason and Bradbury, 2006, 2008) or cooperative inquiry (Heron and Reason, 2006). It brings together 'action and reflection, theory and practice, in participation with others, in the pursuit of practical solutions to issues of pressing concern to people, and more generally the flourishing of individual persons and their communities' (Reason and Bradbury, 2008: 1). Mahoney similarly describes collaborative action research as action research that brings together a group of individuals 'who have mutual interests and work together to study those interests' (2014: 238). Thus the aim of collaborative action research is to improve the situation for a group of people affected by an issue shared by all (Pavish and Pharris, 2012).

In describing cooperative inquiry, Heron and Reason explained how the traditional, individual researcher role is replaced by a cooperative relationship: 'so that all those involved work together as co-researchers and as co-subjects" (2006: 144); participation by the researcher and the participants is fundamental. For Habermas (1974) and Kemmis et al. (2013), what they term 'practical' action research, goes beyond the technical and requires cooperative and collaborative relationships between researcher(s) and participants. The process involves working together using cooperative or collective effort. Herr and Anderson (2005: 3) describe action research as 'inquiry that is done by or with insiders to an organization or community, but never to or on them'. They explain that 'changes occur either within the setting and/or within the researchers themselves' (2005: 3).

Our conceptualisation of collective action research in the coaching setting borrows from these earlier approaches. It is similar to cooperative action research in that it involves a group of researchers cooperating to explore the same problem, but we have observed how it differs because the researcher still has a different status from the other members of the group. In such cases the researcher, although a 'native' (Brannick and Coghlan, 2007), still has ultimate responsibility for the project, although the participants have an active professional and personal involvement in it too.

One of the main differences between evolutionary action research, as discussed earlier, and collective action research is the level of involvement of others in the research project.

In the evolutionary mode of action research, the research question might not be as relevant to the participants as it is to the researcher; the research process is aimed at finding generic theories and models that can be applied in many cases, rather than focusing on developing a real practical outcome that would benefit the participants. The collective mode of action research, by contrast, is about the group of participants/co-researchers who have a shared interest in formulating the purpose, approach and outcomes of the research. Collective action research may still involve personal inquiry and the evolution of a model or practice, but the dimension of the collective is added.

The process of collective action research may vary. The first example we offer involved a group of colleagues benefiting from receiving coaching from one of the researchers, whereas the second involved a group of colleagues researching their own coaching practice and coming together to share results. In the first study, the participants provided feedback on how the coaching was working to improve their joint situation. In the second, the researcher and participants worked together as each other's critics in the process of generating the data of for the study. Both studies resulted in enhanced practice for both the researchers and the participants as a collective.

Box 9.7 Case study

In the first example, the action researchers focused on improvements in group understanding and practice within an existing organisational system. In this study a longitudinal coaching intervention was designed to help improve psychosocial skills for a group of retail support workers in the mobile communications industry in the UK. Cox and Patrick (2012) described how an action research methodology was designed to explore a year-long combined coaching/group-coaching intervention. The authors suggested that the action research approach adopted most resembled the Industrial Action Research (IAR) described by Kemmis and McTaggart (2000) which is humanistic and individualistic rather than critical and is typically consultant driven, but includes 'collaboration between researchers and members of different levels of the organization' (Cox and Patrick, 2012: 38). Underpinning the intervention was a social constructivist epistemology since the authors believed employees

(Continued)

create meaning through interaction with each other and their workplace and that meaningful learning is a social process that occurs through dealings and relationships with others.

In the study there were two action researchers and participants were a group of fifteen retail employees, including the core support team and a number of closely allied employees. However, unlike in inquiry action research or evolutionary action research, where research is undertaken solely by an individual practitioner-researcher and participants are normally only representative of a target audience, the participant employees in this study formed a collective with an active interest in their own development.

Box 9.8 Case study

In the second example, Harding (2006) trialled a coaching model that explored the ways in which a group of coaches could use Gardner's Multiple Intelligences (Gardner, 1999) in their practice with university staff in the UK. In this master's study, six coaches, including the researcher herself, participated and devised interventions to introduce the multiple intelligences through a coaching process. These coaches met in three action learning sets at the beginning, middle and end of the study and meetings were recorded and transcribed as data. Concurrently, each coach met for six coaching sessions with clients/learners over a period of four months. Reflective diaries were completed during this process and also used as data. The study concluded that by emphasising a range of multiple intelligences during the coaching process learners were inspired to learn. Furthermore, advances were made in coach understanding, encouraging the group to take risks in designing other experiential interventions (Harding, 2006). Thus, the emphasis in Harding's study was not evolution of the multiple intelligences model, but the collective development of the participant coaches.

Collective action research studies necessarily emerge in response to shared participant dilemmas, where the aim is to improve collective understanding and development of a shared interest. In Cox and Patrick's research and in Harding's study the researchers and the participants had equal interest in the research and worked as co-researchers. This involvement is different from the involvement of participants in evolutionary action research. Collective action research, as we have conceptualised it, implies a stronger emotional connection to the research for all the participants involved – they are not simply participating at a representative level. Another key distinction between the evolutionary and collective modes is that participants may never meet in an evolutionary action research study, they are not a collective and so do not necessarily collaborate with each other. In the collective mode, the collaboration between participants is fundamental.

Transformative action research

The fourth mode captures the form of action research that has a transformative and emancipatory purpose. An emancipatory outcome is central to many definitions of action research: Carr and Kemmis (2003: 203) explain how 'in emancipatory action research, the practitioner group takes joint responsibility for the development of practice, understandings and situations and sees these as socially-constructed'. More recently, the kind of action research that emphasises participants as co-researchers and also includes personal and social transformation, has been referred to as transformative participatory action research (Mertens, 2014).

In her description of transformative participatory action research, Chilisa (2012) positions participants as co-researchers but the emphasis is also on personal and social transformation and emancipation where researchers are committed participants as well. Researchers thus align with whatever ideals of social responsibility and engagement are needed to develop a sense of individual and shared accountability within the action research project. The guiding principle of this framework, according to Chilisa, is 'decolonisation': 'a process of conducting research in such a way that the world views of those who have suffered a long history of oppression and marginalisation are given space to communicate from their frames of reference' (Chilisa, 2012: 23).

This emphasis on relief from oppression is a key part of the history of action research where it has been seen to be a significant way of supporting grassroots activism (Freire 1972). Groups of people were encouraged to change their circumstances and overcome difficulties through working together. Thus there was a substantial agenda relating to social responsibility and/or social justice. This action research 'movement' began by understanding the context and then working with people to design actions that might alleviate problems or find solutions. The action was then reviewed together and changes made to what was needed to move to the next phase. For McCarthy and Simon (2016) this is transformative action research. These authors claim that in post-positivist research, there is a requirement to *change the site of inquiry* through the doing of research' (2016: 175, our emphasis). They suggest that researchers should 'not only declare their bias but put it to work and offer rich transparency as rationale, background and learning for the study', arguing that this involvement 'connects to concerns expressed by oppressed and colonised groups of people who have been researched and had all manner of falsehoods, intentional or otherwise written about them which have often led to the development of policies which have served to oppress these groups further' (McCarthy and Simon, 2016: 175).

The transformative action research mode therefore involves mutual action, research and participation, and also necessitates changing the status quo within the site of inquiry. The focus is on individual perspective transformation (Mezirow, 1991), as well as the transformative and emancipatory improvement of the participants' social, work, political or other systems. It is involved with the 'big issues' (Reason and Bradbury, 2008: 696). So although transformative action research might involve individual change for the researcher (inquiry), and development of new theories and models (evolutionary), and even help with practical solutions to current challenges for the participants (collective), this is all done from the fundamental standpoint that the structural reality of the participants needs to be critically examined and challenged.

Box 9.9   Case study

In Shoukry's doctoral research into 'Coaching for Emancipation', a critical theory epistemology was used. Critical theory upholds that our reality is influenced by 'social, political, cultural, ethnic, economic, and gender values that are crystallised over time' (Shoukry, 2016: 19). The action research approach chosen as a counterpart to critical theory in this study was cooperative inquiry (Heron and Reason, 2006), which involved the researcher 'working collaboratively with a group of co-researchers, reflecting on their direct experience with the studied environment' (Shoukry, 2016: 20). To achieve the collaborative working, Shoukry recruited a group of twelve human development specialists in Egypt, each of whom implemented the emerging coaching for emancipation model with their coachees. Following each of three implementation cycles, the researcher and the group jointly analysed journals and reflections at reflective workshops.

   This study, although designed as a collaborative or collective action research study, had the potential to take a transformative direction. The coaches and coachees were Egyptian subjects each with their own experiences of oppression in their country and Shoukry's findings suggest similarities between the emancipatory journey experienced by coachees and elements of Mezirow's (1991) theory of transformative learning. Shoukry explained how many coachees appeared initially powerless: 'they did not believe in their ability, did not feel in control of their lives, and could not make sense of their experiences' (2016: 20). He went on to explain how coaches can empower coachees not only to reclaim empowerment and agency, and to transform their beliefs, but also to take action to change their social condition.

Within the transformative action research conceptualisation there are also elements of participatory action research. For example, as Gibbon (2002: 547) reports, in participatory action research the 'outsiders' (researchers) and 'insiders' (respondents) are partners, sharing and learning together in a process where the outsider researcher is able to develop the research capacity of the insiders. To enable these activities to take place, it is argued that there has to be a balance between safety and risk taking and an atmosphere of critical reflection and confidence building. Certainly in Shoukry's study this was in evidence. The research problem originated in the community and the solution was defined and analysed by the community of coaches. A further transformative element might have been added had it also been possible to involve the coachees in the design and analysis of the coaching programme.

There is a distinct contrast between the transformative action research mode discussed here and the collective action research mode described earlier. In collective action research the action remains at the level of practice improvement, or situation improvement for the group involved – it does not necessarily promote significant transformation or engender wider social action. Transformative action research, on the other hand, has the potential to transform situations and systems. It involves total commitment by all participants to their shared societal or organisational goal. Another important distinction is the emphasis in transformative action research on ensuring that the research approach, and relationships within the group, are emancipatory in their own right: being critical and fully aware of all internalised biases, while empowering all participants to challenge the status quo.

Although Shoukry used a critical theory epistemology allowing examination of social, political, historical and cultural antecedents of context, a social constructionist epistemology might also be appropriate in order to understand mankind as a social product and transform the jointly constructed understandings that form a basis for participants' shared assumptions about reality (Cunliffe, 2008).

Evaluation

Action research enables researchers to gather rich data about how interventions progress within organisations and, as we have argued here, can contribute to the development of both practical and theoretical understanding of the developmental and relationship processes involved in coaching and related interventions.

In this chapter, we have explored action research as a family of research approaches for developing the evidence base for coaching and, potentially, other organisational interventions. We began by noting the close affinity between action research and coaching where knowledge results from 'the combination of grasping and transforming experience' (Kolb, 1984: 41). We also recognised the wide variety of existing action research approaches and identified an inherent confusion in the action research literature that sometimes hinders students' choice of research design. Then, using our own experience with practitioner-researcher development in the higher education sector, we presented examples of studies conducted by master's or doctoral students which, for us, suggested four distinct modes of action research that are being used in coaching research contexts. We differentiated these four modes by distinguishing their distinctive purposes and outcomes, and discussing the research challenges and different levels of participant and researcher involvement.

In Figure 9.2 we summarise the four modes across two dimensions: Researcher–Community (as the key drivers of the purpose or intent of the action research), and Practitioner–Praxisioner – a word used by Bruna (2014) to mean someone who uses reflection and action to transform structures, as per Paulo Freire (1972). The Practitioner/Praxisioner dimension highlights the personal versus professional emphasis of the four modes.

Figure 9.2   Four modes of action research

As educators, we are keen not to let the potential of action research for developing the coaching field slip between the confusions caused by theoretical idealism and the realities of action research practice. We always advise students to think explicitly about the outcome of the study before they commence the design of their action research. With the identification of the four action research modes, we are now able to advise on purpose, the different characteristics of participant involvement and researcher role – and possibly also offer suggestions for epistemological alignment. These are the challenges of action research which have been under-theorised so far, but which should help students and practitioner-researchers to design more robust studies, not only in the coaching arena, but also in other disciplines, such as Human Resource Development, where practitioner involvement is key.

We acknowledge that the typology of modes introduced here is still in its theoretical infancy. Further research is needed to explore particularly the following aspects:

1. Potential overlaps between modes. For example, in evolutionary action research, while the researcher is intent on developing a theory or model of practice, the participants could be using the same opportunity to engage in inquiry action research (developing themselves as individuals). Thus the different participants involved in the research

may have different agendas from those anticipated by the researcher in the choice of a particular mode.

2. The process of data collection and analysis methods for the four modes. Are methods merely the choice of the researcher or are there specific methods that fit the modes more readily? Data analysis, in particular, was an area that challenged many students. They felt discussion of various analysis approaches was lacking in current literature and in need of significant development and explication in the action research field.

3. Whether different epistemologies can be recommended for each mode. It could be that each mode may support a specific epistemology, driven by the purpose of the research and the strategy employed.

Further reading

Herr, K. and Anderson, G.L. (2014). *The Action Research Dissertation: A Guide for Students and Faculty*. Thousand Oaks, CA: Sage Publications.

Outlines the choices that students need to make when choosing to undertake action research. It includes explanations and examples and discussions of the challenges students may face when conducting an action research project for their thesis or dissertation.

Kemmis, S., McTaggart, R. and Nixon, R. (2013). *The Action Research Planner: Doing Critical Participatory Action Research*. New York: Springer Science & Business Media.

Provides a guide to developing and conducting a critical participatory action research project. Five in-depth examples of this type of action research study are incorporated, together with numerous resources for planning critical participatory research, including establishing an action research group and identifying a shared concern, research ethics, protocols for collaborative work, advice on keeping a journal, gathering evidence and reporting.

Discussion questions

- Since the values and procedures linked with each mode are different, what happens when participants have different agendas for the research?
- There seems to be very little transformative action research. Why should this be the case?
- How might data collection and analysis be best conducted for each mode?
- Is it possible to align a specific epistemology to each of the four modes of action research?

References

Brannick, T. and Coghlan, D. (2007). 'In defense of being "native": The case for insider academic research'. *Organizational Research Methods* 10 (1): 59–74.

Bruna, K.R. (2014). 'The spiral of science (mis)education, Parker's "multiple influences," and missed opportunities'. *Cultural Studies of Science Education* 9 (2): 335–42.

Carr, W. and Kemmis, S. (2003). *Becoming Critical: Education Knowledge and Action Research*. London: Routledge.

Chilisa, B. (2012). *Indigenous Research Methodologies*. Thousand Oaks, CA: Sage Publications.

Cochran-Smith, M. and Donnell, K. (2006). *Practitioner Inquiry: Blurring the Boundaries of Research and Practice*. London: Routledge.

Coghlan, D. and Brannick, T. (2014). *Doing Action Research in Your Own Organization*. London: Sage Publications.

Cohen, L., Manion, L. and Morrison, K. (2013). *Research Methods in Education* (7th edition). London: Routledge.

Cook, J. (2011). 'The effect of coaching on the transfer and sustainability of learning: Coaching for leaders, a collaborative action research study'. DCM thesis, Oxford Brookes University.

Cook, J. (2016). 'Collaborative action coaching for leaders: A way of enabling transfer and sustainability of learning for all external coaches?' *International Journal of Evidence Based Coaching and Mentoring*, Special Issue 10: 76–83.

Cox, E. and Patrick, C. (2012). 'Managing emotions at work: How coaching affects retail support workers' performance and motivation'. *International Journal of Evidence Based Coaching and Mentoring* 10 (2): 34–51.

Cunliffe, A.L. (2008). 'Orientations to social constructionism: Relationally responsive social constructionism and its implications for knowledge and learning'. *Management Learning* 39 (2): 123–39.

Dziuban, C.D., Picciano, A.G., Graham, C.R. and Moskal, P.D. (2016). *Conducting Research in Online and Blended Learning Environments: New Pedagogical Frontiers*. New York: Routledge.

Freire, P. (1972). *Pedagogy of the Oppressed*. Harmondsworth: Penguin.

Gardner, H. (1999). *Intelligence Reframed: Multiple Intelligences for the 21st Century*. New York: Basic Books.

Gibbon, M. (2002). 'Doing a doctorate using a participatory action framework in the context of community health'. *Qualitative Health Research* 12: 546–58.

Habermas, J. (1974). 'Introduction: Some difficulties in the attempt to link theory and praxis'. In J. Habermas, *Theory and Practice*. London: Heinemann, pp. 1–40.

Harding, C. (2006). 'Using the Multiple Intelligences as a learning intervention: A model for coaching and mentoring'. *International Journal of Evidence Based Coaching and Mentoring* 4 (2): 19–42.

Heron, J. and Reason, P. (2006). 'The practice of co-operative inquiry: Research "with" rather than "on" people'. In P. Reason and H. Bradbury (eds), *Handbook of Action Research: Concise Paperback Edition*. London: Sage Publications, pp. 144–54.

Herr, K. and Anderson, G. (2005). *The Action Research Dissertation: A Guide for Students and Faculty*. Thousand Oaks, CA: Sage Publications.

Hodge, A.A. (2014). 'An action research inquiry into what goes on in coaching supervision to the end of enhancing the coaching profession'. Doctoral dissertation, Middlesex University.

Ives, Y. (2011). 'Goal-focused coaching: Theoretical foundations and practical implications'. PhD Thesis, Oxford Brookes University.

Kemmis, S. (2012). 'Researching educational praxis: Spectator and participant perspectives'. *British Educational Research Journal* 38 (6): 885–905.

Kemmis, S. and McTaggart, R. (eds) (1988). *The Action Research Planner* (3rd edition). Geelong Waurn Ponds: Deakin University Press.

Kemmis, S. and McTaggart, R. (2000). 'Participatory action research'. In N.K. Denzin and Y.S. Lincoln (eds), *Handbook of Qualitative Research* (2nd edition). Thousand Oaks, CA: Sage Publications.

Kemmis, S., McTaggart, R. and Nixon, R. (2013). *The Action Research Planner: Doing Critical Participatory Action Research*. New York: Springer Science & Business Media.

Kolb, A.Y. and Kolb, D.A. (2008). 'Experiential learning theory: A dynamic, holistic approach to management leaning, education and development'. In S.J. Armstrong and C.K. Fukami (eds), *The SAGE Handbook of Management Learning, Education and Development*. London: Sage Publications, pp. 42–68.

Kolb, D.A. (1984). *Experiential Learning: Experience as the Source of Learning and Development*. Englewood Cliffs, NJ: Prentice-Hall.

Mahoney, M. (2014). 'Engaging with industry: Collaborative action research as a useful tool in facility management, knowledge and learning'. In V. Dermol, M. Smrkolj and G. Ðaković (eds), *Human Capital without Borders: Knowledge and Learning for Quality of Life – Proceedings of the Management, Knowledge and Learning International Conference*. Celje, Slovenia: ToKnowPress, pp. 237–44.

McCarthy, I. and Simon, G. (2016). *Systemic Therapy as Transformative Practice*. Farnhill: Everything Is Connected Press.

McIntyre, A. (2008). *Participatory Action Research*. London: Sage Publications.

McLaughlin, M. (2012). 'Coaching for brave leadership: An action research study'. Doctoral thesis, Oxford Brookes University.

McLaughlin, M. (2013). 'Coaching for brave leadership: An action research study'. *International Journal of Evidence Based Coaching and Mentoring* (S7): 125–39.

McNiff, J. (2013). *Action Research: Principles and Practice*. London: Routledge.

Mertens, D.M. (2014). *Research and Evaluation in Education and Psychology: Integrating Diversity with Quantitative, Qualitative, and Mixed Methods*. London: Sage Publications.

Mezirow, J. (1991). *Transformative Dimensions of Adult Learning*. San Francisco, CA: Jossey-Bass.

Newton, T., Deetz, S. and Reed, M. (2011). 'Responses to social constructionism and critical realism in organization studies'. *Organization Studies* 32 (1): 7–26.

Pavlish, C.P. and Pharris, M.D. (2012). *Community-based Collaborative Action Research: A Nursing Approach. Methodology Unfolding*. Sudbury, MA: Jones & Bartlett Learning.

Reason, P. and Bradbury, H. (eds) (2006). *Handbook of Action Research: Concise Paperback Edition*. London: Sage Publications.

Reason, P. and Bradbury, H. (eds) (2008). *The SAGE Handbook of Action Research: Participative Inquiry and Practice* (2nd edition). London: Sage Publications.

Robson, C. (2002). *Real World Research* (2nd edition). Oxford: Blackwell.

Shoukry, H. (2016). 'Coaching for emancipation: A framework for coaching in oppressive environments'. *International Journal of Evidence Based Coaching and Mentoring* 14 (2): 15–30.

Titchen, A. (2015). 'Action research: Genesis, evolution and orientations'. *International Practice Development Journal* 5 (1): 1–16.

Torbert, W.R. (2001). 'The practice of action inquiry'. In P. Reason and H. Bradbury (eds), *The Handbook of Action Research: Participative Inquiry and Practice*. London: Sage Publications, pp. 250–60.

Torbert, W.R. (2004). *Action Inquiry: The Secret of Timely and Transforming Leadership*. San Francisco, CA: Berrett-Koehler Publishers.

Torbert, W.R. and Taylor, S. (2008). 'Action inquiry: Interweaving multiple qualities of attention for timely action'. In P. Reason and H. Bradbury (eds), *The SAGE Handbook of Action Research: Participative Inquiry and Practice*. London: Sage Publications, pp. 239–51.

Whitehead, J. and McNiff, J. (2006). *Action Research: Living Theory*. London: Sage Publications.

Wood, L., Seobi, A., Setlhare-Meltor, R. and Waddington, R. (2015). 'Reflecting on reflecting: Fostering student capacity for critical reflection in an action research project'. *Educational Research for Social Change* 4 (1), 79–93.

Zachariadis, M., Scott, S.V. and Barrett, M.I. (2013). 'Methodological implications of critical realism for mixed-methods research'. *MIS Quarterly* 37 (3): 855–79.

Zuber-Skerritt, O. (1992). *Professional Development in Higher Education*. London: Kogan-Page.

Zuber-Skerritt, O. (2002). 'A model for designing action learning and action research programs'. *The Learning Organization* 9 (4): 143–9.

Zuber-Skerritt, O. (2015). 'Participatory action learning and action research (PALAR) for community engagement: A theoretical framework'. *Educational Research for Social Change* 4 (1): 5–25.

PART III

THE IMPACT OF RESEARCH

10

The experience
of research

Elaine Cox and
Peter Jackson

Introduction

Over thirty years ago Reason and Marshall (1987: 112) identified how all
good research produces outcomes in three distinct areas: *'for me, for us* and
for them' (author italics). *For them* is the traditional research contribution to
the fund of knowledge about a subject; *for us* is a contribution from the
research that is relevant and timely or, in today's parlance, has 'impact'; and
for me is the contribution to the researcher's own personal and professional
development. This chapter is concerned with the third of these areas – how
the experience of research affects the researcher both as a professional and
as an individual.

Because coaching is still quite a nascent discipline, particularly in relation
to research, we believe it is important to capture the developmental experiences of doing research in the field. In this chapter therefore we include first-
hand accounts of how doing doctoral research has affected some of our former
students, how it has influenced their engagement with the discipline and has
helped them reconsider or expand their professional practice. With the objective of presenting individual case studies and drawing out pertinent themes,
we invited doctoral alumni from Oxford Brookes University to share their

experiences of doing coaching research. We received feedback from six alumni working in a range of coaching contexts and below we share how their research has impacted their professional lives and their personal development. In presenting the cases we have used pseudonyms to aid confidentiality.

We hope that by drawing together doctoral candidates' experiences of research in this chapter we will be able to share how students working on coaching topics identify and confront the various benefits, risks and challenges that doing a doctorate presents.

Student 1 – Savannah

Savannah is an experienced executive coach and supervisor and her research topic was directly related to her work at that level. She had identified a lack of guidance and research on how to obtain direct client feedback to support her professional development as a coach and so her research was focused on designing a feedback instrument to address this problem.

There were two strands to the research: a qualitative strand undertaken with a small number of clients to develop the instrument, followed by a quantitative strand where the instrument was surveyed with a larger number of coaching clients.

Savannah explained how undertaking doctoral research had affected her work as a coach.

During her study she uncovered how clients of other coaches were both willing and able to provide developmental feedback to their executive coaches. Involving participant clients in the development of a feedback instrument for executive coaches had surfaced an expectation of professional transformational learning actions and empathic behaviours. It also encouraged the inclusion of these two outcomes as part of the feedback discussions subsequently initiated with survey participants. Thus, specific findings were implemented in practice; indeed the addition of these two elements to the feedback instrument was found to relate to the strength of the working alliance and the generation of new insights. At the same time, the feedback instrument developed with participants did not include many goal setting and monitoring behaviours, nor was it related to the achievement of goals. Rather than taking the need for goal setting for granted, Savannah decided to ask participants in the survey whether they were interested in receiving support for goal setting purposes.

The findings stimulated Savannah to actively seek developmental feedback from her own clients and systematically suggest topics to them as potential feedback domains.

As well as the impact on practice, Savannah also shared the ways in which she considered her doctoral research had impacted the discipline and her understanding of the discipline. She explained how one of the issues she encountered at the beginning of the research was the absence of relevant literature relating to client feedback in executive coaching. As a result, she says:

I explored the theory of feedback in related disciplines such as management and helping disciplines. I also explored various theories of coaching to find out which one would be suitable to support a theory of client feedback. This allowed me to explore in depth two theoretical domains that are core to my practice, thus equipping me with explicit theoretical foundations to continue developing my own practice and supporting those of my supervisees.

Savannah has also been influenced both personally and professionally as a result of the research experience. She noted how she found out during the literature review that the competency models she used to train and accredit coaches are generally not explicitly related to a theoretical framework. This inspired her to join the research committee of the American professional body 'Graduate School Alliance for Education in Coaching' and support the ongoing development of their academic standards. In her practice, she learned to critically review coaching models and make decisions about adopting them based on the rigour of the research behind them rather than based on sponsors' request or popularity within my coaching communities. Finally, the research experience inspired her to teach coaching skills in an academic setting.

We have seen in this example how the choice of research question can be directly linked to work as a coach. For Savannah this link was vital: her motivation for the study was fuelled by the lack of research into client feedback and the identification of the potential impact she could have on the discipline itself. Following her doctorate, Savannah felt moved to contribute to the development of others and to the improvement of academic standards for coaches – all based on her felt need for rigour in the field engendered through the research.

Student 2 – Leon

Leon is an experienced coach with a background in therapy. His critical realist research explored the experiences of insight of coaches and their clients during coaching sessions.

Leon reported that he had no doubts whatsoever that his understanding of the discipline had been improved: 'Having read the amount of coaching literature, having discussed coaching in differing cohorts and attended conferences, I have become aware of so many papers and research results within the industry.' He also confirmed how the critical thinking promoted by doing a doctorate has forced him to think about deeper and differing ways of being: 'Firstly, there is an increased awareness of the self; then, there is an increased desire to consider the client at a deeper level and to understand more about the client's unknown philosophical beliefs in order to understand how they are describing differing issues and questions.'

Leon reported that during the research phase of the project his coaching activity continued as previously. However, he noted that once the analysis phase was complete, he was keen to attempt to identify whether the results of the research would manifest in coaching sessions. Leon reflected on this delay in applying findings to practice and asked himself whether he was 'giving my all to the client or if I was adding value'. So Leon now asks himself: 'What are they seeking and from what perspective?' He is implementing the results of the research in order to operate as a better practitioner.

One of the additional outcomes Leon had not considered was the underlying pressure he felt to maintain 'the professional expectations and standards expected as a person holding the title of Doctor of Coaching and Mentoring and also as a member of the doctoral community'. This is something that was mentioned by a number of students.

In summary, Leon's coaching practice appears to have deepened by undertaking his doctorate. His understanding of the topic has resulted in him exploring areas in greater depth with clients, rather than, as he puts it, taking things for granted. Like, Savannah, Leon's view of himself has also changed. He seems very aware of an uplift in expectation by clients and others towards someone who has reached doctoral level.

Student 3 – Pearl

Pearl's interest was in how creative writing could be integrated into coaching. Her biggest insight was around the discipline of coaching and the discovery of its complexity despite the 'wider perception as to its simplicity for those who focus simply upon coaching skills'.

Additionally, Pearl found that her Heuristic Self Search methodology, involving the use of her own experience as data, supported 'healing and growth and, critically, a shared but unique perspective with co-researchers'. She explained how her reflexive diary was 'invaluable in terms of my growth and development throughout the research process and my appreciation of the experience and learning I had garnered'. Pearl thus shared with us what she calls the 'riches gained from the research experience in terms of skills and competencies'. She now knows that she is 'instinctively a reflexive practitioner' and that the research brought forth enriched perspectives of self.

Pearl considered that she had developed a 'greater breadth and depth of insight' which underpins her communication and understanding of the discipline. She highlighted how her research brought forth key contributions in the areas of 'identity' as a coach; moving 'beyond personal narrative' into a more reflexive practitioner and the 'craft of becoming', recognising that these are possible areas of focus for dissemination of the research.

For Pearl, the reflexivity involved in doctoral research provided a realisation that learning is ongoing and describes this as a 'gateway into the possibilities of becoming; the idea that there is always the potential for more; the notion that becoming is about evolving and progressing towards the fulfilment of potential and that everything can contribute to learning and growth subject to the willingness of the individual to commit to enhancing capacity and capability'. She recalled how throughout the heuristic research process her ability to differentiate between her approach to her work and that of others increased. This differentiation was partly 'grounded in a deeper and richer appreciation of coaching theory' which enabled her to be clearer about her offering when talking with clients. She also explained how these considerations remain 'invaluable, influential and enduring' acknowledging that the research process has contributed to the enrichment of personal and professional credibility. Pearl considered that this level of engagement requires 'practice, effort and courage and a willingness to embrace the notion of development as an ongoing process rather than a fixed destination (or qualification)'.

Once her studying was completed, Pearl noted how she missed the academic resources that were available during the doctorate: 'I miss access to the University library and the academic portals available to me during my doctoral studies and find myself challenging myself as to how I am going to keep abreast of developments within coaching and related fields.'

In relation to how her doctoral research had impacted the field and her understanding, Pearl conceded that her research had only made a small contribution to the field: 'One of the things to emerge very clearly from my coaching research is how much there is to learn – an exciting and daunting idea but one which is also stimulating and encouraging. A critical piece of learning for me throughout my research was that my research contribution is a crumb the size of a pinhead but that it is no less valuable for that scale.'

Like Leon, Pearl also commented on her new identity as a doctor: 'My doctoral title gives evidence as to the rigour and discipline of my approach and supports ongoing clarity of self and personal approach to coaching. Practically, it took about six months post viva to feel worthy of my new identity and to incorporate it into my being. Congruity between identity, professional credentials and delivery has secured new client work.'

Pearl's experience was similar to Savannah and Leon in that she also found that completion of her doctorate provided her not only with a deeper understanding of theory but also the opportunity to become more reflexive. The doctoral journey has impacted her view of herself, supporting 'a richer, deeper me to emerge – a more measured and considered individual with a stronger richer sense of self which supports enhanced self-belief and confidence'. Finally, and enduringly her research facilitated understanding: 'a greater sense of how little I know, a greater appreciation of the breadth and depth of my field of practice alongside a curiosity and a humility to learn more and to find ways to share and apply my insights'.

Student 4 – Mollie

Mollie has been a project manager and self-employed coach and she reports how undertaking doctoral research had been time consuming and had 'hampered the creation of new possibilities from a time perspective'. However, her study did force her to think about what she was doing: 'it highlighted the importance of philosophy'.

Mollie also explained how because of the research process she has slowly softened all her opinions to be more accepting of different positions. For example, previously she would have said that without the contracted coaching conversation a coaching culture can easily embed hierarchy/power. Now she would say 'it depends on the context'. However, although the research process can have individual impact, she suggested that it may be hard for any doctoral research to impact the discipline overall because the meaning of coaching is so idiosyncratic: 'different for each client'.

Mollie also confirmed that the research had encouraged her to read more than she would otherwise have done. For example, she now has a better understanding of different discourses. She identified how much she has been influenced as a result of the research experience. Research has made her engage more in thinking and argument. However, Mollie realises that she still is not a natural theorist. She considers that this may have hampered her career and understanding: 'I'm thinking I've had practical knowing rather than theoretical knowing and I might have been less good at the practical if I'd spent more time on the theoretical.' She stresses that the time taken to complete a doctorate, whether a professional doctorate or a regular PhD, should not be underestimated.

Student 5 – Ava

Ava was clear that she felt much more confident as a coaching supervisor and as a supervisee following her doctoral research: 'As a coach – I feel more up-to-date about the latest thinking in coaching. I read a lot more books about coaching and leadership than I did before.' She feels she has 'stepped into' her authority as a coach, writing articles and speaking at conferences. She has also become a partner in a coaching organisation and takes a significant role in the CPD activities there: 'I have increased my fee rates as a coach and supervisor.'

Following her doctoral study, Ava is now involved in two new areas of research in the coaching field (on coaching women leaders and chemistry sessions and matching processes). She acknowledges that she feels confident in her abilities as a researcher and attends a lot more conferences. She also confirms that the doctoral research has 'deepened my understanding of the discipline. For example, I understand more about the supervisee perspective and I am more aware of the power dynamics and feelings of fear that are present in coaching supervision.'

Ava explained how the research had made her feel differently about her professional self, describing how she had incorporated her findings into how she works as a supervisor and as a supervisee: 'I feel that my research added to the scant body of knowledge about the supervisee perspective in coaching supervision and I frequently get asked to contribute to conferences, share my findings with organisations, write articles and contribute to books on the subject.'

Ava explained how she is now involved in two new areas of research in the coaching field as a result of her research, namely coaching women leaders and chemistry sessions and matching processes. She feels confident in her abilities as a researcher and attends a lot more conferences. She is also more conscious of the importance of academic and empirical evidence in coaching and coaching supervision and so is more able to critique research and articles. Overall the doctorate has increased her confidence.

Most students agreed that undertaking the doctorate enabled them to be more informed in relation to theory. Ava also felt she had become more authoritative and has begun disseminating findings in writing and speaking engagements. Similar to the other students she observed how she had grown in professionalism, but she also notes how it has 'given me a sense of my signature presence as a supervisor'.

Student 6 – Alfie

Alfie commented on how the research had affected his practice as a coach on a number of levels: 'The most obvious is that I have had a rare opportunity to undertake a collaborative inquiry into a phenomenon that seems to be inter-twined with the very essence that everything that coaching, and being a coach, means (certainly from a relational standpoint).'

Alfie explained how he became 'highly sensitised' to the concept he researched and how presence is 'expressed and experienced from the perspective of both coaches and their clients'. Through the research process, Alfie explains how he met people from outside his regular network 'who have been willing to work with me to make sense of what many see as being a slippery and nebulous concept'. He considers that this exploration and consequent development of a practical model has been invaluable to his own practice.

Alfie also came to appreciate 'the interrelationship between coaching practice, research and learning from the research of others' and recognises now 'having contributed my own grain of sand to the beach of knowledge, I now feel a responsibility as an active member of this community'. He confirms how researching at a doctoral level has taken existing good continuing professional development habits to a new level with new ones being developed during the process of becoming a researcher: For instance, he says, 'with search engines like Google Scholar at my fingertips, my whole discipline of reflexive practice has been enhanced through being able to access the wealth of coaching research. It's a bit like having a virtual supervisor to hand to help with reflective insights after a coaching session.' Alfie gives examples of this new ability:

> If I had an experience where there was a sense of rupture with a client because I had challenged too strongly, I might find some research on 'critical moments' and understand more of what other coaches have felt and done about this. If I felt a sense of flow during a coaching session, I might find a paper on flow in coaching and how it affects practice. Whilst this doesn't necessarily provide clear-cut answers or solutions, it adds to my appreciation of the wider system or field of intelligence that I can access to make sense of my coaching experiences.

Alfie confirmed how many of the insights that he drew from the research have found their way back into his practice: he confirms that he has been able to experiment with new ways of being and build a different type of relationship with his clients following a study of presence in the coaching relationship. As a result, he prepares differently, coaches differently and reflects differently:

> For example, I spend more time at the start of a session allowing myself and my client to come into presence with each other by listening with an aware compassion, noticing my breathing, sitting upright in my chair and trying not to let my mind jump into problem-solving mode. I am more aware that my presence impacts my client on a conscious and sub-conscious level so I have developed habits to cultivate presence, including meditation (a research finding was that clients felt when a coach wasn't fully present with them and that this affected the strength of their relationship and their ability to trust and show vulnerability). I am more attuned to the power of silence, allowing it to be an active part of the coaching process and I value my role as a witness or observer when a client is recounting a narrative of an event or issue (because client research partners reported the value of this role to them). These are examples of a wealth of new, practical knowledge arisen directly from the research that have informed new practices, attitudes and ways of being and which I believe, have helped me to be a more effective coach.

Alfie explains that during and since the research: 'There have been many moments of insight and many more gradual shifts in my appreciation of coaching. For example, one further fascinating aspect that arose during the research was the frequent use of metaphor by research partners when trying to make sense of their experience of presence.' The study identified sixteen different metaphors and further investigation into these has led to a more informed understanding of the concept of tacit knowledge and the process of eliciting and expressing this kind of knowledge so that it can find language and meaning which can then be communicated. 'This awareness has direct relevance to the coaching process and I am now more highly attuned to the use of metaphor and more actively work with it.'

Alfie's experience of the research process is profound. He explains in some detail how the process has contributed to a depth of understanding about his own philosophy and consequently his approach to his professional work:

> The research process has broadened my thinking and helped me to understand more deeply my philosophy as a coach. Previously, I had only a vague awareness of the ontological and epistemological stances that underpinned my worldview and my preconceptions of who I was as a coach. I remember it took me some months of exploring my professional and personal identity before I became comfortable with taking a constructivist stance and choosing to undertake a phenomenological inquiry.

> Coming to this position was a challenge and a journey and in doing so, I have realised that the congruence I feel (and can now better express) between who I am as a person and who I am as a coach, is also reflected in who I am as a researcher. The common ground is that I try to value all perspectives of clients or research partners as equally valid and stay true to an inductive, dialogic process. I view meaning-making as a mutual process unique to our particular time and place, informed by our individual histories and the histories we bring into the room with us. My focus as a coach and a researcher is on listening with all my being on a physical, emotional and mental level, to hear beyond the words and also to contribute fully to the meaning-making dialogue that happens between us. It has been a gift to really

clarify this in my own mind and then to practise a phenomenological approach to research, which then deepens that same stance as a coach and vice versa. It's as though one hand washes the other.

Alfie also identifies that the close relationship between being a coach and becoming a researcher was evident right from the start of the research journey and continued to develop over the years of the doctorate: 'I have evolved as a coach since experiences in one domain have informed experiences in the other. The key to making sense of it all has been a much deeper reflexive practice as a both researcher and coach. This to me, really brings home the meaning of what it is to be a researcher-practitioner.'

Summary

A doctorate in coaching is most likely to be rooted in the professional practice of coaching and, whilst recognising and explicitly embracing academic research as an integral component, will also be concerned to develop and test new theories, practices and knowledge in that professional context. Consequently, the completed research will often have direct professional significance for the student, their work situation and, importantly, the professional field. Writing about their experiences with professional doctorates in the education sphere, Burnard et al. (2018: 41) also confirmed that, through research, the identity of the researching professional can change:

> Whether situated as an insider or in-betweener, encountering new ideas, and embracing a willingness to accept one's identity as being fluid through engagement in a professional doctorate programme involves risk-taking; the outcomes of ongoing reflexive self-interrogation may be uncomfortable, personally, professionally, culturally and methodologically. The impact may be difficult to predict or control.

In this chapter we have shared how the experience of doing coaching research has affected six doctoral researchers working and studying in that field. The chapter considered the effect of the research process on students and the outcomes for their professional lives and for their clients. It revealed several themes that were common to all students despite differing ages, backgrounds and applications of coaching.

One noteworthy theme is the insights gained into the practice of coaching. Over the years, many students have commented that they had not realised that the theoretical understanding and research rigour employed, particularly in a doctorate, could have such a significant impact on practice. Most students confirmed that they now have a different type of relationship with clients following their research.

Another significant theme relates to how students took on the mantle of 'doctor'. One student referred to it as stepping into her authority, another said he felt a responsibility and yet another referred to waiting to feel 'worthy'. This process of identity formation, or of 'becoming doctor' (Barnacle and Mewburn, 2010), has tended to be overlooked in education research, but the credibility that the doctorate confers to these student coaches is plainly vital to their identity not only as a researcher but as a professional coach.

In the quote above, Burnard et al. (2018: 41) point out that being open to new ways of thinking and being can be 'profoundly challenging and unsettling'. This certainly appeared to be the case for Mollie and most of the other students who shared their experience with us.

As noted earlier, critical thinking stimulated by doctoral research forces students to think deeper about not only the topic area, but also their practice and for many, their whole way of being. For doctoral researchers, and especially for professional doctorate researchers, the influence of the process on the profession and on the researcher him or herself is seen as particularly important. This chapter, as well as highlighting relevant propositional knowledge, therefore considered the influence of the research process on the researcher and highlighted their developmental experiences.

Further reading

Gupta, R.K. and Awasthy, R. (eds) (2015). *Qualitative Research in Management: Methods and Experiences*. New Delhi: Sage Publications.

This book explores a diverse range of qualitative approaches through the in-depth, lived experience of researchers in the management field.

Sverdlik, A., Hall, N.C., McAlpine, L. and Hubbard, K. (2018). 'The PhD experience: A review of the factors influencing doctoral students' completion, achievement, and well-being'. *International Journal of Doctoral Studies* 13: 361–88.

This paper presents a comprehensive review of the factors, such as success, satisfaction, time management and well-being, that influence the experiences of doctoral students.

References

Barnacle, R. and Mewburn, I. (2010). 'Learning networks and the journey of "becoming doctor"'. *Studies in Higher Education* 35 (4): 433–44.

Burnard, P., Dragovic, T., Ottewell, K. and Lim, W.M. (2018). 'Voicing the professional doctorate and the researching professional's identity: Theorizing the EdD's uniqueness'. *London Review of Education* 16 (1): 40–55.

Reason, P. and Marshall, J. (1987). 'Research as personal process'. In D. Boud and V. Griffin (eds), *Appreciating Adult Learning: From the Learner's Perspective*. London: Kogan Page, pp. 112–26.

11

The dissemination and implementation of research-based coaching knowledge

Peter Jackson and Elaine Cox

Introduction

People do coaching research for a number of different reasons. They may do so out of pure intellectual curiosity, to fulfil a course requirement, or for some instrumental reason associated with a career in academia or elsewhere. As we highlighted in Chapter 10, they may do research 'for me, for us and for them' (Reason and Marshall, 1987: 112). Ultimately, however, the key characteristic of research in an applied discipline is that it creates something that eventually might be applied in some way to the practice of that discipline, so 'for us and for them'. This is the underlying purpose of everything we have discussed in this volume up to this point.

This chapter is intended to complete the cycle of the process of knowledge creation in coaching. In Chapter 1, we outlined evidence-based practice as a rationale for undertaking research and as a motivator to do it in a robust way. We discussed the underpinning theoretical foundations of the research process in Chapter 2, and the planning of a research project in Chapter 3. The chapters in Part II of this volume explored a selection of appropriate research strategies to investigate coaching problems, bringing us full circle to the question of knowledge creation and its transfer into practice.

How then do the insights generated in academic research come to be enacted in practice? At a superficial level, it would seem that the process of turning research findings into practice would consist of two elements: dissemination, via various written or oral means; and implementation, which requires adoption of theories or recommendations by relevant stakeholders. Yet, this process appears to be difficult to put into practice: among other challenges, researchers find it difficult to produce research findings that are both acceptable to academia and that transfer easily into practice. Historically there are a number of obstacles or barriers.

In health sector research, Glasgow and Emmons (2007) identify four categories of barriers to dissemination: these include characteristics of (i) the intervention (the recommendation is expensive, complex or not customisable); (ii) the target settings (needs of clients, limited time, prevailing work practices, lack of support); and (iii) the research or evaluation design itself (not representative because of sample size or target sample, failure to evaluate reach or to assess implementation); Glasgow and Emmons also note that, (iv) there are interactions among the first three categories.

Similarly, Guldberg (2017) writes about the form the gap between research and practice takes (this time in the field of studies on autism). She identifies 'the methodological readjustments that are needed, recognising that broader discussions around "what works" have been problematic in both practice and theory, as well as in methodology' (Guldberg, 2017: 150).

Guldberg sees part of the problem as 'translational' where research dissemination is viewed as 'a linear, top-down transmission model from which practitioners should draw knowledge' (Guldberg, 2017: 160). Research is imagined to flow from dissemination via a journal or conference into practice with very little engagement by practitioners. This model elevates the researcher to the position of 'expert' and the practitioner becomes merely the vehicle for delivering the intervention.

Given that Wall et al. (2016) have demonstrated that similar barriers exist in relation to the dissemination and implementation of coaching research, we can now consider what more coaching researchers can do as part of their programme of research to help transfer findings into practice. Drawing on Glasgow and Emmons (2007), three interrelated areas are discussed: the design of the study; the dissemination challenges; and application and implementation.

Creating research that communicates to practice: The research design and methodology

It may not be immediately obvious to the student researcher how research design and methodology affects dissemination. However, Glasgow and Emmons (2007) demonstrate how this can be the case. They argue that there are tensions for example between broad policy changes with small impacts on individuals and more targeted interventions that have a significant impact on particular populations. Correspondingly, researchers may tend towards designs which look at particular or idiosyncratic populations in order to demonstrate significant impact in their study. In this case, the specificity of the study population may lead to findings that are poorly generalisable to wider populations, resulting in poorly targeted interventions. Conversely, the effect size reported by larger scale studies using broader populations may look to the practitioner to be so small as to be irrelevant to a specific case. Although practice in the coaching field is less influenced by policy, similar issues arise: highly contextualised findings may be difficult to apply where it is not clear what features of the client's specific situation have most influence; while broad generalities may simply not apply to an individual case. We can easily imagine, then, that the pathways of dissemination and implementation will be different for evidence emerging from different methodologies.

Establishing a link between research evidence and practice in the field is often expressed in terms of evidence-based practice. It is important to examine this concept critically because it can be articulated in simplistic ways which privilege certain research approaches over others.

Forms of evidence-based practice appear in a whole range of applied disciplines. Stober and Grant (2006: 5) describe the roots of evidence-based coaching specifically in the fields of medicine and social science-based practices. They describe how in medicine there is an assumption of a definitive evaluation of 'good' versus 'bad' treatments. The core of the concept is essentially the knowledge of what is the best course of action. In medicine, however, it is arguable that there is a very clear theory of knowledge, centred around clearly definable outcomes, and a consensus on which methods of knowledge production are valued. Therefore, in a field where the evidence concerned arises essentially from hard science, methods attuned to the creation of confident and generalisable knowledge on specific topics are privileged: hence the characterisation of randomised controlled trials, identified as primary by the Canadian Task Force on the Periodic Health Examination (1979: 1195), as a kind of 'gold standard' (Grant, 2016: 76).

Stober and Grant (2006: 5) note, however, that 'coaching engagements are not medical interventions that follow prescribed or manualized treatment regimes'. In place of the relative predictability of biochemistry, coaching deals with the infinitely variable behaviour of autonomous individuals with free will. As a participant in Maxwell's research on coaching supervision colourfully notes:

people don't turn up for coaching sessions with just their business issues. They turn up with their hang ups and their brains … the whole damn human being. That messy thing turns up and sits in the room. (Maxwell, 2009: 85)

Another response to the nuanced and complex nature of evidence is to emphasise the role of the practitioner as the conduit of knowledge and expertise. Lane and Corrie (2006) describe, for example, the history of the concept of the scientist-practitioner. Here again, the founding premise was the strength of positivist empiricism, though Lane and Corrie come to a position that emphasises the importance of the ongoing development of criticality in the practitioner. In the same volume, Cavanagh and Grant (2006) associate this discriminating capability specifically with the psychologist's training, whilst also acknowledging psychology's historical preference for hypothetico-deductive approaches to knowledge production. In the context of coaching psychology, this presents a limitation as:

The unique, dynamic adaptive nature of the system formed in coaching relationships means that coaching (along with most practical psychological interventions) is a radically unpredictable, almost iterative process in which the next step is informed, in large part by the conditions immediately preceding it. (Cavanagh and Grant, 2006: 155)

More recently Bachkirova et al. (2017) have clearly articulated the implications of this complexity for the training and education of coaches, arguing for a constructive-developmental approach to training in preference to definitive competencies.

Each of the writers on evidence-based practice cited above conclude that practitioners need to approach disciplinary knowledge in more nuanced and practical ways, thinking about the best available evidence (Barends et al., 2014), or how evidence can trigger experimentation in practice. This in turn makes the researcher's role in producing evidence more complex. It is no longer a case of following good practice in a particular methodology in order to produce findings that are valid and generalisable.

How then does this affect the design choices of individual researchers who may be looking across a wide range of methodological strategies, whether interpretive or objectivist in character?

First and foremost, there is a need to meet the requirements of the target audience for the research. (We have been discussing mainly the implementation of research findings in practice, but the same is true of theoretical work. Many journals require a strong theoretical contribution.) As practitioners ourselves, and having worked with hundreds of coaching students, we would argue that evidence needs to be clear, trustworthy and meaningful. In explaining these criteria we will refer back to the high level recommendations for how to design the research project set out in Chapter 3.

Finding focus and describing the problem. Many doctoral research proposals in their draft stages identify a research question which the researcher finds inherently interesting. This is a great motivator for the researcher, but the relevance to other potential users of the research is often neglected at this stage. We may need to ask ourselves here whether a different (or usually a tighter) scope would be appropriate: a particular coaching approach; a particular coaching application; a particular population of clients. A single piece of research is very unlikely to tell us anything robust, valid and significant across a whole field of study. A clearer, more specific focus for a study often results in greater practical impact even if it appears to apply only to some practices in some circumstances. The tension between generalisability and sensitivity to context is well rehearsed in the methodology literature. However, as Glasgow and Emmons (2007: 417–18) note, this is just one of a number of tensions between different products (that is, types of evidence) emerging from different research approaches; they identify the following:

> tacit and explicit, quantitative and qualitative, process and outcome, biological and patient centered, quality improvement and controlled trial, intended and unintended consequences data, internal and external validity, efficacy and feasibility, cost and implementation, and adoption and sustainability evidence.

This list reminds us of how many dimensions are in play when the researcher decides what their research is 'about'.

Literature review. As a reminder, the aim of the literature review was described in Chapter 3 as being 'to locate all relevant research undertaken on the chosen topic to date and to marshal it into a useful review that exposes a gap in the research' (Cox, Chapter 3, this volume). It very clearly defines key terms and situates the research question in the context of existing knowledge. Alongside the parallel activity of situating the results in the context of existing knowledge (that is, the discussion chapter), this should therefore help specify the area in which the research is aiming to make a contribution. Furthermore the discipline of articulating this as a theoretical framework should enable the researcher to hold on to a very clear concept of what their research (eventually) says about the discipline. In a world of information overload, and where claims may be made for all sorts of reasons other than for the furtherance of knowledge (for example, marketing bespoke products and services), it is difficult for the practitioner to sift reliable knowledge from hearsay or propaganda. Communicating effectively the boundaries of knowledge claims may be extremely helpful in dissemination, but this message will be confused and confusing if the researcher is not clear in their own mind.

Identifying a relevant research approach (including designing participation, data collection and data analysis, consideration of ethics and quality). Each of the contributors in Part II of this book has identified the kinds of questions for which the approach they describe might be appropriate. Aligning the research strategy with the research question is at the very heart of creating useful knowledge. Yet this is only the start of the process of making methodological choices: equal attention needs to be paid to the recruitment of participants, the methods of analysis, validity, reliability, reflexivity and the role of the researcher (depending on the strategy deployed). These are important because both the quality and the transparency of these decisions determine the extent to which knowledge claims can be understood and evaluated. Clough and Nutbrown (2012: 21) advise that:

> The final difference between a persuasive and a merely sufficient methodology is that the convincing one takes little for granted. It worries endlessly at its own terms and is not content to justify its decisions largely by reference to other research.

Recall that we are aiming here for clear, trustworthy and meaningful research. The specific issues relevant to each approach will not be repeated here as they are outlined in the respective chapters of Part II. However, regardless of the specific methodology, progress towards these aims can be made by a critical engagement with what each step and stage of the process represents in terms of the research question and the field of study, what Clough and Nutbrown (2012: 26) call 'radical enquiry'.

Managing dissemination challenges

Earlier, in Chapter 3, we discussed researchers' desires to make a difference in the world through their research. We have noted that the initial choice of research is important as it can be the critical factor in whether or not the findings of the study will make a valuable contribution to theory and/or practice. The choice of research topic needs to be of interest to the coaching professional and/or make a significant contribution to the theory of coaching.

One way of ensuring the relevance of the topic was discussed in Chapter 3. In that chapter we saw how Montuori (2005) stressed that the literature review process enables researchers to engage in a creative process of finding their 'own voice' through exploring current trends. This offers the chance to locate an original niche which can then be tapped when it is time to disseminate the findings of the research. Montuori suggested that researchers should see themselves 'in dialogue' with the research community so that they can 'go deeper into that community' (2005: 378). We suggested that this 'going deeper' might relate to discipline, culture and the paradigm, or organisational logic: it follows therefore that the depth of connection also informs the dissemination of the research.

Assuming that the value of the research has been identified from a range of relevant literature, then reaching and sharing with the academic and professional communities might take several forms. It can comprise the publishing of research findings in an organisational or in-house setting; publishing findings in academic or trade journals (national or international); and/or presenting at conferences, meetings of professional associations, or in community and other stakeholder groups. Each of these modes of dissemination presents its own challenges for researchers, but the paramount task is to get on the same 'wave length' as the publisher, reader or listener. Much time and effort can therefore be spent considering how to present findings to a chosen audience: as Spronken-Smith et al. (2013: 107) point out, 'learning to communicate complex ideas without recourse to discipline-centred terminology and jargon requires significant skill development'.

This difficulty in communicating and achieving take-up of ideas is inherent in Land et al.'s (2016) adoption of the term 'threshold concepts'. They use this term to describe a way to achieve epistemological participation in a discipline: threshold concepts are perceived to act as 'portals' that people pass through in order to change their understanding of something. Researchers might likewise seek out appropriate threshold concepts to use when discussing or presenting their findings, in order to ensure that audiences reach portals of understanding. Adler-Kassner et al. (2017: 18) define threshold concepts as 'concepts critical for participation in communities of practice, the formally or informally defined sites where participants share common rituals, values, and stances'. They explained how 'within communities of practice, participants also share beliefs around what ideas are most important—threshold concepts—and the ways in which these concepts shape members' perspectives'. It might be therefore, that researchers can tap the 'rituals, values and stances' of practitioner audiences when sharing their ideas. To take an example, imagine a researcher who explores empirically coachees' experience of being coached using Beisser's (1970) 'paradoxical theory of change' as a model. Key concepts here are 'Gestalt', 'Beisser', 'paradoxical theory of change' and 'coaching'. Most coaches without an existing interest in Gestalt might ignore material expressed in these terms. But what if we talk about the same material in terms of goals, goal achievement and perhaps the GROW model and when it gets 'stuck': an alternative when we face the (recognisable) scenario of a client not really knowing their true goals, or perhaps playing along superficially with the GROW process.

In relation to our dissemination challenge, the idea of threshold concepts has some relevance as a form of 'intellectual scaffolding'. As Adler-Kassner et al. (2017) would concur, writing is always all about context: the context of the author (in this case the researcher); the context of the content of the writing (the research); and the context of the reader. If researchers understand how to evaluate and analyse the different contexts they wish to impact by identifying the threshold concepts inherent in the findings of their study they can then make them accessible and appropriate to the audience for the research. This in turn will enable them to successfully commute their rhetorical choices as writers. This process can be started in the conclusion to a dissertation or thesis and continued effectively when the research is disseminated via different journals and conferences. As Adler-Kassner et al. (2017: 41) suggest, just as important as epistemological participation in a discipline, is 'the ability to repurpose knowledge across the different writing situations within and beyond that discipline' in order to reach new audiences.

Adler-Kassner et al. also point out that reflection is critical for writers' development and must become an 'integral part of the writing process, making it more than an after-the-fact activity, a practice in revision, or an act of self-assessment' (Adler-Kassner et al., 2017: 29). These authors argue that, as a mode of inquiry, reflection 'prompts writers to recall, reframe, and relocate their writing knowledge and practices'. Accordingly, reflection can assist the process of framing and reframing writing in order to 'relocate knowledge in effective and meaningful ways in different contexts' (Adler-Kassner et al.,

2017: 29), which is effectively what identifying threshold concepts also tries to do. Regular, intentional reflection then can help researchers with the dissemination of their findings to others. For example, a researcher could consider how to address particular audiences at different professional body conferences and later reframe and relocate that knowledge for an academic journal article. In this way reflection can be seen as both process and product: when researchers enter new writing situations, they can reflect in order to assess what is needed to construct 'new rhetorically situated responses' (Adler-Kassner et al., 2017: 291).

Fillery-Travis and Cox (2018: 530) have looked at the often-difficult task of disseminating in academic journals. They identify that there is a growing number of coaching journals that publish quantitative and qualitative research, but that a problem arises when 'as journals mature and seek a more elite status ... they cease to acknowledge the value of publishing exploratory, qualitative studies'. This they see as a difficult situation for an applied field like coaching:

> a disjunct occurs between theory and practice. Papers with a clear exploratory stance and some practical application can sometimes be rejected by journals on the grounds that they do not have a large enough sample size or have not used a control group. (Fillery-Travis and Cox, 2018: 530)

For researchers aiming from the outset to disseminate and publish in academic journals, it is important to consider how the design of the research can be made robust and satisfy the criteria of the more established academic journals.

We have discussed here the principles of disseminating research for which academic journals may be the first stage. For practitioner-oriented research, much more can be done and there are consequent issues to be considered concerning the media and strategy of dissemination. A familiar route is to turn the material towards practitioner media (online and physical magazines and newsletters), blogs, professional fora and educational and networking events. Project research blogs can be particularly useful to users of the research, especially if they meet a critical mass of content and currency. Social media is a fast-developing and already complex area. Readers are referred to Carrigan (2016) and Mollett et al. (2017) where the effective use of social media and its complexities are discussed in detail.

Rickinson (2017) urges researchers to think of the challenge as one of learning rather than telling. He suggests outputs that are varied in format, interactive and usable (for example, by translating material into practice tools and methods – 2017: 991). He identifies a range of opportunities to help potential users of research outputs:

- Telling key audiences about the outputs well before completion.
- Linking the outputs to well-known topical issues or initiatives.
- Timing the distribution of outputs carefully for target audiences.
- Getting support for the outputs from respected opinion formers.
- Emphasising how and why the outputs could help end-users.
- Publicising the outputs via relevant networks and social media. (Rickinson 2017: 993)

Researchers with an organisational career background may note that Rickinson's recommendations evoke classic models of organisational change strategy.

From a more constructivist perspective, Rieger and Schultz (2014) explore a variety of arts-based communication strategies, for example, dance, drama, poetry and photography. They argue that such strategies, 'embrace the complexity of contextual knowledge, promote communities of practice, enhance practitioner engagement, and draw on practitioners' tacit knowledge to extend the impact of research evidence' (Rieger and Schultz, 2014: 133–4). Keen and Todres (2007) offer three specific case studies of qualitative studies whose authors carried the knowledge beyond academic journals in novel ways, in particular drama. Dramatic presentations, whether reproduced live, made available as recordings, or presented for example as forum theatre (see Boal, 1979), bring the immediacy of human narrative to an audience.

Implementation challenges: The practitioner's role

Iordanou and Wall (2017) have identified how the words 'practitioner' and 'researcher' are frequently used in a variety of formal and informal coaching settings. What is surprising, they say is that 'when we use these terms, an inferred and invisible barrier seems to be erected between the two, as if there is a silent dichotomy that distinguishes those who "*do*" from those who "*ponder*"' (2017). This section, therefore, discusses some of the implementation challenges that both coaching researchers and professionals face when trying to introduce and embed new research ideas into practice.

Challenges for the researcher

Implementation is an important issue for researchers if they want their findings to have application in the real world. It involves the acceptability of research-led, evidence-based suggestions for practice by practitioners.

However, in the health sector, Neta et al. (2015: 49) identified a major challenge in implementation in that 'most evidence-based interventions are not ready for widespread dissemination'. These authors suggest there are many reasons for this, some of which are relevant to the coaching field including the fact that research methods and reporting may not appear relevant to the actual situations faced by practitioners.

One of the important components of research that Neta et al. (2015) identify is context – a vital element of any study that has implications for implementation. They explain how 'context is multilevel, and cuts across domains including economic, political, social, and temporal factors' yet, the majority of research only captures the basic characteristics of context, often just demographic information of participants and population size. This information is usually not enough to justify the outcomes of studies and Neta et al. explain how such characteristics 'fail to capture other important contextual factors that may greatly influence adoption, implementation, and sustainment such as organizational capacity for change, presence of an opinion leader, communication and feedback strategies, and the nature of the provider–end user relationship' (2015: 50). Consequently, it may be that researchers need to highlight these issues at the point of dissemination in order to stimulate implementation.

Challenges for professionals

In Cox (2013) it was acknowledged that the transfer of new understanding and enhanced expertise into coaching practice and workplace situations involved overcoming several interrelated external and internal barriers. The external barriers might relate to organisational culture issues that interfere with implementation intentions through unpredicted problems, tasks and reactions in the environment. Internal barriers, on the other hand, could be related to energy and motivation and the challenge of changing entrenched habits or priorities.

Difficulties in practitioners' use of research knowledge can also be related to the perceived needs of clients, limited time, lack of practical or financial support, or prevailing work practices (Proctor and Rosen, 2008). In addition, as Proctor and Rosen point out, practitioners may lack an understanding of research processes, be unaware of the relevant literature or they may not be practised in critical thinking, bringing instead their lay modes of thinking into professional practice. However, as these authors also maintain, 'knowledge use, or implementation in practice, can no longer be ignored or dismissed from the agenda of research' (Proctor and Rosen, 2008: 4).

> The purpose of knowledge use, the characteristics and organization of the knowledge to be used ... the decision-making processes involved in implementation, and the contingencies affecting the knowledge-using agency and the knowledge-using practitioner (including, of course, client characteristics) all need to be considered part of knowledge use and be integrated into the profession's knowledge development enterprise. (Proctor and Rosen, 2008: 4)

Research evidence as described above is, according to Mullen et al. (2005), just one of three key elements of professional expertise (the other two being appropriate interventions and client preferences) and 'failure to use this valuable resource leaves [a] profession with unacceptable alternatives, such as basing policy or practice on opinion, conjecture, or ideology' (Mullen et al., 2005: 80). However, these authors argue that professionals need also to be trained to find and use the evidence critically. Professionals may lack the time and the research skills to avail themselves of the information on offer, despite computer-based searching becoming easier each year and the volume of information increasing. So, there is an implementation challenge which needs to be recognised by researchers.

It therefore befits the coaching researcher to ensure that dissemination includes information about what Proctor and Rosen describe as the:

potential decision-making processes involved in implementation, and the contingencies affecting the knowledge-using agency and the knowledge-using practitioner. (Proctor and Rosen, 2008: 287)

Thus, in order to reach professionals and encourage them to apply the new coaching knowledge, researchers need to understand the work context and be able to address the specific needs of the profession in that context.

In the conservation field where implementation is a considerable problem, Pietri et al. (2013) have developed a summary of key strategies, tasks, benefits and challenges for researchers working to bridge the research–implementation gap. They conclude that 'the more active a stakeholder's role in interpreting information presented to them, the more likely the information is to be incorporated into their beliefs and attitudes, potentially leading to concomitant behavioral change' (Pietri et al., 2013: 7–8). These authors see approaches such as workshops and community forums as useful for building stakeholder knowledge and ultimately disseminating and implementing research findings.

Conclusion

We started this chapter by emphasising the necessity of research to make a contribution to knowledge. Although the contribution may be theoretical, the emphasis in an applied discipline such as coaching is likely to be on practice. We learn from other applied disciplines that the transformation from research knowledge to practice knowledge is not straightforward. There is a suggestion that traditional concepts of evidence-based practice have tended to privilege methods modelled on those that work best in the physical sciences and that emphasise generalisability. Rather, we suggest, the more fruitful challenge is to ensure that methodology is well suited to answer a well-structured question. The foundation stone of effective dissemination and implementation is sound research.

The management of the process, as described in Chapter 3, and a good understanding of the implications of methodology (for example, those described in Part II of this book, among others) create high quality raw material for dissemination. Then we argued that the research needs to be both inherently relevant to practice, and to be made evidently so for practitioners, for example by leveraging threshold concepts. When it comes to implementation, there are a number of barriers to changing practice: access to knowledge created through research; having the time to develop the skills and expertise that might be implied by the outcome of that research; having the time to understand the research in the first place; the impact of career, commercial or job-role related pressure to perform rather than to experiment. Understanding these barriers can help researchers to design the communication of their research outcomes in ways that fit recognisable contexts, contribute to recognisable challenges, and wherever possible, to yield recognisable benefits.

As educators we are involved in promoting the understanding of research amongst practitioners, including encouraging them to gain first-hand experience of creating research. The various professional bodies also provide fora, conferences, including research conferences, and accreditation schemas which all encourage the sharing of knowledge. There is more to be done and more to be said about this side of the equation. In this chapter, however, we have focused on dissemination and implementation as a stage of 'Doing Coaching Research'

Further reading

Brownson, R.C., Colditz, G.A. and Proctor, E.K. (eds) (2018). *Dissemination and Implementation Research in Health: Translating Science to Practice*. Oxford: Oxford University Press.

This book provides an in-depth exploration of a range of dissemination and implementation issues in the clinical and public health sector. Some of the challenges of translating research into practice may be relevant to coaching researchers.

Kelly, B. and Perkins, D.F. (eds) (2012). *Handbook of Implementation Science for Psychology in Education*. Cambridge: Cambridge University Press.

This book explains implementation science and then provides case examples of how to implement interventions effectively in real-world educational contexts.

References

Adler-Kassner, L., Clark, I., Robertson, L., Taczak, K. and Yancey, K.B. (2017). 'Assembling knowledge: The role of threshold concepts in facilitating transfer'. In C.M. Anson and J.L. Moore (eds), *Critical Transitions: Writing and the Question of Transfer*. Fort Collins, CO: The WAC Clearinghouse and University Press of Colorado, pp. 17–47.

Bachkirova, T., Jackson, P., Gannon, J., Iordanou, I. and Myers, A. (2017). 'Re-conceptualising coach education from the perspectives of pragmatism and constructivism'. *Philosophy of Coaching: An International Journal* 2 (2): 29–50.

Barends, E., Rousseau, D.M. and Briner, R.B. (2014) *Evidence-Based Management: The Basic Principles*. Amsterdam: Center for Evidence-Based Management.

Beisser, A. (1970). 'Paradoxical theory of change'. In J. Fagan and I.L. Shepherd (eds), *Gestalt Therapy Now*. New York: Harper & Row, pp. 77–80.

Boal, A. (1979). *Theatre of the Oppressed*. London: Pluto Press.

Canadian Task Force on the Periodic Health Examination (1979). 'The periodic health examination'. *Canadian Medical Association Journal* 121: 1193–254.

Carrigan, M. (2016). *Social Media for Academics*. London: Sage Publications.

Cavanagh, M. and Grant, A.M. (2006). 'Coaching psychology and the scientist-practitioner model'. In D. Lane and S. Corrie (eds), *The Modern Scientist-Practitioner: A Guide to Practice in Psychology*. Abingdon: Routledge, pp. 146–57.

Clough, P. and Nutbrown, C. (2012). *A Student's Guide to Methodology*. London: Sage Publications.

Cox, E. (2013). *Coaching Understood: A Pragmatic Inquiry into the Coaching Process.* London: Sage Publications.

Fillery-Travis, A. and Cox, E. (2018). 'Researching coaching'. In E. Cox, T. Bachkirova and D. Clutterbuck (eds), *The Complete Handbook of Coaching* (3rd edition). London: Sage Publications, pp. 518–35.

Glasgow, R.E. and Emmons, K.M. (2007). 'How can we increase translation of research into practice? Types of evidence needed'. *Annual Review of Public Health* 28: 413–33.

Grant, A.M. (2016). 'What constitutes evidence-based coaching? A two-by-two framework for distinguishing strong from weak evidence for coaching'. *International Journal of Evidence Based Coaching and Mentoring* 14 (1): 74–85.

Guldberg, K. (2017). 'Evidence-based practice in autism educational research: Can we bridge the research and practice gap?' *Oxford Review of Education* 43 (2): 149–61.

Iordanou, I. and Wall, T. (2017). 'EMCC Policy Provocations Report: Extended Conversations 8 of 10'. Available at: www.linkedin.com/pulse/emcc-policy-provo cations-report-extended-8-10-dr-tony-wall/ (accessed 30 September 2019).

Keen, S. and Todres, L. (2007). 'Strategies for disseminating qualitative research findings: Three exemplars'. *Forum: Qualitative Social Research* 8 (3): Article 17.

Land, R., Meyer, J.H. and Flanagan, M.T. (eds) (2016). *Threshold Concepts in Practice*. Rotterdam: Sense Publishers.

Lane, D. and Corrie, S. (eds) (2006). *The Modern Scientist-Practitioner: A Guide to Practice in Psychology*. London: Routledge.

Maxwell, A. (2009). 'How do business coaches experience the boundary between coaching and therapy/counselling?' *Coaching: An International Journal of Theory, Research & Practice* 2: 149–62.

Mollett, A., Brumley, C., Gilson, C. and Williams, S. (2017). *Communicating Your Research with Social Media*. London: Sage Publications.

Montuori, A. (2005). 'Literature review as creative inquiry: Reframing scholarship as a creative process'. *Journal of Transformative Education* 3 (4): 374–93.

Mullen, E.J., Shlonsky, A., Bledsoe, S.E. and Bellamy, J.L. (2005). 'From concept to implementation: Challenges facing evidence-based social work'. *Evidence & Policy: A Journal of Research, Debate and Practice* 1 (1): 61–84.

Neta, G., Glasgow, R.E., Carpenter, C.R., Grimshaw, J.M., Rabin, B.A., Fernandez, M.E. and Brownson, R.C. (2015). 'A framework for enhancing the value of research for dissemination and implementation'. *American Journal of Public Health* 105 (1): 49–57.

Pietri, D.M., Gurney, G.G., Benitez-Vina, N., Kuklok, A., Maxwell, S.M., Whiting, L. and Jenkins, L.D. (2013). 'Practical recommendations to help students bridge the research–implementation gap and promote conservation'. *Conservation Biology* 27 (5): 958–67.

Proctor, E.K. and Rosen, A. (2008). 'From knowledge production to implementation: Research challenges and imperatives'. *Research on Social Work Practice* 18 (4): 285–91.

Reason, P. and Marshall, J. (1987). 'Research as personal process'. In D. Boud and V. Griffin (eds), *Appreciating Adult Learning: From the Learner's Perspective*. London: Kogan Page, pp. 112–26.

Rickinson, M. (2017). 'Communicating research findings'. In D. Wyse, N. Selwyn, E. Smith and L.E. Suter (eds), *The BERA/SAGE Handbook of Educational Research*. London: Sage Publications, pp. 973–97.

Rieger, K. and Schultz, A.S.H. (2014). 'Exploring arts-based knowledge translation: Sharing research findings through performing the patterns, rehearsing the results, staging the synthesis'. *Worldviews on Evidence-Based Nursing* 11 (2): 133–9.

Spronken-Smith, R.A., Brodeur, J.J., Kajaks, T., Luck, M., Myatt, P., Verburgh, A. and Wuetherick, B. (2013). 'Completing the research cycle: A framework for promoting dissemination of undergraduate research and inquiry'. *Teaching and Learning Inquiry* 1 (2): 105–18.

Stober, D.R. and Grant A.M. (eds) (2006). *Evidence-Based Coaching Handbook: Putting Best Practices to Work for your Clients*. Hoboken, NJ: John Wiley & Sons.

Wall, T., Hawley, R., Iordanou, I. and Csigás, Z. (2016). *Research Policy and Practice Provocations: Towards Research That Sparks and Connects*. Brussels: European Mentoring and Coaching Council.

Index

Abstract Conceptualisation 150
Accelerating Difference (AD) programme 139
action learning 149
action research 43, 148–65
  collective action research 152, 153,
    158–60, 164
  data collection and analysis methods 165
  distinctive features of 149–50
  emancipatory 155
  emancipatory outcome 161
  evaluation 163–5
  evolutionary action research 152, 153,
    155–8, 159, 164
  four modes of 163–4
  inquiry action research 152, 153, 154–5, 164
  participatory action research 162
  practical 155
  practical issues 152–3
  purposes of 151–2
  role of researchers and participants 150–1
  technical 155, 156
  transformative action research 152, 153,
    161–3, 164
  uncertainty surrounding 149
action research cycle 149–50
action research design 116
action researchers, roles
  change agent 151
  group designer/facilitator 151
  participant 151
  practice designer/developer 151
  research facilitator 151
action science 149
Active Experimentation 150
Adams et al. 95
Adler-Kassner et al. 187
aims and objectives of research projects 36–7
analysis issues in quantitative research 123–4
Anderson, L. 96, 100
Andreanoff, J. 116, 121
Anfara Jr, V.A. and Mertz, N.T. 67
ANOVA ('Analysis of Variance') 119
anti-positivists 26
applicability of research 44
appreciative inquiry 149
arts-based communication strategies 189

Atlas.ti 68
auto-ethnography 96–7
autoethnographic vignettes 104–5, 107, 108
autoethnography 7, 93–108
  challenges 101, 107
  coaching and 103–4
  comparison with other ethnographies 98
  critical moments 107
  definition/description 94–6
  distinctive features 94
  evaluation 106–8
  Liam's story (vignette) 102–6
    key learnings 106
  memory and recollection 105
  origins of 96–8
  practical issues 99–102
    autoethnographic practices 99–101
    researching the self 99
  relational ethics and writing 101–2
  researcher-as-subject 97
  subjective nature of 107
autonomy 9

Bachkirova et al. 10, 184
Bachkirova, T. and Smith, C.L. 11
Baskarada, S. 129, 135
Bauwens et al. 42–3, 43
Beattie, R.S. 133
Beisser, A. 187
Belli, G. 11
Bennett, J.L. 9, 10
blind spots 104
Bonneywell, S. 139
Booth, A. 39
bracketing 78
Brannick, T. and Coghlan, D. 150
Brinberg, D. and McGrath, J.E. 44
Bruna, K.R. 164
Bryant, A. and Charmaz, K. 55
Bryman, A. 23, 24, 26
Bryman, A. and Bell, E. 132–3
Burnard et al. 179, 180
Burrell, G. and Morgan, G. 24, 26

Carmichael, Terri 63
Carolan et al. 129, 135, 137

Carr, D. 9
Carr, W. and Kemmis, S. 156, 161
Carrigan, M. 188
case, definition 130
case method 130
case records 130
case study approaches 43, 116
Case Study Observational Research
    Framework 135
case study research 128–43
  data collection methods 132
  definition 131
  distinctions between different theoretical
      stances 132–3
  distinctive features of 129–32
  evaluation 141–3
  goal of 132
  interviews 142–3
  misconceptions about 142
  misunderstandings about 142
  practical issues 135–41
    articulating research philosophies 136
    case studies 139–41
    data analysis 137
    data collection 137
    determining case and design 136–7
    presenting findings 138–9
    writing up 138–9
  rigour 132
  six-step process 135
  and theory 134
  value of 133–4
  wide usage of 129
Case Study Research and Applications (Yin) 131
categorical data 118
causality 26
Cavanagh, M. and Grant, A.M. 183–4
Chang, H. 95
change agent 151
Charmaz, K. 54, 59, 60, 65
  literature and theoretical sensitivity 61
Chi-squared tests 118, 119
Chilisa, B. 161
classic grounded theory 54, 59
  causality 67
  characteristics of 56–8
  definition 55
  differences from constructivist grounded
      theory 57–8
  literature integration 68
  qualitative data 61
Clough, P. and Nutbrown, C. 186
clustering research 39–40
co-created meaning 88
coaching 10
  evidence-based practice 107

human action and interaction 74–5
and phenomenology 74–5
professional recognition of 10–11
subjective experiences of clients 75
as a systemic practice 104
coaching speak 81
Cochran-Smith, M. and Donnell, K. 154
codes of ethics 48
Cohen et al. 156
coherence theory of truth 26
collaboration in grounded theory method 66
collaborative action research 149
collaborative inquiry *see* collective action
    research
collaborative meaning-making 88
collective action research 152, 153, 158–60, 164
  case studies 159–60
  contrast with transformative action
      research 163
collectivism 62–3
comparative coding in grounded theory
    method 67
concept mapping 67–8
concepts 67
conceptual encounter 6, 76, 77
  accent of description 86
  accent of interpretation 86
  case study 86–8
  challenges of researching using 88–9
  parallel process 86–7
  researcher influence 88
conceptual frameworks 41–2
Concrete Experience 150
confidentiality in research 47
confirmatory design 115–16, 116
consciousness 78
consistency in research 44
constructionism 23
constructivism 21, 21–2, 22, 27
constructivist grounded theory 55, 59
  characteristics of 56–8
  differences from classical grounded
      theory 57–8
  literature integration 68
  qualitative data 61–2
constructs 67
context-dependent knowledge 142
context-independent knowledge 142
convenience sampling 122
Cook, Janice 8, 151, 156–7
cooperative inquiry *see* collective
    action research
correlation 118
correspondence theory of truth 26
Cox, E. 190
Cox, E. and Ledgerwood, G. 12

Cox, E. and Patrick, C. 159
Cox et al. 40
Creswell, J.W. 42
critical participatory action research 149
critical realism 28, 29
critical theory 22, 27, 28, 162
Cronbach's Alpha 120
Cronin, C. 129
Crotty, M. 20, 24, 25, 27–8, 86
culture in literature reviews 40
Cunningham, G.B. and Sagas, M. 118
Custer, D. 101

Dasein 78
data analysis for case study research 137
data analysis in grounded theory method 64
data coding in grounded theory method 66–7
data collection in case study research 137
data collection methods in research design 43
data gathering in grounded theory
      method 62–4
Data Protection Act (2018) 122
data, safety of 47
data storage 137
   issues in quantitative research 122
de Rivera, J. 88
decolonisation 161
Denshire, S. 100
Denzin, N.K. and Lincoln, Y.S. 42
DESCARTE model 135
description vs explication in
      phenomenological research 81–2
descriptive case studies 134
designing research projects 33–40
   aims and objectives 36–7
   ethics 46–8
   focus 33–6
   legitimation 43–4
   literature reviews 38–42
   participant selection and access 45–6
   problem statements 34–6
   qualitative research, importance of research
         approach 42–5
   representation 43, 44
   writing a proposal 36–8
      challenges 37–8
developmentalism 10
Dewey, John 26
discipline in literature reviews 40
dissemination and implementation
      of research-based coaching
      knowledge 181–92
   barriers 182
   focus and problem description 184–5
   implementation challenges 189–91
      context 189
      external barriers 190
      for professionals 190–1
      for the researcher 189–90
      internal barriers 190
   literature review 185
   managing dissemination challenges 186–9
   relevant research approach 185–6
   research design and methodology 183–6
   target audience 184
   threshold concepts 187, 188
documents for data collection 137
Doloriert. C, and Sambrook, S. 99, 107
dualist/objectivist epistemological position 26
Duberley et al. 30
Dul, J. and Hak, T. 130, 131
Dupagne, M. and Garrison, M. 133

educational action research 149
effect size 120
Eisenhardt, K.M. and Graebner, M.E. 134
Ellinger, A.D. and Kim, S. 10
Ellis, C. and Bochner, A.P 96
Ellis et al. 95, 97, 100, 101
Ellram, L.M. 130
emic 59
empiricism 117
epistemological relativism 78
epistemology 20, 21, 22, 28, 42
   holistic outlook 30
   systemic position 30
   terms to describe 25–7
epoche 78
ethical issues in quantitative research 121
ethical training 48
ethics
   in designing research projects 46–8
      codes 48
   in grounded theory method 66
ethnographic authority 97
ethnography 6–7, 97, 98
etic 59
European Mentoring and Coaching
      Council (EMCC) 11
evaluative case studies 134
Evans, L. 9, 10
Evetts, J. 9
evidence-based coaching 12
evidence-based practice 12, 107, 183
evidence, definition of 113
evolutionary action research 152, 153,
      155–8, 159, 164
   case studies 156, 157, 157–8
   collaboration 156–7
   participatory 157–8
experience of research 171–80
   case studies 172–9

chemistry sessions and matching
processes 176–7
coaching women leaders 176–7
creative writing 174–5
doctorates in coaching 173–9
feedback instrument 172–3
insights of coaches and clients 173–4
presence 177–8
process of becoming doctor 179–80
research process 172–9
theory 175–6, 177
experiential learning cycle 150
explanatory case studies 134
exploratory case studies 134
exploratory design 115
externality 29

factor analysis 119, 124
Fillery-Travis, A. and Cox, E. 13, 188
Finlay, L. 65, 66
Fishman, D. 29
Flyvbjerg, B. 142
focus in research projects 33–6
for me research outcome 171
for them research outcome 171
for us research outcome 171
foundational trilogy 131
Freire, Paulo 164
Fried, R.R. and Irwin, J.D. 119
Friese, S. 68

Garvey, B. 12
General Data Protection Regulation
(GDPR) 122
generalisability 112
Gergen, K.J. and Gergen, M. 30
Gestalt 187
Gibbert et al. 129, 141
Gibbert, M. and Ruigrok, W. 141, 142
Gibbon, M. 150, 162
Gill, A. 140
Gillham, B. 130
Giorgi, A.P. 83
Giorgi, A.P. and Giorgi, B.M. 82
Glaser, B. 54, 59, 61, 67
see also grounded theory
Glasgow, R.E. and Emmons, K.M.
182, 183, 185
Global Code of Ethics (2018) 101
Google Scholar 177
Graduate School Alliance for Education in
Coaching 173
Grant, A. 113
grassroots activism 161
Gray et al. 10, 116, 133
Griffin et al. 118

grounded theory 6, 43, 53–69, 157
definition 55
see also classic grounded theory;
constructivist grounded theory
grounded theory method 55, 67
appropriate uses for 55–6
coding the data 66–7
concurrent data gathering and
data analysis 64
criticism of 69
data gathering 62–4
distinctive features 56–8
integrating the literature 68–9
literature and theoretical sensitivity 60–1
memos and reflexivity 64–6
practical issues 58–61
ontology and worldview 58–9
role and positionality of
researchers 59–60
theoretical sampling 64
unstructured interviews 63–4
qualitative data 61–2
self-awareness and other-awareness 59
theory development 67–8
writing up 58
group designer/facilitator 151
GROW model 187
Guba, E.G. and Lincoln, Y.S. 21–2, 23,
26, 27, 86
Guldberg, K. 182

Habermas, Jürgen 158
Hamlin et al. 133
Handfield, R.B. and Melnyk, S.A. 53–69
Harding, C. 160
Hawthorne effect 116
Haynes, K. 95, 100
health sector research 182
Heideggerian phenomenology 75
Heider, K.G. 96–7
hermeneutics 83
Heron, J. and Reason, P. 150, 158
Herr, K. and Anderson, G. 158
heuristic research methodologies 76, 77
Heuristic Self Search methodology 174
Hoare et al. 61
Hodge, A.A. 155
Hofstede, G. 62–3
Holman Jones et al. 94–5, 100
Holt, N.L. 96, 100
Houghton et al. 141
Howell, K.E. 24
Humphreys, M. 96, 107, 108
Husserl, Edmund 78, 81–2
Husserlian phenomenology 75
misunderstanding and clarification 78–9

Hwang et al. 118
hypotheses 142

idealism 24
idiography 83
imaginative variation 78
immateriality 29
implementation of research findings *see*
    dissemination and implementation of
    research-based coaching knowledge
independent T tests 118
individualism 62–3
inductive theory 134
Industrial Action Research (IAR) 159
inferential statistical tests 118
inquiry action research 164
    case study 155
inquiry active research 152, 153, 154–5
inquiry in phenomenological
    approaches 80–1
insiders (respondents) 162
intellectual scaffolding 187
intentionality 80
interaction data 88
International Coaching Federation (ICF) 11
International Coaching Research
    Forum (ICRF) 11
interpretative phenomenological analysis
    (IPA) 76, 77
    case study 82–5
    challenges in research and coaching 84–5
        data volume 84
        participants' articulation of
            experiences 84
        reflexivity 84–5
    Heideggerian influence 83
    idiography and hermeneutics 83
interpretive case studies 134
interpretivism 26, 27
interpretivist paradigm 78
interpretivist theoretical stance 133
intersubjectivity awareness in grounded
    theory method 66
interval/ratio data 117
interviews 43, 63–4
    for data collection 137
intransitivity 29
introspection in grounded theory
    method 66
Iordanou, I. and Wall, T. 189
Iphofen, R. 46, 48
ironic deconstruction 66
Ives, Y. 157

Johnson, P. and Duberley, J. 24
justifiable interventions in research 46

Keen, S. and Todres, L. 189
Kelle, U. 61
Kemmis et al. 12, 155–6, 158
Kemmis, S. and McTaggart, R. 150, 159
Kempster, S. and Iszatt-White, M. 95
Kempster, S. and Stewart, J. 95
knowledge 26
    co-creation of 65
    legitimacy of claims 18, 19, 30
knowledge use 190
Kolb, A.Y. and Kolb, D.A. 150
Kolb, D.A. 163
Koning, J. and Ooi, C.S. 107–8
Kotte et al. 11–12
Kruskal-Wallis test 119
Kuhn, T. 21, 142
Kvale, S. 75

Lai Fong Chui 149
Land et al. 187
Lane, D. and Corrie, S. 183–4
Lane, D.A. 9
Lane et al. 9, 10
language deconstruction in grounded
    theory method 66
language in phenomenological approaches
    80–1, 89–90
legitimation in research design 43–4
Leonard-Cross, E. 116
Likert scales 117
Lincoln et al. 22, 27
Lincoln, Y.S. and Guba, E.G. 21, 23, 27
literature in grounded theory 60–1
literature integration in grounded theory
    method 68–9
literature reviews 185
literature reviews in research projects 38–42
    clustering the research 39–40
    culture 40
    discipline 40
    ongoing literature searches 38–9
    paradigms 40
    summarising the theoretical framework 40–2

Mahoney, M. 158
Mann-Whitney test 119, 123
Maxwell, A. 183–4
Maxwell, J.A. 29
McCarthy, I. and Simon, G. 161
McLaughlin, M. 157–8
memories for autoethnography 105, 107
memos in grounded theory method 64–6
Merleau-Ponty, Maurice 75–6
Merriam, S.B. 129–30, 130, 131, 133, 134, 135
    three-step approach for writing case
        studies 138

Merriam, S.B. and Tisdell, E.J. 137
metaphors 178
    in autoethnography 101–2
metaphysical paradigms 29
methodology 20, 21, 22
methods 20
Mezirow, J. 162
mixed method design 116
Mollett et al. 188
Montuori, A. 39–40, 42, 186
Morgan, D.L. 29
Morgan et al. 135
Morgan, G. and Smircich, L. 24, 26–7
Mullen et al. 190
Multiple Intelligences (Gardner) 160

naturalist 21, 23
Neta et al. 189–90
neutrality in research 44
Newnham-Kanas et al. 119
Newsom, G. and Dent, E.B. 119
NHS (National Health Service) 46
nominalism 24
non-research case studies 130
Noon, Roger 86–8

objectives of research projects 36–7
objectivism 23–4, 24, 25, 63
observations for data collection 137
O'Connell, C. 89–90
Olivero et al. 116
Olsen, W. 117
online surveys 121
ontological realism 78
ontology 20, 21, 22, 28, 42
    and grounded theory method 59
    holistic outlook 30
    systemic position 30
    terms to describe 23–5
ordinal data 117–18, 118
organisational autoethnography 98
organisational ethnography 98
outsiders (researchers) 162

p values 119–20
paired T tests 119
Paley, J. 80, 85
Palmer, A. and McDowall, S. 10–11
paradigm wars 19
paradigms 20
    epistemological questions 43
    in literature reviews 40
    methodological questions 43
    ontological questions 43
    terms to describe 27–9
    see also research paradigms

paradoxical theory of change 187
parametric statistical tests 118–19
participant 151
participants in research 45–6
    ethical safeguards 46–7
participatory action research 162
Peirce, Charles Sanders 26
phenomenological approaches/research 74–90
    comparison of methodologies 77
    conceptual encounter 76
    conceptual encounter case study 86–8
        challenges of researching 88–9
    distinctive features 76–82
        description vs explication 81–2
        inquiry, language and sampling
            issues 80–1
        role of theory 81–2
        suitable questions 79–80
        variations of methodologies 82
        viable knowledge and role of the
            research 76–9
            epoche 78
    evaluation 89–90
    heuristic research methodologies 76
    interpretative phenomenological
        analysis (IPA) 76
        case study 82–5
    language 80–1, 89–90
    making a case for 74–5
    plural 76
phenomenological philosophy 75–6
phenomenological psychology method 77
phenomenological reduction 78
phenomenology 6, 74–5
    ontological and epistemological positions 78
    underlying aim 79
phenomenon 81
pictorial representations 118
Pietri et al. 191
Pike, K.L. 59
Polkinghorne, D.E. 63
popular case studies 130
portals 187
positionality in grounded theory method 65–6
positive self-regard 53
positivism 21, 21–2, 26
positivist research 44–5
post-positivism 21, 22, 27
postmodernism 27–8, 97
power relationships in grounded theory
    method 66
practical action research 158
practice designer/developer 151
practitioner research 11–12
practitioner researchers 12–13
pragmatic epistemology 26

pragmatic relativism 29
pragmatism 28
pragmatist perspectives 28–9
Principal Component Analysis 124
prior experiences/assumptions in grounded
    theory method 66
probability distribution 119
problem statements 34–6
procedural ethics in research 46–7
    challenges 47
Proctor, E.K. and Rosen, A. 190, 190–1
professional bodies 11
professional codes of ethics 48
professionalisation 8, 9
professionalism 9, 10
project research blogs 188
propositions 67
psychology 40

Q-sort technique 88
qualitative case study research 131
qualitative data in grounded theory
        method 61–2
qualitative research
    importance of research approach in 42–5
quantitative data 117–18
quantitative data analysis 118–20
quantitative research 112–26
    analysis issues 123–4
    case study 124
    data storage issues 122
    designs 115–16
        action research 116
        case study 116
        confirmatory 115–16, 116
        exploratory 115
        mixed method 116
        quasi-experiment 116
    distinctive features of 113–15
    empiricism 117
    ethical issues 121
    evaluation 124–5
    factor analysis 119, 124
    methods 117
        questionnaires 117
    mixed-method design 113
    objectivist ontology 115
    positivist epistemology 115
    positivistic tradition 114
    practical issues 120–1
    pragmatic paradigm 115
    quantitative data 117–18
    quantitative data analysis 118–20
    research questions 114
    sampling issues 122
    strong evidence 113

quasi-experiment design 116
questionnaires for quantitative research 117
questions for phenomenological study 79–80

randomised controlled trials 183
rank data 117–18
ready-made research approaches 44–5
realism 20, 24
realist theoretical stance 133
reality 78
Reason, P. and Marshall, J. 171
Reed-Danahay, D.E. 96
Reed et al. 121
Reed scale 121
reflection 187–8
Reflective Observation 150
reflective practice 104
reflexive practice 88
reflexive writing 65
reflexivity 80, 84–5, 104, 107, 174
reflexivity in grounded theory method 64–6
regression 118
relational ethics 101–2
relativism 24
relativist theoretical stance 133
reliability 120
representation in research design 43, 44
research
    definition 12
    mastery of 18, 30
    quality of, criteria for understanding 18, 30
research approaches 42–5
research facilitator 151
research knowledge 8–11
research outputs 188
research paradigms 21–3
research proposals, writing 36–8
research questions 114, 117, 173
researcher-practitioners 12
researchers
    objectivist-orientated 63
    role and positionality 59–60
retroductive analysis approach 158
return on investment (ROI) 112, 115, 117, 124
Rickinson, M. 188–9
Rieger, K. and Schultz, A.S.H. 189
Rogers, Carl 53
Rose, Alison 80, 82–5
Runfola et al. 142

sample size estimators 122
sampling issues in phenomenological
        approaches 80–1
sampling issues in quantitative research 122
Sartre, Jean-Paul 75
Saunders et al. 28

scale data 117, 118–19
scales for quantitative research 120–1
scientific revolutions 21
self-awareness in grounded theory
    method 65–6
self-development 10
self-indulgence of autoethnographers 104
self-reflection 85
semi-structured interviews 64
service 9
Shoukry, H. 162
Siggelkow, N. 134
six-stage case study process 135
Smith et al. 83, 85
snowball sampling 122
social media 105–6, 188
sociology 40
Spearman correlation 119
Spence, G.B. 9
Spronken-Smith et al. 186
Stake, R.E. 131, 133, 135
STARLITE process 39
statistical approaches *see* quantitative
    research
statistical tests 118–19
Stenhouse, Lawrence 12
Stober, D.R. and Grant, A.M. 183
strong evidence 113
Structure of Scientific Revolutions,
    The (Kuhn) 21
subjective bias 142
subjectivism 63
subjectivity 78

teaching-practice case studies 130
technical action research 155, 156
theoretical foundations of research 17–31
   key debates and differences 23–9
     epistemologies, terms to describe 25–7
     ontologies, terms to describe 23–5
     paradigms, terms to describe 27–9
   research paradigms 21–3
   theoretical landscape 19–20
   theoretical thinking 18–19
theoretical frameworks 41–2
theoretical perspective 27
theoretical sampling 64
theoretical saturation 64
theoretical sensitivity in grounded
    theory 60–1

theoretical thinking 18–19
theories
   characteristics of 53–4
   concepts and 67
   see also grounded theory
theory-building 67
Thomas, G. 27
threshold concepts 187, 188
Torbert, W.R. 154
Torbert, W.R. and Taylor, S. 154
transactional/subjectivist epistemological
    position 26
transformative action research 152,
    153, 161–3, 164
   case study 162
   contrast with collective action
     research 163
transformative learning, theory of 162
transparency in research 47–8
triangulation 85
truth value in research 44

universities, research ethics procedures 46

Vagle, M.D. 76, 80
validity 44, 120
van Manen, M. 80
Van Veggel, N. 12–13

Wall et al. 182
Whitehead, J. and McNiff, J. 150–1
Wilcoxon 119
Willig, C. 29, 80, 81, 83, 89
Willis, J.W. 133
Winkler, I. 95, 96, 100, 101, 104, 105, 107
Wood et al. 155
working titles in research projects 34–5
worldviews 59
   awareness of 59
Wotruba, S. 140–1
writing case studies 138
writing in autoethnography 101–2
writing research proposals 36–8

Yazan, B. 131
Yin, R.K. 42, 129, 130, 131, 132, 133, 134,
    135, 136, 137, 138

Zahavi, D. 75, 82
Zuber-Skerritt, O. 149, 155